# Improving Purchase Performance

Russell Syson

Pitman Publishing
128 Long Acre, London WC2E 9AN

A Division of Longman Group UK Limited

First published in 1992

© Russell Syson 1992


**British Library Cataloguing in Publication Data**

A CIP catalogue record for this book can be obtained from the British Library


ISBN 0 273 03233 X

Typeset, printed and bound in Great Britain

# Contents

# Introduction

For over half a century it has been received wisdom within purchasing circles that the function of purchase and all those other aspects of storage and supply associated with it does not receive the respect due to it. Its importance in all forms of enterprise and more especially in manufacturing has never been adequately recognised. For a long time, the arguments deployed by purchasing people rested upon the value of spend and, in particular, upon that value as a proportion of total cost.

It has to be admitted that there were intrinsic weaknesses in the case made, since many procurement decisions were made outside the purchase function, which was for the most part characterised as essentially reactive and clerical. Today there are still organisations where such a view could be advanced but they are relatively few and becoming fewer. Purchase has developed first by emphasising its commercial dimension and second by becoming the beneficiary of exciting developments such as supply chain integration and by being an agent of change in the move towards out-of-house manufacture.

The organisation, lying at the heart of the strategic triangle interfaces and interacts with customers, competitors and suppliers (see **Fig. i**). Purchase plays its part in this relationship by adding the search for innovative ideas, the development of greater flexibility and a major participation in the drive for total quality, to its traditional roles (see **Fig. ii**). It does this through partnership, involving carefully chosen suppliers at an early stage in design and development, through increasing integration of information systems and through continuous improvement programmes. To achieve these things, purchase is becoming much more proactive, with each of the key elements in a new form of purchase system being subject to ongoing development (see **Fig. iii**).

It is the hallmark of the new purchasing that there must be a close

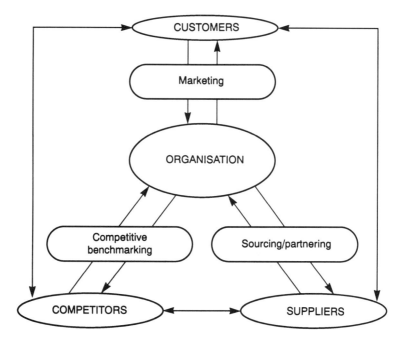

**Figure i** The strategic triangle

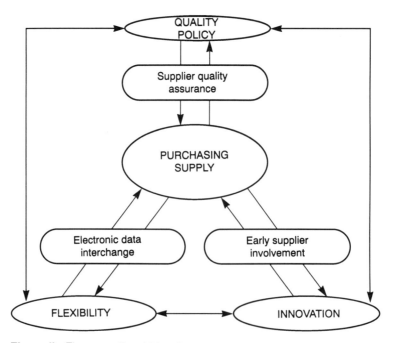

**Figure ii** The operational triangle
Source: A. van Weele

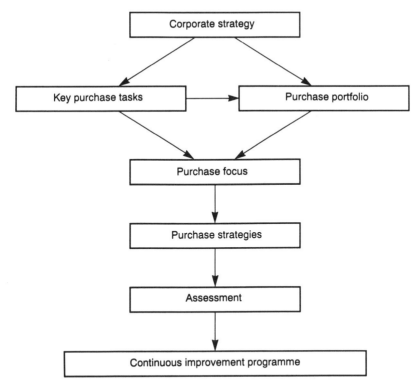

**Figure iii**   The purchase system

relationship between a number of major elements:

- Corporate strategy.
- The five key tasks of purchase of the supplier portfolio.
- Departmental focus.
- Measures of accountability.
- A programme of continuous improvement.

The purpose of this introduction is to indicate in outline the nature of these factors and the way in which they relate to each other.

Purchase cannot exist in a vacuum any more than can any other function. That it sometimes appears to do so is a reflection of its traditional reactive role, providing a linkage from origin to satisfaction of need.

This remains an important task, but one that needs to be placed in an altogether wider context. In fact, it represents only one of the five primary purposes of purchase today (see **Fig. iv**). These purposes are

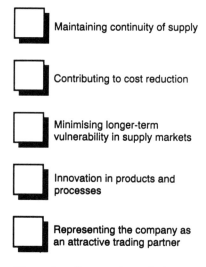

**Figure iv**  Key purchase tasks

common to all organisations but with widely varying practices and weightings.

Each task features a different time horizon and is the product of natural evolution and planned changes. *Ensuring short-term continuity of supply* is historically the function's primary mission, achieved in the past by multiple sourcing, by the use of competition wherever possible as a stimulus or threat, and by high insurance premiums in the form of stock. Today's approach sees, in contrast, the use of a smaller number of carefully selected nurtured suppliers as the key to high service levels, without the need for the heavy deployment of expensive working capital. This places a premium upon active management of the supply portfolio, taking a longer-term view and wherever possible integrating logistics.

The second task is one that has an overriding appeal to all who are, by their nature, commercial animals. It is the *ability to manage costs*. This may imply cost avoidance or reduction. Indeed in some industries – for example white goods – competition in the end market may make cost reductions in real terms essential. Increasingly, however, it is not the initial purchase prices that are important but 'whole of life costs', which include quality, reliability and service elements. Trading, and an adversarial approach to suppliers, is, as a result, giving way to the closer relationship of partnership purchasing.

The *requirement to minimise vulnerability in the supply market* has longer time-scale implications. A much greater insight into the characteristics of the purchase portfolio is now called for. Considerations of competitive demand, of the structure (in market terms) of the supplying industry, of profitability, technological change and barriers to entry assume greater importance. They must be ranged against the strength of the purchase organisation and the implications of leverage. Strategic alliances and supply chain management may be the outcomes requiring, almost inevitably, a more mature approach to the task of negotiation.

It makes possible a departure from older practice, which is to place a *premium upon innovation in both products and processes*. This is a natural consequence of the shortening of product life cycles and of the search for differentiation as a key competitive element in many more markets. Purchase decisions are increasingly pushed backwards into the research or design stage, whilst supplier involvement as part of a team alters the whole concept of the management of this interface.

Finally, *the total quality imperative* makes it necessary that everyone play a part in presenting the organisation as a desirable and attractive trading partner. This will effectively underpin closer relations with suppliers, since it emphasises and gives greater prominence to the responsibility of purchasers towards what are, in effect, external customers.

The changes of emphasis that are detectable amongst these tasks, find a clear reflection in the buyers' approach to *portfolio management*. No longer can this be simply a consequence of actions but rather the basis for active management. A well-structured portfolio is a must for professional buyers, a view implicitly recognised by all who talk of rationalising their supply base. There is little sense in reducing the number of suppliers unless this is carefully planned against well-formulated objectives.

Peter Kraljic of McKinsey management consultants was one of the first to recognise the value of *matrix analysis* as applied to supply markets, identifying as it does the operational factors and strategic thrust (see **Figs. v** and **vi**).

A newer concept is that of *purchase focus* (see **Fig. vii**). This reflects a department's essential orientation, bringing together as it does both the five key tasks and the external supply environment – see **Fig. viii**. Focus must relate to organisational requirement and it must also, whatever it may be, achieve the characteristics needed to achieve excellence in its mode.

This implies *measurement*. No topic in purchase brings forth more diverse views but this lack of agreement upon what should be measured derives in part from a failure to appreciate the importance to be attached to focus. Each of the five types of focus – clerical, transactional, commercial, logistical and strategic – calls for different performance measures.

Bottleneck items
Avoid
Insure

Strategic items
Seek long-term
alliances

Any market
complexity/
risk

New critical items
Rationalise
Systematise

Leverage items
Exploit flexibly

Purchase strength/impact on value added

**Figure v**  Purchase portfolio: operational factors

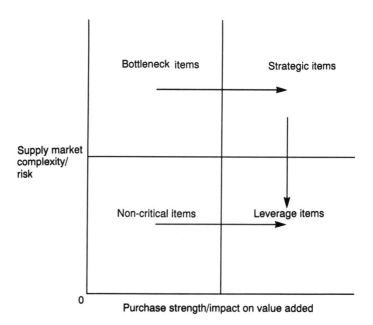

Bottleneck items

Strategic items

Supply market
complexity/
risk

Non-critical items

Leverage items

0

Purchase strength/impact on value added

**Figure vi**  Purchase portfolio: strategic deconstruction

**Clerical / transactional**

**Commercial / logistical**

**Strategic / proactive**

**Figure vii**  Purchase focus

| Focus | clerical→transactional→commercial→logistics→strategic |
|---|---|
| Key element | procedures→systems→price/quality/delivery→integration→ |
|  | sustainable competitive advantage |
| Evolutionary | reactive and service ──────────→ proactive and |
|  | driven          market driven |
| Orientation | efficiency ──────────→ effectiveness |

**Figure viii**  Purchase focus and time

Once this is understood, it becomes possible to identify key performance areas and to devise standards (see **Figs. ix** and **x**).

Comparison against benchmarks, ideally based upon best practice of competitors or allies, is the essential prelude to structured change.

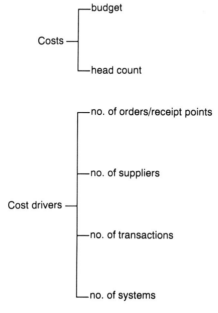

Costs ─┬─ budget
       └─ head count

Cost drivers ─┬─ no. of orders/receipt points
              ├─ no. of suppliers
              ├─ no. of transactions
              └─ no. of systems

**Figure ix**  Assessment: efficiency

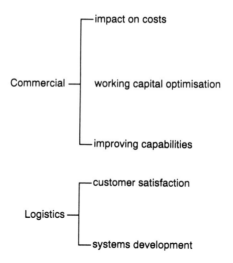

**Figure x** Assessment: effectiveness

Continuous improvement is the hallmark of total quality and of the drive towards excellence. Cost – whole of life cost – will always be a priority area, as will efforts to optimise the use of working capital. A newer concept is customer focus and the need to develop and maintain essential competencies. All of them relate to the survival and prosperity of the organisation as a whole. It is this total view that characterises the *new purchasing*. Short-term advantage is not enough in the last years of the twentieth century. Purchasing's overriding aim is to contribute to the full to the maximising of sustainable competitive advantage.

# 1

## The role and scope of purchase

● Introduction

The purchasing function has evolved slowly and unevenly. From the aspirations of 1931, to proactivity and the positive purchasing of the 1990s has been a gradual progress. Our purpose here is to examine aspects of this progress to decide how far natural evolution must be supplemented by development programmes in order to obtain the appropriate match between the purchasing function and the wider organisation that it serves. As a starting point, it may be appropriate to examine the development of the function.

● Development of the function

For many years any serious discussion of the purchase function has begun by examining and, as appropriate, reassessing its role and scope. A common view, is that purchasing has the task of obtaining material, components, equipment, services and supplies at the right price, to the agreed quality standard, in the right quantities and at the appropriate time. These objectives were to be achieved in the most advantageous way for the company, and are typical of many remits to the function. Frequently, although by no means universally, there is a clear statement requiring the mandatory use of the services of the purchase department from origin of need, through supply and storage, up to and including issue to user.

   As an approach this is indicative of the short-run perspective that many apply to the function, seeing it as essentially a reactive operational area. Changes in the nature of the competitive environment, however, have called the subordinate nature of this role into question, and it is increasingly recognised that important changes must be made if purchase is to be able to discharge its ultimate obligation to make the maximum possible contribution to sustainable competitive advantage.

## An early view of purchasing's role and scope

As long ago as 1931, in the *Handbook of Business Administration* produced by the American Management Association (AMA), the purchase role was described in terms that correspond to what would be regarded today as the most basic form of department; one which is essentially clerically or transactionally oriented. It was claimed in 1931 that in the United States, some 57% of the total cost of manufacturing industry was incurred in the purchase of materials. This is almost identical to the statistics advanced by the proponents of professional purchasing in the late 1980s as evidence of the function's growing importance.

In order to cope with this important cost segment, the AMA recommended that the model purchase department should address six major aspects.

### 1. Administrative aspects

Administration was seen as an essential part of any purchase department. Its role was to approve requisitions and contracts and to maintain contact both with internal customers such as operations and engineering and also with the outside market. This recognition of the importance of customer focus was indeed quite prophetic and has re-emerged as a major issue in recent years. In 1931 the emphasis was of course different, but the description of this particular part of the purchase role does show clear recognition of the service nature of the function. It also shows that concern with process, and in particular with authorisation procedures, while essential to all purchase activity, is pre-eminent in bureaucracy or in areas with a highly developed sense of public accountability. It is perhaps unfortunate that such a preoccupation can all too easily be ridiculed as a consequence of inertia and a characteristic of very low level activity. It is in fact a prerequisite of any purchasing operation that some such fundamental underpinning be in place.

### 2. Ordering

The second principal section of the department had the responsibility of placing orders and should, it was argued, be organised on commodity lines – another characteristic of the contemporary scene. The work of this section was clearly characterised by the need to achieve efficiency. Particular stress was again placed upon the importance of correct procedures, and appropriate levels of authorisation were seen as an element of the highest importance. The order division also had responsibility for expediting and there is clear evidence at this time of a preoccupation with lead times and of anxiety regarding the ability of suppliers to maintain strict schedules. However, the prime role was formally to commit an organisation to expenditure and to commence a process capable of withstanding scrutiny by audit.

### 3. Payments and accounting

At the end of this process, when goods or services had been legally and physically transferred, what was described as the accounting division had responsibility for the reconciliation of orders, advice notes, goods receipt notes and invoices. Whilst payment against agreed deliveries is part of all purchase, it is not difficult to discern, in the description of this activity, a slightly supercilious attitude, and the *Handbook* does indeed refer with condescension to the fact that in terms of staffing this process requires no more than good clerks. Today we can too easily take for granted the existence of well-validated systems using powerful hardware and software packages. Yet major errors still occur and problems of double payment may still be sufficient to exercise the attention of purchasing's most senior levels of management, even in well-ordered departments within front line companies.

### 4. 'Economics'

It is a little difficult to identify precisely where, in 1931, the true focus of the 'Economics' division was felt to lie. There was reference to responsibilities for the maintenance of records but in some ways the 'Economics' division has characteristics that would today seem to be appropriate to purchase research departments. It was stressed that market structures were in need of continual analysis, that the elements of cost in the price of a product must be carefully analysed and areas of potential savings identified. The *Handbook* did, however, in this latter context state that

'Economy in purchasing is not a matter of selecting the lowest of a number of bids but of knowing that the material bought is adapted for requirements effectively produced and bought at a price that represents a fair profit to the seller.'

3

The notion of fair profit to the seller, although undefined, is one that remains contentious. It is highly relevant to modern theories of supply chain management with its emphasis upon single source and long-term commitment. It is also, if not alien to, certainly difficult to reconcile with, adversarial negotiations and heavily leveraged situations.

## 5. Inspection

The authors of the *Handbook* stressed the absolute necessity of strict conformity to specification. This was linked with emphasis upon the merits of standardisation and it may be seen that herein lies the beginning of early focus upon quality. The inspection division was explicitly charged with drawing up, maintaining and revising standards, and in parallel, was called upon to investigate both new sources and new materials. This work, which can be proactive in nature, subsequently, in many industries, became overwhelmed by routine or tended to pass either to research or design departments. It has, however, re-emerged of late as a major innovative factor in some organisations, since it has been recognised that many sourcing decisions are effectively made at the design or development stage, and that supplier involvement has both a functional and a commercial dimension.

## 6. Salvage

Scrap and salvage was a key area for purchasing in 1931. The value of reclaimed materials was important in the corporate scheme of things and this has continued to be the case. In the Saudi Arabia Petrochemical Company, to cite but one example, the commercial disposal of obsolete or reclaimed material is a major area of work even though the operating plants are little more than ten years old. At the end of 1988, approximately one fifth of the total inventory was either surplus to requirements or stock for which there was no foreseeable use. A recovery of 10–25% of the original purchase cost was an attractive alternative to holding in stock, subject only to analysis of the market and in particular of the cost of having to repurchase the material should it ever be needed in the future. Such items were often acquired as spares, scalings obtained against manufacturers' initial recommendations. What was different was that technological change significantly reduced the time horizons in question. Obsolescence might no longer be a matter of 30 or more years but of a single decade or less.

These divisions thus formed the basis of an appropriate departmental structure, deemed to operate according to clearly defined principles,

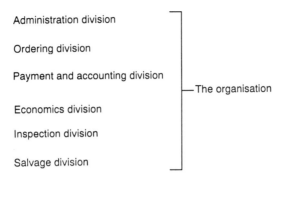

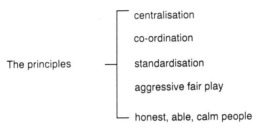

**Figure 1.1**   Purchasing in 1931

which were enunciated to cover resources and product, organisation, people, goods, and the approach to buyer/seller relationships. Many aspects are equally relevant today albeit with rather less certitude than was apparent 60 years ago (see **Fig. 1.1**).

### 'Essential principles of 1931'

The first essential principle of purchasing, emphasised as fundamental to the whole situation, was that *centralisation was the key to success*. Centralisation alone would ensure that 'everything was handled by the Purchasing agent', the one individual with both responsibility and authority. That this aspiration was very unlikely to be fulfilled does not seem to have occurred to the authors. Even today the purchase department of a typical manufacturing company may effectively be responsible for the sourcing of less than half of the total spend, with land, buildings, computer installations and software and many services excluded. Additionally, raw material purchases are frequently handled elsewhere. In the UK, the Central Electricity Generating Board's purchases of fuel were not part of the purchase portfolio and this is by no means an isolated case.

In the scenario described in 1931, the purchase agent, possessed of 'absolute and definite' authority and control, might seem to have formidable power. In fact, however:

'In a broad sense the determination of what to buy is not a purchasing function. The need for and specification for goods arises outside the Purchasing Department and must be expressed before the Purchasing Department begins to function.'

Only then can purchasing begin to search for appropriate sources of supply, its role confined to the right to ask questions and make suggestions. Its abilities to do so were much enhanced by, indeed depended upon, centralisation, for this alone could ensure adequate knowledge, common standards and sound specifications, price records and the insight that would facilitate any necessary substitution.

*Adequate personnel* were seen as the second key element in successful buying and this remains a perennial problem for purchase management. Essential personal qualities were honesty, technical and manufacturing knowledge, a comprehensive understanding of economics, and an ability to reason calmly and logically. Formal qualifications were deemed unnecessary and different entry levels not perceived as important. The purchasing professional was possessed of 'executive ability' and had, above all, a capability for dealing with people. This was because he was a key figure in co-ordinating the major units of the organisation, ensuring corporate success by combining the technical skills of engineering with his own commercial skills.

The third principle related to the goods to be bought. In the context of standardisation, underpinning all successful buying operations, there was a need for *detailed and accurate specifications*. Wherever possible these were to conform to national standards defining exactly the characteristics of that which was sought and detailing precisely the type and degree of inspection to be applied. The cost of quality was clearly a concept yet to be developed but there was an awareness that this was an issue of importance that directly impinged upon purchasing effectiveness. That standardisation appeared desirable as an aid in itself was, perhaps, not surprising as this was the age of mass production with consumer choice subordinated to availability at low cost.

Finally came stress upon *sound ethics*; ethics enshrined within a 'courteous and fair policy' and applied within a framework of relationships with dependable sources of supply. Fairness was alleged to be the order of the day, but the purchasing professional was urged to 'know what you buy' and to be 'aggressive in negotiations'. Many would not demur from this basic advice today, although fairness is not the most frequent topic of conversation amongst either buyers or sellers.

In its conclusion, the *Handbook of Business Administration* contained the assertion that purchasing was no incidental or subordinate function. Co-ordinated with product development, professional buying would stabilise conditions (this was, of course, the period of the Great Depression) by producing an equitable relationship between production cost and selling price. Its progress would ensure and hasten a new age, and the *Manual* concluded its advice by sounding this clarion call:

'The universal application of scientific purchasing will lead to greater efficiency, greater economy, and hence greater prosperity throughout industry.' (*The American Management Association Handbook of Business Administration*, 1931)

Why has this historic view been quoted at some length? Today, purchasing is a very different activity, certainly in the form that matches its aspirations. But many cases remain where the role of purchase fits without undue difficulty into the 1931 mode. Clerically oriented models abound in the public sector, and in manufacturing, examples still remain, even in major corporations, where the efficiency with which the function operates rather than its effectiveness remains the paramount consideration. The movement towards positive or proactive purchasing assumes efficiency and targets effectiveness. The question at issue is how to blend these two elements and relate them in an appropriate way.

## ● Forces for change in the role of purchase

### Sustainable competitive advantage: the aim

In the 1960s, the key to successful corporate enterprise was the identification and development by companies of their unique and distinctive competence. Upon this depended the answer to the key question '*why do my customers come to me?*'. Peter Drucker was the leading promulgator of a doctrine that saw in customer focus the difference between those who prospered and those who perished. The simplicity of this central concept has ensured its survival – the language may have changed but the underlying idea remains intact. Today's enterprises are concerned with sustainable competitive advantage and, in the face of intense, often global competition, with new ways of achieving it. One such way is to recognise that in the purchase field the adoption of entrepreneurial and directional attitudes of the type more frequently associated with marketing is now an essential. Leading edge purchasing directly impacts upon profitability not just because more and more items are bought in rather than made, but because more frequent product change cannot be achieved without harnessing the creative abilities of the whole supply base.

## Global competition

### The spread of industrialisation

For many years the term 'the industrialised nations' could only have been reasonably applied to Western Europe, North America and small areas in the Southern Hemisphere. In the two decades following the Second World War, demand far outstripped supply and the effects of competition amongst the industrialised countries were mitigated by the variety of consumer and capital demand. The development of manufacturing capacity outside these areas in regions of low labour cost such as the Pacific Rim, was not perceived as a threat since its characteristics were those long abandoned by the western world. Technology levels were low, product appeal was based primarily upon price, and designs were licensed, borrowed or copied from the west.

However, much has now changed. New aspirations, new abilities, the development of new technology, and above all of new attitudes have meant that it has become increasingly apparent in the last 15 years that world trade has become much more global in its competitive nature. The principal manifestation of this has been the rise of the Far East as a manufacturer no longer competing at the low cost end of the mass market but as a producer of sophisticated high margin products. Backed by the planners of the Ministry of International Trade and Industry, Japanese industry has overwhelmed whole sectors of western manufacture. Systematic penetration has been backed by massive funding of research and development and by an emphasis upon innovation combined with competitive pricing. From early successes in auto engineering – the Honda 50cc motor cycle was not originally perceived as a threat – to electronics and financial services, the Japanese have swept forward into a position of market domination.

In the Middle East also, rapid industrialisation has taken place based upon rich endowments of natural resources. SABIC, the Saudi Arabia Basic Industries Corporation, was established by Royal Decree in 1976, charged with creating a new industrial base in Saudi Arabia by converting natural gas, the product of crude oil production, into basic

• **Table 1.1**
Globalisation of business

---

*Engineering plastics* (1)
High value speciality products for aerospace, automobiles, defence, factory machinery and
domestic products: price $3,000–$30,000 per tonne

Annual value: £15 billion
Growth rate: 8–10% pa
Properties: strength heat resistant
Market Strategy: tailor specific materials by varying production conditions to meet
individual customer needs

---

| | *m tonnes* | *Europe* | *USA* | *Far East* |
|---|---|---|---|---|
| Polypropylene | 4 | ICI DSM | | |
| Acrylonitrile butadiene styrene (ABS) | 2 | | General Electric Dow Monsanto | ChiMei (Taiwan) Lucky (S Korea) |
| Polyamide (Nylon) | 1 | Hoechst BASF ICI | Du Pont | Mitsubishi |
| Polycarbonate | 1 | Bayer | General Electric Dow | |
| Thermoset epoxy resins | 1 | Shell Ciba-Geigy | Dow | |
| Polyacetyl | 0.5 | Hoechst BASF | Du Pont | |

---

*Joint teams, for specific applications*
  Dow: Sikorsky
  General Electric: Volkswagen: Ford
*Alliances*
  Polycarbonate:Idemiton:DSM
  Polycarbonate:Sumitomo:Dow
  Polyphenylene sulphide:General Electric:Toso
  Polyphenylene sulphide:Hoechst:Kureha

---

Source: *Financial Times*, 1991

industrial products. Previously these gases, mainly ethane and methane
had been flared since it was uneconomical to exploit them. By 1986,
SABIC was selling over 9,000,000 tons of products to some 65 countries
and generating revenues of over £600 million. It had developed within
a new functional infrastructure based upon Al Jubail and had achieved

a high technology quantum leap with the aid of companies such as Shell, Mobil, Exxon and Mitsubishi Gas Chemical Co.

Through joint ventures as much as through changes in the nature of communications, world trade has changed its shape and become more truly global. Improved logistics have simplified the problems that are normally posed by distant markets: no longer can inefficient industries shelter behind geographical boundaries.

*Suppliers as a source of cost reduction*

In order to survive, the management of western industry has been forced to look for severe cost cutting and for improvements in efficiency. A high value of purchase input has made suppliers a most valuable source of cost reduction and innovation, the need for which is clearly demonstrated in the electronics field (see Table 1.2). Without both factors it is impossible today to compete in many consumer markets and it is observable that, as product life cycles shorten, purchasing assumes a wider importance. In manufacture the doctrines of zero defect and of low inventory, pull-style production have gained ground. *Just-in-time* has gained wide acceptance as a competitive strategy although its effective implementation would in many cases have been easier had management more clearly understood its meaning and reality. Flexibility of response has led market leaders like IBM to move from integrated production to long-term component sourcing whilst General Electric has claimed that careful use of supplier know-how can cut the development costs of complex products by up to 60%. Organisations such as Timex have placed a premium upon low-cost component sourcing with frequent changes reflecting the price sensitivity of the end product in the context of world-wide competition.

## Economic changes

Attitudes towards purchasing cannot be insulated from macro-economic movement. The years since 1970 have seen periods of recession, recovery and further recession in the western economies. Amongst causal factors can be counted the longer-term effects of the ending of the Vietnam War, changes in the scope of space exploration and major fluctuations in the price of oil consequent upon Middle Eastern political instability. Third World debt, the Islamic movement and above all the collapse of communist regimes and the ending of the cold war are elements whose impact is likely to be even greater. Opportunities in Eastern Europe and the development of the German 'super power' will all impact directly and fundamentally upon the purchase scene.

● **Table 1.2**
Cost reduction and innovation: prices and features

| 1985 | | 1989 |
| --- | --- | --- |
| £299<br>Turntable | *Microwave* | £299<br>Turntable<br>Microwave/convection oven<br>  combination<br>Auto defrost<br>Auto start<br>Touch controls<br>Digital display<br>Temperature probe |
| £350<br>Remote Control | *Video Recorder* | £350<br>Remote control<br>Stereo<br>LCD programmable handset<br>Slimline<br>Front load<br>Twin speed recording and<br>  playback<br>Teletext |
| £1,200<br>Autofocus/zoom<br>Separate recorder/Camera<br>Bulky VHS machine | *Camcorda* | £699<br>Autofocus/zoom<br>Integral recorder/Camera<br>Lightweight<br>High speed shutter<br>User friendly |

Source: Annual Report, Dixons plc, 1989

All major changes in world economic conditions, whether in the demand for advanced materials or in substitution, alter the nature and the volume of industrial activity (see Tables 1.3 and 1.4). Changes in the utilisation of capacity, in the attitudes of governments towards protectionism and in the development of regional trading groups radically alter the nature of the buyer's job. These differing pressures are enhanced by shifts in the perspectives of senior management. When activity increases and pressures upon the supply market are to the fore, purchase departments are often expanded at a more than pro rata rate. It is paradoxical then that it is at this time that so many of the fundamental disciplines of supply – keen prices, high quality and reliable delivery – have historically tended to go by the board in the scramble to maintain output. As a corollary, it is equally paradoxical that at

- **Table 1.3**

World market for advanced materials

|  | 1986 billion ECU | Average annual growth in real terms (%) 1986–1988 |
| --- | --- | --- |
| New iron and steel products | 50 | 2.3 |
| Engineering thermoplastics | 10 | 8.3 |
| Engineering duroplastics | 15 | 5.5 |
| New metals and non-ferrous alloys | 13 | 3.8 |
| Composites | 12 | 8.7 |
| Structural ceramics | 7 | 13.9 |
| New glass-based products | 4 | 9.3 |
| Functional materials for electronics | 14 | 12.0 |
| Total | 125 | 6.4 |

USA, Japan and EEC aggregated; USA accounts for 42.5% of total in advanced materials production; the EEC for 30%; Japan for 27.5%.

Source: OECD, 1988; one European accounting unit – ECU – is worth about £0.66

times when the purchase contribution might be of particular benefit, when falling demand or organisational trauma places great strains upon cost structures, management easily adopts a short-sighted and detrimental view. Instead of mitigating current difficulties through seeking the benefits that would come from a higher purchasing profile, management forces contraction both in terms of head count and the type of work undertaken. Schlumberger and Rolls Royce are amongst illustrious names that have, at different times and for different reasons, trodden this path, whilst in developing countries the substitution of expatriate staff by local nationals is but an aspect of the same syndrome. It would appear, then, that corporate management in many cases does not see flexibility in purchase's role nor opportunity in its work, but tends to stereotype the activity. Development of the profession directly relates to the perceived benefit derived from it. It demands that senior management be made more aware through both education and intensive marketing of its potential for sustainable competitive advantage. This potential is equally valid at all levels of economic activity. It is the job of purchase managers to highlight it.

## Countertrade

Barter and countertrade is a widespread form of doing business. American government sources point to some 50% of industrial trade

● **Table 1.4**
Substitution between materials

*Old and new: production in Japan*

|  | 1983 $m | 1990 $m | Annual growth (%) |
|---|---|---|---|
| *Advanced materials* |  |  |  |
| Fine ceramics | 1,670 | 6,315 | 19 |
| New polymers | 1,800 | 4,210 | 13 |
| (Engineering plastics) | 1,100 | 2,736 | 14 |
| New metals | 710 | 2,315 | 18 |
| (Amorphous metals) | 12 | 147 | 42 |
| Composites | 105 | 631 | 29 |
| (Carbon fibres) | 63 | 160 | 14 |
| Total | 4,285 | 13,471 | 18 |
| *Conventional materials* |  |  |  |
| Steel | 67,676 | 80,000 | 2 |
| Non-ferrous metals | 29,200 | 35,790 | 3 |
| Ceramics | 36,324 | 44,210 | 3 |
| Chemicals | 80,955 | 101,052 | 3 |
| Textiles | 3,945 | 40,000 | 2 |
| Pulp and paper | 29,730 | 34,526 | 2 |
| Total | 277,830 | 335,578 | 3 |
| *Advanced materials as % of conventional material* | 1.5 | 4.0 |  |

Source: Industrial Business Inc; MITI for price of conventional
materials; 1990 figures are forecasts expressed in 1983 dollars

being conducted upon this basis by the 1990s. This reflects not just trade between the west and what used to be called Eastern Bloc or Third World trading partners, but also amongst western nations themselves.

Countertrade cannot be explained simply in terms of shortages of hard currency or economic mismanagement. It is rather a political and commercially expedient solution to structural imbalances in the world economy caused by the regulating activity of governments motivated by political as well as economic considerations. In essence, countertrade may or may not involve the transfer of funds across boundaries or intermediaries. Even where funds are not transferred across boundaries the money value of goods as expressed in international currency on international markets forms the basis of the deal, being termed the *'shadow price'*.

Countertrade usually takes one of the following forms and gives rise to the growth and employment of specialising agencies.

- *Direct matching* of sales and purchases between the parties. This may take the form of simple barter or the payment of monies, which are immediately paid back for the purchase of other goods. The range of items covered in this way can extend from sophisticated weaponry being paid for by Saudi oil to Pepsi obtained by the USSR against submarines, valued at $150,000 each, to surface ships and even field mice skins.
- *Intermediary action* in which a third party is responsible for the provision of compensating goods from the country that has problems in funding. Normally the exporting party transfers his obligations to a specialist trader or broker with the possibility that at some stage in the transaction money will change hands.
- *Buy back agreements* are a variant upon direct matching. In such an agreement, installation of plant or capital equipment is paid for by new product from the plant. Distribution channels and outlets for this product will normally have been pre-established, which can be favourable to the equipment supplier involved.
- *Offset*, when not used as an alternative name for countertrade in general, usually refers to direct matching or intermediary action where the initial goods supplied are of a capital or high unit value nature.
- *Switch trading* is the term used to describe the year end discounting of residual balances on bilateral accounts. These credits in the clearing account currency arise when substantial and unforeseen imbalances arise between the partners to a bilateral agreement. This purchasing power attracts no interest and in the nature of the type of partners who subscribe to such agreements may be subject to significant depreciation. Switch trading may involve a multi-partner transaction in order to find a user of the credit either in exchange for other goods or for cash.

As a strategy, countertrade is often viewed as a marketing activity. A market for compensating goods must be sought and the supply function may have to play an important role. Trade missions by US multinationals to Common Market countries usually include a purchasing executive since countertrade obligations may be used, perhaps by necessity, for raw material sourcing. The purchase organisation must therefore have up-to-date awareness of the potential of bilateral partners in sourcing terms. Frequently this is of a relatively low order. Most buyers faced with perennial questions of quality and delivery reliability, needing to explore just-in-time in order to derive maximum benefit from flexible manufacture, can do without this type of complication. But it exists and could become more significant in the future.

## Fundamental technological change

The term *'industrial revolution'* has, in the past, been used to describe fundamental change. This may have involved new power sources, or steam, electricity and nuclear power. Equally the term has been applied to parallel activities in the field of organisation for production, such as the division of labour. What is significant about the revolution of the latter part of the twentieth century is that it is not simply scales of output or rates of production that have been affected. It is the whole strategy of manufacture from raw material through the supply chain to the end market. Advances in technology such as injection, extrusion or moulding, play a fundamental role in the development of new materials. The world market for such advanced materials shows sustained real growth with significant substitution between materials. Consequently, generations of managers brought up in traditions that can be traced back to Adam Smith have found themselves in the midst of the greatest economic and technological revolution of all. They have had to face the implications of what McKinsey has termed the *'economies of scope'*. These economies encompass small-batch manufacture within the same cost parameters as previously applied only to large-scale production. They encompass reduced lead times and short product life cycles. Customisation becomes a practical reality with differentiation the principal competitive thrust. Quality of performance and attractive, whole of life costs are regarded as normal.

*Impact upon purchasing*

Such a change implies that the role of purchase be modified. With large-scale manufacture, standardisation and rationalisation are key factors. Stable planning, possibly through Materials Requirement Planning, is essential to volume oriented business. The disciplines implied by formal systems are paramount and must frequently be imposed upon lower level personnel. Emphasis upon lower inventories finds reflection in supplier selection with delay factors a major evaluation factor. Centralisation becomes a dominant organisational form. Stability is the keynote of the function.

With a move towards differentiation, the role of purchase changes. Continuous market scanning to identify design excellence and sources of innovation becomes important and the trade off against experience curve benefits crucial. The accent is upon creativity. Manufacture assumes many of the characteristics of the job shop with decentralisation and flexible planning viewed favourably. Higher level personnel are needed and the key equation is based upon maintaining leverage whilst achieving greater flexibility. The new technologies go hand in glove with much enhanced needs in terms of worker involvement and with programmes of continuous improvement.

From the purchase point of view, the rate of progress towards software-dominated manufacture is of vital importance. Lending itself to end market orientation, this type of activity inevitably leads towards functional integration. Purchase must work much more closely with marketing and with design, just as it must also work with manufacturing. Crucial decisions move to the design phase and enormous pressure develops to reduce the design to product launch lead time. The development of project teams, with multi-functional origins, becomes a major organisational priority as does the ability to accept and use information systems with substantial transparency and with shared ownership. Extensions of teams beyond institutional boundaries, to suppliers and customers, calls for new skills and makes good supplier selection purchase's number one priority. Success in this area effectively preempts other problems and is the hallmark of the professional buyer.

## Change in the environment

In broad terms the effect upon purchase of environmental or macroeconomic factors will vary and depend upon the interplay of other elements. The criticality of purchase in terms of the firm's competitive position is perhaps the most fundamental. This may be derived from the relationship between manufacturing and supply lead times, and from that, between material costs and the value of the company's total production. Where this latter proportion is high, purchase becomes a concern of top management as, for example, in the food industry, in aerospace or the automobile industry.

Purchase emphasis can also arise from supply side complexity and it is in this context that environmental elements may most directly lead to a change in organisational position.

These factors are additionally impacted both by industry maturity and by company profitability. As industries move along their life cycles, the need to maintain market share through more effective competition on price grows. In such a situation the opportunity to decrease costs may lead to a reorientation of purchase role. In consequence there is a significant difference in purchase focus between companies with frequent product change and enhancement such as computing, and those whose principal problems are those of severe price competition. Even here, however, as in the manufacture of electrical white goods, segmentation by perceived quality or feature can be successfully followed. Companies such as ASEA can attract and hold customers on a price differential of up to 100% by virtue of their claims to maintenance-free longevity.

However, there is another factor that, whilst interrelated, is also dominant. This is the quality, the ambition and the purpose of purchase management. Perhaps alone among the major functions, purchasing draws heavily upon other functions – marketing, finance and manufacturing in particular – for its senior managers. Drawn in, sometimes for periods of three or four years only, such managers often provide the catalyst that is needed for change. It is a reflection upon the relative lack of glamour of purchasing in the past and upon its potential today that this should be so. There is every reason why purchase, from what is often a low base, should be capable of rapid strides; given ambition, talent and an eye for opportunity.

**The keys to sustainable competitive advantage**

Sustainable competitive advantage is today a well-known concept. As long ago as 1987 it was identified as the theme of MCE's International Purchasing, Logistics and Materials Management Conference in Brussels. Its achievement was characterised by excellence, innovation and partnership. Separately, each has power. Together, they constitute three keys to the achievement of success in the world of global players (see **Fig. 1.2**).

*Excellence*

Excellence as an overriding business aim has been widely publicised. The message conveyed by Tom Peters is that to be successful in the market-place, organisations require commitment and understanding:

- A commitment to build a powerful competence in the company.
- An understanding of how to build an appropriate distinctive competence – clearly Drucker, two decades on.
- An understanding of the part that must be played by top management in the competence building process.

| Excellence | | Sustainable |
|---|---|---|
| + innovation | = | competitive |
| + partnership | | advantage |

**Figure 1.2** A strategy for the 1990s

The Peters' philosophy focuses upon total customer satisfaction through superiority of product or service and through giving value for money. It demands development of an enterprise culture stimulating an entrepreneurial drive upon the market-place.

For the purchase function, the achievement of excellence poses a variety of problems. In many companies purchase is seen as a reactive service function, with performance and criteria of attainment remaining the same even as the organisation's distinctive competence changes. This is clearly to fail to recognise that differing corporate strategies must elicit varying responses from the materials area. It is a failure to recognise that product superiority and real value may themselves be purchase dependent, resting upon the role and upon the quality of the purchase function, upon a quality defined not simply in commercial terms, but also in the ability to provide competitive edge through the exercise of entrepreneurial talent in the supply place.

A second major question is one of perspective. Purchase's historical view has been upstream towards the supplier. Too many purchasing people have little or no knowledge of the end user market, and are unable to relate supply characteristics to the distinctive competence claimed for or required by the product. The function in some ways appears to operate in a capsule insulated from and unrelated to the competitive demands of the end user market.

Purchase excellence requires a clear sense of purpose devised to further organisational goals and clearly harmonised with corporate strategy. This implies an understanding of company priorities and the crucial role of purchase in their determination. In turn, senior managers, and in particular those with business unit responsibilities, need to have a heightened perception of the potential of the purchase function and of the scope for gains as a result of a greater emphasis upon proactivity.

## Innovation

Innovation means change. It is one of the most overworked words in today's management vocabulary. It implies greater pace, increasing the tempo in order to benefit, by offering to the customer that which is different. Well over a generation ago, Joseph Schumpeter saw innovation as the source of real profit and alleged that as competitors imitated a product or service, so the margin on sales changed from profit to return on capital.

Today innovation fulfils a similar role. It lies at the opposite end of the competitive scale to low price. It is the key to higher than normal margins, to the enhancement of value added. But to create the new requires

a highly specific culture. It is rarely found in bureaucracies and historically frequently wanes as enterprises mature and become complacent.
It is the devastating impact of competition, particularly from Japan,
allied to advanced manufacturing technology, which has awakened customer expectations of product improvement and turned the spotlight
upon shortening product life cycles and, as a consequence, on to the
need to reduce the lead times for new product introduction. Innovation
matters once again. The microwave features listed in **Table 1.2** show the
degree to which product enhancement has overtaken an area of activity
previously dominated by products of great longevity such as the simple
gas or electric cooker.

The implications for purchase are twofold. Shortening product life
cycles not only makes it necessary to seek or develop suppliers able to
accommodate technical enhancement; it also places a premium upon
suppliers with design capability and upon the buyer's ability to sell his
or her own company as a desirable partner with whom to do business.
Secondly, it requires organisational change. The development of project
teams is a feature of more rapid product introduction. Purchase needs
to be involved in this process since more and more sourcing decisions,
many implying sole supply, are made at this stage. Epson, the world's
leading producer of personal computer printers, is part of the Japanese
Seiko watch empire. Together with companies such as Minolta, Sony,
Nissan and the typewriter and sewing machine maker Brother, Epson
has seen the project team approach as the key to more rapid product
development. Halving the time that it takes to develop a new printer,
aiming to get it down to under a year, is seen as a major weapon in
staying in front of the competition. Described by Hideaki Yasukawa,
senior managing director of Seiko Epson, as a way of 'putting pressure
on our engineers and doing more group work', the project team
approach involves a hand-picked multi-disciplinary team. Design to
market time is reduced by a process of overlapping with, for example,
the design of production tooling going on at the same time as product
development.

For purchase this has important consequences. With a printer having
an effective life of 12 to 15 months, the window for 70% of purchase
shipments may be only five to six months. Purchase must therefore
acquire the skills and attitudes demanded by the integrative approach.
To a function that has historically trained its personnel in techniques
based upon competition and confrontation, such internal integration
can pose a challenge to well-established mind sets. As Deloitte, Haskins
and Sells pointed out in their survey of 100 large British enterprises
(*Innovation: The Management Challenge for the UK* (1988)), 'new ideas are

**19**

apt to get stranded ... unless innovation becomes an attitude of mind that pervades the organisation and commits everyone in it to making things happen'. With 75% of all products now on the market either new or being offered in a different form from ten years ago, the implications for purchase are clear.

## Partnership

The third ingredient in achieving a greater purchase impact on competitive advantage is the notion of partnership. The quest for total quality has shown the importance of good supplier selection. Analysis of the cost of quality equation has clearly demonstrated that prevention of defect is the most effective way of increasing consumer satisfaction. Quality of product or service is no longer a competitive weapon but an admission ticket to the market-place. Suppliers must therefore be chosen who have a proven capacity for nurturing and developing the modern quality ethic. Such suppliers are not to be found through the traditional methods such as competitive tendering, and as vendor rationalisation programmes reduce the supplier base and create more sole source situations, the need for the new long-lasting relationships becomes more apparent. With vertical integration no longer perceived as an attractive strategic option in view of its vulnerability to downturn or recession, purchase must pioneer new patterns of supplier relationship.

Hence the move towards the partnership of fully integrated supply chains based on long-term agreements negotiated with selected suppliers. This process has received wide publicity and is the preferred mode of European subsidiaries of Japanese companies and of companies operating across a variety of consumer durable fields. There is, however, a significant cultural barrier, which has its roots in the traditional buying belief in the virtues of competition. Temperamentally, many western buyers are adverse to what they see as a surrender of power. New skills must be learnt, in particular indepth supplier appraisal, as a prelude to selection and the win/win approach to negotiation. The danger is that their blanket application in inappropriate situations will discredit their wider use.

# 2

---

# Strategy

## ● Introduction

There is a need for a close relationship between purchasing and corporate strategy. Purchasing must, in its different forms, reflect the overall competitive posture of the organisation and must be consciously tailored to meet the altering demands placed upon it. Many difficulties that do in fact arise may be traced directly either to a failure of adjustment or to an inadequate view of the overall corporate strategy.

## ● Purchasing and industry life cycles

Applying conventional life cycle theory may be a useful starting point in determining purchasing's strategic needs. The evolution of industries, moving, like products, through phases of development and growth, maturity and decline, generates different forms of dominant competitive thrust, and requires differing purchase response (see **Fig. 2.1**).

### Purchase in the growth phase

In the first stage it is the development of new products or processes that is the anvil upon which success is forged. Where the customers' assessment of perceived value is great, margins are high and, as volume increases, substantial profits accrue. However, risks are also high and it is essential that the purchase strategy focuses upon flexibility and speed of response. Sales projections are difficult to make and both volume and product specification are subject to rapid and unpredictable change. End markets are not price sensitive and the success of purchase depends upon the extent to which, in spite of great volatility, good quality and

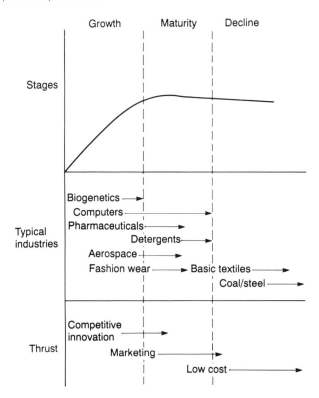

**Figure 2.1** Purchase's strategic role

speedy delivery can be assured. Frequently nominated suppliers are the order of the day with key sourcing decisions moving to the design stage. Under such conditions purchase effort can easily be diffused, with consequent loss of leverage. The function as such may easily lack the focus that is necessary in order to extract the most benefit from the supply market.

Schlumberger EPS, in Petit Clamart, is a highly respected provider of leading edge, high tech products, destined, for the most part, for the oil industry. A continual search for new high quality products and the application of newly researched technologies meant that this organisation characterised those where innovation dominates the way in which the supply market is addressed. The very strong emphasis upon research and upon product development lead to a need for frequent accessing of suppliers and subcontractors by personnel acting outside the control or orbit of the purchase function. As a result, supplier relations were neither controlled nor co-ordinated by the purchase department. The subsequent weakening of the Schlumberger presence in the supply market was a direct result of the fact that several different purchasing centres had come into existence. Within operations there was a purchase focus in planning and control but major purchase activity also fell within mechanical manufacturing. In addition a significant number of purchase subcontract items were outside the remit of either of these two areas. Development contracts let by engineering were substantial in volume and by their nature conditioned and determined much subsequent purchase activity.

This type of approach to the purchase function is typical of organisations at this particular stage of the cycle. The implication is that there is no adequate reflection of the importance of supplier relations to the company. There is much scope for performance improvement, particularly in leverage, whilst the purchase function has difficulty in rising above a purely clerical role. Its organisational standing does not reflect that proportion of total cost represented by bought in parts and materials. When many parties deal as of right with suppliers there is inevitably a consequent loss of purchasing identity. Symptomatic of such loss is weakness in price determination and inadequate control over both quality and price. The technical compensations of this phase of the cycle and the lack of significant price sensitivity in the end market do not of themselves justify an excess degree of decentralisation. Purchase expertise lies in knowledge of supply markets and in superior negotiating abilities, and as a generalisation it is quite wrong for it to be the case that major purchase agreements could be concluded without the involvement or the knowledge of any part of the purchase function.

In addition, under such circumstances, it is unrealistic to suppose that the supplier portfolio can be actively managed. This can imply excessive supplier vulnerability to fluctuations in the levels of the purchaser's business and to a leveraged impact upon profit margins, which can, under some circumstances, actually prejudice survival.

A further characteristic of companies at this stage of the cycle and often also of others who are supplying components, is that the emphasis upon creativity can be accompanied by a failure to develop adequate systems. Delivery problems can become a dominant purchasing feature. Amongst the causes of poor delivery performance are, first, that the specifications can be uncertain. Technical data may be inadequately understood, which can easily result in the quoting of unrealistic lead times. In the second place, such suppliers frequently have problems in terms of realistically assessing their capacity and in getting the workload on to the shop floor. Adequate planning and control systems are noticeable by their absence, and poor delivery performance is an almost inevitable result. A survey of subcontractors in the Paris area showed the widespread nature of this problem. In terms of supplier evaluation, specific attention must be paid to planning and control systems, to the ability of suppliers to be able to make last minute changes and to the quality of people involved in the management of processes.

Purchase must receive sufficient professional attention to develop appropriate logistic responses. Without this it is not possible to meet in an appropriate way the procurement needs of the organisation.

## The purchase needs of mature organisations

As organisations begin to move into the second phase – that of maturity – so in broad terms competitors emerge, offering similar products. The competitive edge of innovation is eroded. This leads to a fall in margins and to the strategies of competition becoming more marketing led. There is heavy promotional expenditure offsetting any fall in the direct costs of manufacturing or experience curve effects. Whilst demand might remain relatively inelastic, price competition does become increasingly important. Historically, there has been an emphasis at this stage upon economies of scale, with volume becoming a key factor. In purchase terms, this can lead to a need for quantity insurance in the supply market. Demand forecasting and scheduling, and the introduction of MRP systems become more important. Frequently the role of purchase is perceived as essentially to run the function. Efficiency is a major focus for management, and good supplier delivery performance, reducing the risk of production loss, becomes more important. The detergent industry typifies this phase. Market penetration depends to a very large extent upon promotional expenditure and skills. The ability of purchase and sourcing to affect corporate success in a direct and major way is, in this stage, potentially at its lowest point.

## The low-cost product

In the final stage with products that are unsuitable for marketing driven strategies, organisations may seek to compete by being the lowest cost producer. This is the alternative to divestment and leads to an attempt to obtain scale economies through large plants, mass production of standard products, and by the location of manufacture in low labour cost countries. There is normally a demand for stability, for flow, for zero inventory. Standardisation becomes important and purchase needs to be able to guarantee access to critical inputs. There is a need for tight control over materials and for intense pressure upon the price of goods bought.

# ● Choosing the right purchase and logistics strategies

If this form of analysis, based upon the work of Michael Porter, is accepted then the next step is to ensure that a purchase and logistics management system is devised that will support the competitive strategy of the company by recognising the stage of the cycle that is applicable at a particular point in time. If the overall corporate strategy is unclear, then operational management will find it difficult to fit its systems to the task in hand. Where purchasing management has insufficient knowledge or insight into overall corporate thrust, it may adopt strategies inappropriate to that stage of the cycle. It could bring about purchasing characteristics that would reflect differentiation, for example, and mix them with strategies more appropriate to low-cost manufacture. This would give rise to incompatibilities and contradictions. One of the large growth areas in purchasing consultancy in recent years has focused on the attempt to identify the extent to which the purchase organisation has adequately assessed the corporate need and has designed its activities to meet those needs in the most appropriate way. Porter makes reference to organisations that are 'stuck in the middle'.

A typical 'stuck in the middle' company would perhaps have some of the following characteristics: it would have a general management, which seeks to manage the business using quite tight yardsticks of achievement; there would be a controller or controllers continuously evaluating such factors as productivity, efficiency and machine utilisation; and there would be a marketing department, seeking to promote the company and its products as being innovative, creative, flexible, possibly with high technology overlay. The 'stuck in the middle' company might then, however, have a production system organised in a job shop layout but with a rigid production planning department, trying to achieve a frozen master production schedule. Another typical, stuck in the middle, factory might produce standard products to customer order in a job shop organisation attempting to control this by the Kanban pull system[1] with flexible production people who try each day to solve shortage problems. Such scenarios are far from being uncommon, and it is in purchasing that the impact of such contradictions can so often be seen.

To break out from impasses of this type frequently requires a push from top management imbued by the determination to halt the

---

[1] A system, as used by e.g. Toyota, of manufacturing only against orders, received or anticipated, and 'pulling' production through the factory as a result.

seemingly inevitable progression along the life cycle curve. Rejuvenating purchase as part of this process is a task often (perhaps usually) requiring new men and almost always the catalyst of outside perspectives and advice.

Ideally a well-defined and highly competitive firm will have outlined its competitive strategy in such a way that implementation requires systems and policies that reduce cost whilst at the same time increasing the possibilities for differentiation. Alternatively of course, such a firm might find a way to differentiate at a lower cost or level.

The *just-in-time* approach could be perceived as filling the latter case. Just-in-time is more than a purchasing, logistic, or even manufacturing system. It is – or rather should be – a fully blown corporate strategy that effectively, often using new technology, enables a company to regress along its life cycle curve. It seeks to harmonise what could otherwise, in the Porter perspective, be seen as mutually exclusive strategies – low-cost or differentiation. Japanese companies have gone down this road, partially for geographical or economic reasons but also because it appeals to the national temperament. They have devised efficient and effective logistics management, have a good understanding of how to focus their factories, and are highly skilled in matching policies and systems to strategy. Notwithstanding confuting western myths to the contrary, they are innovative and creative, and are often successful at lowering cost whilst increasing differentiation at the same time. Above all, they continuously improve their reliability levels, believing that competitive advantage can never be achieved while there continue to be unreliable processes and unskilled and poorly trained people with, as a consequence, a low range of quality out turn.

It is therefore important to ensure, when the economies of scope become a major factor in an organisation, that the impact of new manufacturing technology or improved methodology is followed by a far reaching review of the purchase strategy and organisation. This implies that supply chain integration based upon partnership with suppliers, becomes a purchase priority. It is simply not possible to meet what amounts to the total rethinking of supply market strategy whilst purchase remains preoccupied with the apparent need continuously to exploit competition or to handle large amounts of routine, day-to-day processing.

The application of life cycle theory is, however, simplistic. Hence it is necessary to look for other reasons to explain why the harmonisation of purchase strategy is, in spite of its importance, often neglected. Specifically, these include the geographical expansion of the supply base, the changing nature of consumer demand, the increasing pace of technological advance and, finally, the increasing importance to management of techniques such as value added analysis.

## ● Expansion of the supply base

The development of world-wide supply bases brings both opportunities for and problems to purchasing. Facets may be illustrated by reference to different companies, their commitment, size and experience.

### 1. Thorn EMI

Colin Southgate, the chief executive of Thorn EMI plc said at the Institute of Purchasing Supply National Conference in 1988:

> 'Whilst we seek the best terms country by country, on a group basis we seek relationships with international suppliers in order to achieve the cost benefits of economy of scale on a country by country basis. In a nutshell, that's purchasing clout'

### 2. British Aerospace

In terms of sheer size, in 1987, British Aerospace was Britain's top exporter with a total export of £3.89 billion. To sustain that effort, total purchases were made of £4.78 billion. The approximate geographical distribution of this saw some three-quarters or £3.58 billion sourced to the United Kingdom, 10% or £0.48 billion sourced elsewhere in the EEC, £0.42 billion or 9% to the United States and £0.3 billion or 6% in the Far East. This spread, with the attendant problems of logistics, demands a proactive purchasing stance.

### 3. Cerestar

Similar patterns emerge in many other companies with overall results that can be seen in a number of different and conflicting ways. In the first place service reliability demands a much greater emphasis upon effective logistics as supply and distribution chains become much longer. Such chains represent an important area of cost generation. Geoffrey Lyon, the logistics director of Cerestar, said in Amsterdam in 1989 that the European logistics costs of his organisation were of the order of 330 million DFL against sales of 2,500 DFL. He pointed out that the impact

**27**

- **Table 2.1**

  Logistics service as a competitive factor

  | Perceived importance of logistics service | |
  |---|---|
  | Product Features | 3.58 |
  | Logistics Service | 3.24 |
  | Brand/Manufacturers' Image | 3.10 |
  | Technical/Sales Advice | 3.02 |
  | Price | 3.00 |

  Max. 5.00

  Source: McKinsey

of such logistics costs is frequently underestimated. Inventory is often inaccurately assessed, handling and transport costs underestimated and those of systems often unknown. With Cerestar, in-borne transportation accounted for some 20% of costs, out-borne transportation for 55%, warehousing and handling 15%, finance of industry 5%, and administration 5%. To reduce cost by integration can be a source of major competitive advantage. In the case of Cerestar, Geoffrey Lyon estimated that savings of some 5–10% were possible; a matter of up to 20 million DFL. To the extent that these are typical figures, it is clear that with wider sourcing, major cost advantages over the inefficient organisation becomes a very real possibility.

## 4. Toshiba Consumer Products (UK) Ltd

A potential area of conflict lies where longer supply and distribution chains can be seen to clash either with some of the requirements of just-in-time or with programmes of localisation. Notwithstanding devices such as consolidators, used for example by Xerox in their transatlantic bridge from Europe to North America, just-in-time does not lend itself to a widely dispersed supply base. Indeed, as a rule of thumb it might be said that one of the prerequisites of a just-in-time supplier is reasonably close proximity to the point of consumption.

The implications for purchase of world-wide supply were discussed at the 1989 Just-in-Time Briefing in Brussels by Peter Bayliss of Toshiba Consumer Products (UK) Ltd. This company was established in Plymouth in the United Kingdom in 1981 to manufacture colour televisions and microwave ovens. All production is sold through a sales company and marketed abroad into Germany, France and Switzerland. Market pressures in the field of consumer durables are very intense in Europe and there is continual pressure to reduce prices whilst providing a very high degree of service to customers. In particular it is important that a high quality product be available at the right time and price. Toshiba has a well-developed, detailed planning system, which leads to a high degree of schedule stability based upon a routine monthly planning cycle. In consequence Toshiba views the preservation of an expediting facility as an unnecessary cost. Once an order is placed and accepted, goods are expected to arrive as required on the specified day. Toshiba has long had a fundamental policy of no goods inward inspection, which has clear implications in terms of quality of component. Additionally, exact quantities must be supplied at all times and there is no count of incoming materials.

When Toshiba was first established in the United Kingdom such attitudes were at variance with the then current orthodoxy, and Toshiba therefore carefully monitored the performance of suppliers in meeting what were to many of them stringent conditions.

It was found that there was a significant difference in the performance of local suppliers when compared with those from the Far East. In terms of quantity, Far Eastern suppliers were much more accurate and if there was any tendency to supply inaccurate quantities, then those in the Far East erred upon the high side whereas those from local suppliers showed a distribution pattern where errors were equally spread about the required quantity. With regard to sourcing policy, there were two major areas of supplier – Far Eastern and local. In the Far East, two major areas in turn were Toshiba and direct suppliers, the latter being located in a number of countries including Japan, Singapore, Malaysia, Taiwan and Korea. Throughout the 1980s, Toshiba made consistent efforts to increase the volume of local purchase, and in financial terms, even allowing for changes in the exchange rate, there has been a major switch into locally sourced products. Toshiba has a localisation programme that is a continuing operation to investigate new European sources of components able to offer consistency with price, quality and delivery performance. The obvious benefits of doing this include protection against fluctuations in the exchange rate, the avoidance of some 30 days' shipping time and possible ten days' customs clearance, a faster response time if problems occur and the avoidance of freight and duty.

There are drawbacks for Toshiba however, which would make it difficult to achieve complete localisation, and indeed during the 1980s made the speed with which their programme was implemented slower than might have been desired. In the first place all the designers were in Japan. This led to the tendency for them to specify suppliers known to them and, in particular, Japanese companies.

Additionally it took time and resources to approve any new source for a component, since this activity was also done in Japan. Finally, for much of the 1980s, components sourced in Japan and the Far East were considerably cheaper than local equivalents. Peter Bayliss pointed out that in some cases there was a gap to be bridged even when freight and duty had been added to the Far Eastern cost. Referring specifically to the impact, in terms of just-in-time, of this dependency upon overseas sourcing, he summed up in the following way. The rapid growth of output placed a considerable pressure on space, particularly in terms of storage capacity of finished goods and purchased materials. Where purchase materials were concerned, an analysis of the situation revealed that for small components it was possible to order by stock number and accept deliveries twice per month. For larger components, such as cabinets or tubes, these had to be delivered on a batch basis, one to five days before production. Finally, for packaging material such as cartons and expanded polystyrene cushions, delivery lead time could be reduced to under a day and in many instances it was possible to operate a true just-in-time operation. By the end of the 1980s, therefore, the Toshiba just-in-time situation was that first, with regard to Far Eastern supply, just-in-time could not be operated, even though exact order quantities could be placed on a monthly basis – shipping schedules made it impossible. In the second place, for local small parts, again monthly deliveries of exact quantities were made but with two deliveries per month and again true just-in-time was not feasible. Where large parts were concerned, batch orders with a lead time of one to five days approached something of the just-in-time concept. With regard to packaging, ordering was again by batch with delivery on the day of production or the day before and in some cases two deliveries per day. Much of this was conditioned by vehicle load sizes. Clearly most appropriate and most economical were deliveries made in full loads, and as far as possible every organisation organises in this way. This can mean that in a number of cases, just-in-time is not applicable, even though lead times have been reduced to an absolute minimum.

The Toshiba case highlights the stresses that can arise when policies are adopted that are to any significant degree incompatible. World-wide source poses not just logistics problems but interacts with corporate policies based upon customisation and small batch manufacture, or upon the drive to integrate within the local community.

## 5. ICL

In other cases, localisation policies take on a different aspect. For example, in communication equipment ICL Information Systems found that by 1990 there was an important need to increase the size of their business volume simply to support their R & D base. The United Kingdom market was too small for this purpose and the company therefore identified a strong and overriding need for pan-European development. At the beginning of this phase, some 40% of all purchases were made within Europe but a target was set to raise this to 70%. The payoff was seen in terms of lower risk and lower cost. In addition, export controls would cease to be a problem whilst the financial aspect of the transaction would take place in relatively stable European currencies. This is a clear case of how purchase strategy reflects corporate need and where the two can be seen to be developing in harmony with each other.

## 6. SADAF

Sometimes localisation policies result from a national rather than a corporate need, emphasising an imperative to develop the local supply base. For example, in Saudi Arabia the purchasing organisation mission statement of SADAF, the Saudi petrochemical company, asserts that the aim is to:

> 'Develop and provide on time effective and efficient purchasing services that contribute to SADAF profitability in a safe, secure, environmentally sound ethical manner, consistent with SADAF's commitments to the Kingdom's industrialisation and Saudisation objectives.'

This Saudisation policy has two principal aspects. In the human dimension it is concerned with the development of Saudi nationals to perform all purchasing functions in a competent professional manner. With regard to suppliers, the policy is to 'promote, encourage and facilitate the utilisation of Saudi suppliers, services, contractors and products'.

In practical terms this found expression in the following goals. Through 1988, Saudisation of staff was to be sustained at a minimum of 75%. In practice, by the end of the second quarter, it had risen to 79%. Excluding imported benzene feed stock and raw materials, some 75% of expenditure during that year was to be committed to companies within Saudi Arabia. In addition, long-term development efforts with Saudi's suppliers were to be initiated whenever those suppliers could be seen as top quality long-term distributors of supplies and spare parts. Wherever possible, national carriers were to be used with a target of 60% of all air and sea freight tonnage. Such a policy can produce a purchasing paradox. The lack of indigenous manufacturers means that for a consumer such as SADAF the net effect is to channel more business through merchants or distributors. Not only does this add to cost but it also introduces an extra link into the information and logistical chain.

## 7. Chip manufacturers

National policies may find expression either in legal or other forms of restriction. These may not simply be national but within regional groupings, and clearly one of the major concerns in respect of the development of globalisation of supply, lies in the possibility that these may seek to inhibit major purchasers from obtaining their supplies abroad either by way of retaliation or by protection.

One area in which there has been a good deal of difficulty and controversy is that of alleged dumping. Let us examine a specific case. The European Community spent some three years examining the dumping of Japanese chips on the European market. An agreement was reached in 1989 between the European Commission and 11 Japanese producers of dynamic random access memory chips (DRAMS) regarding the minimum export price. Under the terms of this agreement, the 11 Japanese producers that together were responsible for virtually all DRAM exports to the European Community, agreed on the minimum price equivalent to average production cost, plus a margin of 9.5%. This was less than the Commission had originally wanted and they had initially thought that a higher ceiling price including a margin of some 20% would be applicable. The reason for this was that the Commission had felt during 1986 and 1987 that there had been serious dumping of DRAMS within Europe. At that time the export prices of DRAMS were several times lower than the domestic Japanese price. As a result there was serious damage to the European producers leading either to unused capacity or to a postponement of the opening of new capacity. The Japanese increased their share of the European market from some 24.6% in 1983 to 70.5% in 1987. The Commission, however, had to argue that minimum import prices did not damage either the semi-conductor user or the final consumer.

Some European chip users felt that the price increase resulting from this move would add to costs and make them less competitive. Some countries, in particular Ireland, objected to the measure on the grounds that it was against the interests of consumers and this has led to delay in the final approval of any scheme.

## 8. BOC British Oxygen Company

It has been said of the renewing and reviving of existing businesses, when technical excellence is regained and new geographic markets are penetrated:

> 'Such herculean feats are certainly impressive. But in today's global economy they are merely qualifications for playing the competitive game – not for winning it.'

Organisational problems of scale and complexity arise from distance, nationality and culture. If they cannot be solved through delegation and profit centres, how can they be tackled? The British Oxygen answer is through the flexibility of interactive networks; being responsive to market differences whilst at the same time expanding from the UK and USA into Asia, the Pacific and Europe, invalidates local self-sufficiency, the traditional pyramid, or a matrix. Networking with centrally facilitated communication and audit is based upon the 'lead ship' approach to technology and operations. The most knowledgeable local unit gives this lead and is responsible for disseminating good practice and ensuring the avoidance of wasteful duplication. According to Richard Giadino, ambiguity and conflict are ever present, and profit and loss benefit is not easily discernible. Co-operation and trust are more important than authority, and new ways of rewarding are needed. The small staff at the UK centre acts 'on occasion as traffic policemen, infrequently as an auditor and very often as a cheer leader'.

What can purchasing learn from this? Networking with local centres of excellence and rapid data communication may provide the answer to sourcing problems, where on the spot knowledge commands a high premium and where the ability to confront crisis or difficulty personally and quickly matters.

It will be seen from these examples that globalisation is highly complex, provoking different responses in varying circumstances. The search for the best supply markets world-wide is a major and continuing activity. It may be concluded that logistics assumes much greater importance, since, as supply chains become longer, both service reliability and effective logistics become crucial for success. Logistics impacts directly upon the savings potential and it is therefore not surprising that the extent to which globalisation of supplies has occurred varies a great deal from industry to industry. In the chemical industry, for example, there is a very high degree of globalisation. This is a process industry with high added value both in sourcing and in distribution, and the purchase function must range world-wide in its search, particularly for items that are basic to the production process. In the food and allied industries, due to extreme market complexity, globalisation is gradual, although it has now extended away from simple commodity sourcing through to the manufacture of key groceries in particular areas (e.g. the concentration of ketchup production in the Netherlands) and to the establishment of world-wide supply networks (e.g. a twice weekly delivery of salad products from the Netherlands via KLM to Saudi Arabia).

Local distribution becomes an important element, with customer service being achieved through the establishment of dedicated distribution networks for particular products. In the United Kingdom for example, Transhield (a British Oxygen subsidiary) are dedicated transporters for the whole of the perishable products for the Marks and Spencer organisation. The operation of Transhield, although technically not just-in-time, does in fact display many of its features. Not least in that there is a real time approach to the demands of the various Marks and Spencer stores, and it is increasingly the expertise of routeing, information transfer and in determining how to match multiple sources with multiple outlets, rather than simply the ability to run transport fleets, which are the key factors in the success of such an operation.

In summary therefore, to extend the supply base on a global scale brings the needs of logistics to the fore. Consumer service is recognised as being in principle a competitive tool. No single function can achieve high standards of service on its own. Hence much greater team-work and functional integration is required, and purchasing must co-operate with those concerned with product development and operational management in selecting appropriate sources. The emphasis is on greater sourcing flexibility and the ability to switch from one supplier to another as various cost parameters change. This implies a need for hands-on experience in the field. It is not possible for today's buyer to be both desk bound and effective. Developing an adequate framework calls for more than the adaptation or extension of traditional forms. Of all the developments in the field, the flexible networks of the British Oxygen Company are validated by commercial success and may prove to be the most appropriate model.

## ● The changing nature of consumer demand

Another major factor that has affected corporate strategy and its relationship with the purchase and logistics function, is the changing and intensifying nature of market-place demands. Today's key to success lies in ensuring that an organisation, through its responsiveness to customers, fully lives up to their expectations. Customers are seeking both reliability and more service; seeking, in other words, not just products but important non-product related features. Perhaps by way of illustration it would be appropriate to consider the changes that have occurred in one major industrial sector – the do-it-yourself market. In order to achieve higher levels of customer service in a strategic sense, it is necessary to improve those factors that link together business success with good logistics, high manufacturing technology, and customer service. These are in fact all bound together by the attitudes of the people in the supplying business. If appropriately developed, these will lead to the derivation of a strategy that will become a powerful competitive edge weapon.

The market for consumer durables in the United Kingdom has undergone rapid and dynamic change within the last ten years. To analyse the situation is to become aware of how customer service as a competitive edge weapon has rapidly gained increasing importance. At the beginning of the 1980s, the distribution of power tools for purposes of home improvement or do-it-yourself in the United Kingdom rested upon a large number of high street hardware stores. These were supported by a significant number of wholesalers, and both retailers and wholesalers operated centralised warehouses in which bulk deliveries were the norm. On the whole, the ways of controlling stock and the systems in operation, both by wholesalers and large retailers, were rudimentary, and stock control was primitive in its application. As a result, major suppliers had a much better picture of what was happening in the customers' warehouses than those customers had themselves. Under such circumstances, the criteria for successful customer service were relatively straightforward; the most important thing being that there was always a stock of any product in the customer's warehouse when that customer wished to replenish the shops. This is a simple framework, but expensive to operate and one that largely ignores the competitive value to be gained by giving a high degree of service to the customer.

During the 1980s, a total revolution in retailing led to the establishment of large, out of town do-it-yourself superstores. This altered the whole framework of the distribution industry. Wholesaling itself became virtually unimportant and there emerged a large network of nationwide chains of do-it-yourself shops. These very large customers made huge new investments in retail floor space. It was necessary as a result to look at the effectiveness of the retail operation with much greater rigour.

Such factors as the working capital employed in inventory, the effective use of shelf space, and the ratio of turnover to stock became much more important. Overriding everything, however, was the fact that these new large customers considered that their particular abilities and competencies lay in different directions from those that had been the preoccupation of the earlier distribution network: the new distinctive competence was in retail skills; retail skills generate turnover; the competence was not in physical distribution.

As a consequence, a whole new pattern emerged. This required that large customers received deliveries to individual stores, many thousands perhaps with locations nationwide. The deliveries themselves had to be closely matched to current sales volumes. Back-up stock was at a minimum – the essence was to replenish the shelves. The implication of this was that there was a movement away from large occasional bulk deliveries to small deliveries once or twice each week to each store. This is a form of service that perhaps could be called just-in-time, if one permitted some degree of licence in the use of this term. This therefore presented a quite different type of logistics problem. Customers would only do business with those suppliers who could meet their particular customer service requirements. Those who were not able to do this were excluded. It is thus the case that to the manufacturers of, for example, power tools, meeting customer service and the demands of customer service, became a matter of survival. Those who could do it better and quicker and more efficiently, gained an advantage. Customer service became a distinguishing feature in competition.

The implication of this for the supplier was that an entirely different physical distribution system was required. The whole company had to achieve much higher flexibility. The principal consequence of this was that manufacturing itself had fundamentally to reappraise its internal systems. In broad terms, lengthy extended programmes had to be changed towards a flexibility that approached a real time and batch of one mode. Responsiveness and the matching need flexibility and this then had to extend to suppliers. In purchase terms it became essential that the quality of everything that happened from suppliers had to increase very significantly. Certainty of outcome was the yardstick of success. It is the speed, the efficiency and the accuracy of data flow that is also significant. Too often this stops short of the supply base, not just in the context of power tools but across virtually the whole industrial spectrum, and with the new consumer demands there will be inevitable pressures for this to be extended. A high degree of integration between purchasing and other functions, in particular product design and manufacturing, is also essential.

In sum, the whole culture of the business needs to change, and the business includes the supply chain. Purchase practices and logistic approaches that were appropriate to the more sedate distribution pattern of earlier times were impaired by a more consumer oriented climate. Not just a commercial but also a strategic element begins to emerge. Purchase evolution has to make a quantum step.

● New technology: its significance for purchase strategy

Reference has been made to the importance, in terms of the new approach to customers, to make the fullest use of technological development, particularly in the information field. It is essential that data can be turned quickly into management information and it should be borne in mind that any technique that can make a company more competitive will sooner or later be implemented by competitors. As there is a limited

**Cost leadership**
- standard products
- flow production
- zero inventories
- accent on productivity
- stable planning
- centralisation
- formal systems
- standardisation
- volume oriented
- low level personnel

**Differentiation**
- customer designed products
- job shop
- slack inventories
- accent on creativity
- flexible planning
- decentralisation
- mutual adjustment
- special components
- order oriented
- high level personnel

**Figure 2.2**  Choosing logistics systems

capacity to test and implement new ideas, it is important that the right ones be chosen, and indeed any right choices represent many different but complementary steps in the same direction. This is the synergy of technological advance.

## Buy rather than make

Let us trace the way in which information technology affects the relationship with suppliers. In the first instance there is a need to make the whole business much quicker and much more flexible in its reactions. Many managers would concur in the view that businesses must become more nimble and focus on their internal distinctive competences – those things that must be done better or at least as well as competitors in the outside world. Establishing what the internal competencies are, in effect makes it possible to isolate other elements that can be done better by those outside the business. These are the things that should be bought in; where suppliers should be used. Taken together with the increasing emphasis upon out-of-house manufacture, the consquence is that purchasing's key role in make or buy is based upon the ability to evaluate the competencies of the supplier base versus in-house capability. As Terry Hogg of Nissan has said, the key purchasing task is finding world class suppliers who will complement the chosen in-house distinctive competencies. Giving this emphasis on the identification and assessment of suppliers and the negotiation of effective contracts, inevitably means the reappraisal of the department's priorities. The need to make an assessment of total supply capability, not just of quality and price but of flexibility and responsiveness and of strategic vision, is an exciting new concept. The purchasing manager is no longer the head of a service department but a business manager in an important part of the supply chain and this implies that traditional mind sets must be altered.

## Reappraising relationships with suppliers

It follows from the emphasis being placed upon the identification and selection of top class suppliers, that relationships with them must be long term. This is not just by virtue of the way in which they are selected, and the efforts involved, but also because of their relative scarcity. It is easy enough to say that long-term relationships are based upon win/win and upon the denial of an adversarial pattern, but precisely *how* this is implemented in practice is a different matter and it can well be that the mutual interest of partners in the supply chain is not incompatible with a degree of adversariality in the process of negotiation. Whilst it is true that the co-operative mode is now one that attracts a great deal of popular support, it must be based, if it is based upon anything at all, upon a realistic assessment of the commercial benefits derived by working together in terms of penetration of the end market. Anything else is an unrealistic way in which to conduct a business relationship. It is the practicalities of mutual advantage that are the foundation of the buyer/supplier contract, not some idealistic vision of what the market-place or the world should really be like.

If the adoption of an overall strategy of the supply chain is based upon long-term partnership, then there is no requirement for a multitude of suppliers of the same component. Multiple suppliers do not guarantee either insurance or safety, and the idea that they do so no longer commands widespread acceptance. In consequence there is inevitably a rationalisation of the supply base and a recognition that along the whole of the supply chain, basic customer wants are virtually identical. As a minimum these consist of the supply to time of high quality reliable products that can be used with confidence and with minimum expense. Everything must be allied to the ability to match what may be highly volatile consumer market demands. This fundamental reappraisal of relationships – this rationalisation – hinges upon one essential factor; the ability to develop an appropriate interchange of information. The key distinguishing element in the integrated supply chain, particularly with a global perspective, is that there is both a willingness and an ability for each customer to give its suppliers real time access to the supply chain programme. This has been described as 'the one critical test of the new purchasing relationship with suppliers'. In order to establish this new relationship there must be a high degree of mutual confidence; indeed there must be a high degree of trust. To establish this throughout the whole supply chain is the most difficult of all the aspects of the new approach. In order to achieve such a free flow of information, not only must relationships be placed on a quite different plane, but systems must be integrated and those obstacles placed by customers upon the better performance of their suppliers (frequently unwittingly) be removed. It is upon these foundations that, ultimately, a consumer driven supply chain is constructed. Without them the whole of the approach will fail.

● New management focuses

The last of the major factors that impinge upon the relationship between corporate strategy and the policies pursued by the purchasing function, may be deemed new management focuses. In particular it is necessary that management have a much clearer understanding than in the past of the significance of the total value added chain and of the various linkages within it.

## Value added

It is generally accepted that there is no single objective or measure of performance with which the merits or otherwise of a company can be assessed. Hence traditional approaches such as return on investment, earnings per share, dividend policy and returns per employee involved, are now reinforced by the concept of value added. Over the long term, the success of a company and its ability to develop and expand, rests upon the degree to which value is added and the way in which it is added. Added value is the means of paying wages and salaries to employees, dividends to shareholders, and of funding new assets and R & D programmes. Every company operates within a particular market structure, which determines both the nature and size of fixed investment. This structure also determines the extent to which outside purchase is important. Additionally, markets vary in the degree to which they are volatile or subject to long-term change. Management therefore needs to be adaptable in its approach both to corporate strategy and to the resultant organisational patterns.

Added value may be determined by subtracting from gross income the sum of bought out materials and services. The three key components of analysis are therefore gross income, added value and profit before tax. The ratio of added value to gross income is an important measure of the effectiveness of a company's operations. It reflects both the company's success in terms of volume and margins in the market-place, and also the impact of make or buy decisions on supply strategies. The nature of the end market will have a significant bearing upon the components of supply chain, and therefore dictates the precise division of added value between the company and those who supply it. This is why added value for any particular segment of industry, when related to gross income, may be expected to fall within fairly closely defined bands. Over the last few years in the United Kingdom, the added value to gross income ratio has changed significantly, with added value decreasing as companies reassess their make or buy policy. The movement towards out-of-house manufacture has indeed been the most potent force affecting the added value situation, and affords a means of comparing the overall impact or implementation of make or buy policies between a company and its principal competitors (see **Fig. 2.3**).

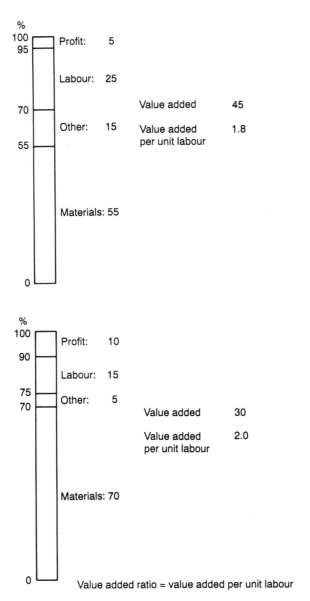

**Figure 2.3** Manufacture out of house: improving the Value Added ratio

Businesses have a choice between seeking to generate margins either at the point of sale or internally within the supply chain. The two are, of course, not mutually exclusive. A company that seeks to develop its margin at the ultimate point of sale normally does so on the basis of a differentiation strategy. Where a product or service is perceived as having unique qualities, the competitive intensity of the market is likely to be much diminished. The company rather than the market-place therefore, is the dominant influence upon the margin and added value. It can dictate prices to its customers and to its sales outlets. Other companies (and Marks and Spencer is frequently quoted as a prime example) seek to establish very high standards of supplier performance and operate a firm control over the purchase portfolio. They are in a position to dictate the margins that are acceptable from that supplier. Faced by falling sales and by the Benetton factor, Marks and Spencer sought to meet the challenge by a reduction in suppliers' margin. The balance of leverage meant that this could be dictated, and that suppliers unable to squeeze costs from their own value added chain inevitably suffered reduced profits. This combination of market situation and a supply chain dominated by the principal manufacturer determines purchase strategy in a manner clearly predicted by the purchase portfolio matrix. Leverage quadrant relationships of this type, however, are far from being the norm since most companies do not have a major advantage either within the supply chain or at the point of sale. The surpluses that they can generate depends to a large extent upon the creation of market niches and of purchase strategies appropriate to this situation.

Where companies primarily depend upon their ability to dominate their end user market, the most important value added ratio is that of profit before tax to gross income. Companies that can command figures in excess of 10% on this scale may frequently have a very strong market presence. Should the figures approach, say, 25% or more, then market dominance is indicated, raising the spectre of legislative intervention to prevent the emergence of a monopoly.

Finally, the amount of leverage possessed by a purchasing organisation is reflected by the ratio of profit before tax to the value added percentage. With the trend to manufacture out of house, comes a lower added value percentage but not necessarily lower profit! The higher the proportion of this value added percentage that becomes profit before tax, the stronger the firm is in terms of determining its own ability to generate value added as opposed to depending on its suppliers and upon their inherent effectiveness or productivity. Ratios of 20% + would indicate front runner status demonstrating either a high influence in the supply market and/or an ability to make the running in terms of the end user market.

The ratio of added value to gross income is the key statistic in terms of the make/buy decision. As more and more items move out of house and become the subject of purchase action, so the added value figure will fall. In consequence it cannot be concluded that the effectiveness of any organisation can be judged simply by the size of this figure. The decision to make or buy becomes increasingly important and it is in this regard that value added analysis can do a great deal to help in the formulation of corporate policy. It enables one to distinguish between those product costs that are produced or controlled by the company and those that are provided by others outside of the company's immediate control. It is possible by using this technique to assess the effect of widely different strategies, varying from those of total assembly to those where an organisation will decide to develop a high degree of competence in some narrow niche and themselves generate a significant number of high value added components. It is upon purchase that the basic impact of a *buy* rather than a *make* decision falls. The longer-term

- **Table 2.2**
  Value chain: steel

| | 1956 | | | |
|---|---|---|---|---|
| | *Japan* | | *USA* | |
| *Purchased inputs* | | | | |
| Coke | 35 | | 13 | |
| Energy | 15 | | 10 | |
| Scrap | 50 | | 18 | |
| Ore | 20 | | 15 | |
| | | 93 | | 56 |
| Capital | 40 | | 15 | |
| Operating labour | 20 | | 52 | |
| Profit | 4 | | 2 | |
| | | 64 | | 69 |
| Transport | 35 | | – | |
| *Total* | | 192 | | 125 |

| | 1976 | | | |
|---|---|---|---|---|
| | *Japan* | | *USA* | |
| *Purchased inputs* | | | | |
| Coke | 47 | | 52 | |
| Energy | 25 | | 35 | |
| Scrap | 20 | | 25 | |
| Ore | 20 | | 40 | |
| | | 112 | | 151 |
| Capital | 66 | | 55 | |
| Operating labour | 50 | | 147 | |
| Profit | 4 | | 1 | |
| | | 120 | | 203 |
| Transport | 36 | | – | |
| *Total* | | 268 | | 354 |

consequence is to impel purchase towards the strategic mode, and no management should make the conscious decision to place more of the value added outside the organisation without reflecting upon the implications for the purchase function.

Value added is a valuable internal tool, but it is equally useful in providing an early comparative study between the American and Japanese steel industries (see **Table 2.2**). The importance of this approach to the value chain is that it is extended beyond the confines of the company itself into the wider supply chain. The period shown covers the revival of Japan as a major competitor to western economies. The dollar analysis shows how, over the years in question, the American cost advantage of $67 per metric ton turned into a Japanese advantage of $86. This is a swing of $153 or more than the total US cost in 1956. The chain analysis indicates the areas in which major differences have occurred and it will be observed that the Japanese advantage has been gained notwithstanding significant transport costs. A similar advantage in the field of consumer products can be seen in **Fig. 2.4** which demonstrates areas

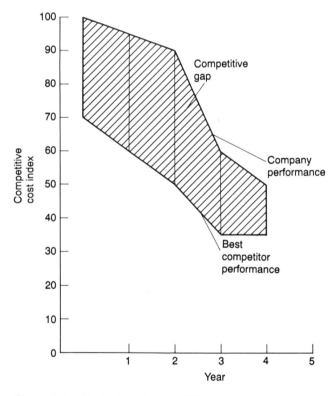

**Figure 2.4**  Product cost competitive gap

of cost leverage in the automotive industry. This example of a value chain is a precursor to the kind of logistic analysis that is now done by companies such as Cerestar. The ability to drive down the wider costs inherent in the supply chain is an important element in increasing value added and improving profit performance.

## Benchmarking

In the process of translating overall strategy into procurement or purchase strategy, a powerful tool that is widely used is that of benchmarking. Benchmarking is a means whereby company performance is related to external or other types of factor. As employed by organisations such as IBM or Rank Xerox, its basis is comparison with best of breed, but it is quite feasible to compare performance with other parts of the organisation. Benchmarking forms part of the process of setting standards, which will become the basis of a programme of continuous improvement. However, it is also a method whereby purchase strategies can be tailored to remedy some of those weaknesses that find expression in the value added chain. Amongst the most commonly used benchmarks are those identifying product cost competitive gaps (see **Fig. 2.4**), which use a competitive cost index to relate company performance of a particular product against that of the best competitor. It will be seen that whereas both companies are achieving a downward movement in their costs, there has been a significant narrowing of the gap between the two organisations. Over the last ten years the real costs of many consumer goods have been significantly driven down partly by improvement in firm efficiency but more notably by pressure upon the supply base. This is what is reflected in product cost strategies such as Nissan's negative pricing, based upon the premise that the cost gains from improved technology must be shared with the end user.

The inventory competitive gap (see **Fig. 2.5**) relates the inventories held to months' supply. This long established method is demand related, and is weakened only to the extent that the choice of number of months' supply held is often subjectively derived and makes insufficient use of modern service function and safety factor analysis. It may also fail to reflect sufficiently the fact that the advent of a highly responsive batch of one manufacturing technology can, by its effect upon lead times, impact to a major extent upon the time related component of risk.

A third benchmark consists of international comparison between a European electronics company and its Japanese parent. As will be seen, initially, in terms of parts per million of product produced in house, the Japanese parent enjoyed something of the order of a 20% advantage. By

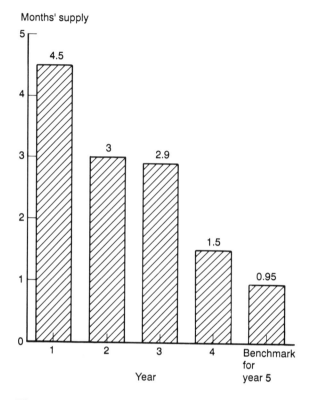

**Figure 2.5** Inventory competitive gap

1987 this relationship of Japanese parent and European offspring had been reversed, and for the first time the European company was enjoying a quality advantage in terms of this parameter (see **Fig. 2.6**). It is worth noting, of course, that in both cases significant improvement had been achieved over previous years, reflecting general quality improvement through more sophisticated approaches to process capability.

● Strategy and organisation

At the Cannes Purchasing Conference, Mike Friedman, managing director of Kepner-Tregoe UK Ltd presented to an audience of pur-chasing directors a view of management needs of the 1990s. This was based upon research into the 'Times 1000' and reflects the need to trans-late corporate strategies into operational measures. Amongst the key

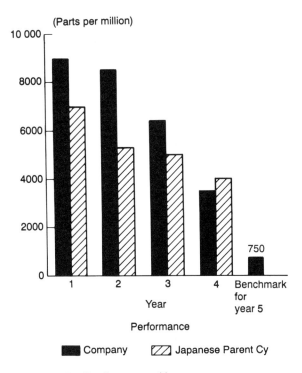

(Parts per million)

Performance

■ Company    ▨ Japanese Parent Cy

**Figure 2.6**  Quality competitive gap

points made was the need for management at all levels and in every function, not just in purchasing, to devote more time and effort to acquiring the skills that are necessary to implement an organisation's strategy. Friedman pointed out that, whilst the ability to generate a strategy was now well established as a process, nevertheless implementation was very different, and that frequently strategy could fail because of a lack of commitment or a lack of ownership. All business areas and functions need to identify a role that is consistent with the overall strategic vision. In the case of purchasing and logistics, the globalisation of the supply market has brought this function much closer to the centre stage in corporate terms. More often than in the past the success of an organisation is more closely related to its skills in the materials area. Hence organisational issues in purchase have today a wider corporate impact. All too frequently the organisational structures of purchase departments have been maintained, notwithstanding changes in the nature of the tasks placed upon them. It is essential that an organisation's structure correctly mirrors its strategic requirements and not the other way around. Too many of them fall into the trap of devising a new structure and then determining a strategy. In addition, a manager needs to acquire greater communication skills so that planning and operational functions can respond to the broader vision.

To a degree, this should be facilitated by the trend towards leaner and flatter organisations. This is a natural consequence of the current emphasis upon pushing responsibility and authority further down the organisation. The devolution of decision power leads to a need to develop those skills that can help to generate creativity, and that make possible the formulation of an environment in which risk taking is a natural and normal process. Rewards must be given and this applies as much to suppliers as it does in-house. The increasing emphasis upon partnership and trust necessarily means that fewer controls will be developed. Where such controls are needed, they should be devised upon a basis that reflects the fact that the tight/loose equation is of paramount importance. This means that management must determine which elements of the function are better centrally managed and which can be decentralised. This highlights one of the key dilemmas of the purchase situation. Historically, purchase departments tended to move towards centralised patterns. The danger of such patterns is that there is a lack of flexibility and commitment at the point of use. The contract between, on the one hand, the need for leverage and upon the other hand, flexibility, is a problem highlighted when strategic business unit models have been adopted. Centralising the commercial aspects of buying whilst devolving operational aspects of logistics, implies that certain elements must of necessity be subject to tighter control than others. Purchasing is not immune to issues varied by the management versus leadership question. As Mike Friedman pointed out:

> 'People don't want to be managed, but they do respect being led and one of the key issues in management development for the purchasing function is how to cultivate leadership skills and how to move away from the notion of centrally determined direction.'

The climate of win/win, usually applied externally along the supply chain, is capable of extension internally, thus minimising adversarial relationships. There is a need to give people greater satisfaction in their current jobs because the spread of the flat pyramid means that they will remain for a longer period of time in that job. The nature of career prospects has changed and as organisations become flatter, so the expectation of career moves is altered. A typical manager may, in the future for example, expect no more than two or three career moves as opposed to six or seven in the past. This does not obviate the fact that the question 'what about me?' must have a sensible answer and that this cannot be couched in conventional terms of promotion. The effect upon personal aspirations of the patterns that are established must be recognised, and alternative ways of both motivating and developing staff devised.

## ● Organisational issues

Mike Friedman of Kepner-Tregoe claimed that the view that organisational patterns could be devised largely independently of the strategy to be followed was surprisingly widespread. Denying the validity of this, he postulated that 'strategy precedes organisation'. This is particularly important in purchase where there is a striking lack of consensus regarding the way in which the function should be organised and where many fundamental problems have their origins in a failure to adapt or evolve. There is a need for much more explicit organisational study, recognising that at this interface both external and internal factors impact and interrelate.

There are three principal organisational issues that dominate the purchase scene. The first of these is what we may term the *organic question*. This is the determination of the appropriate mix between leverage and flexibility. It is organic since all purchase functions will tend to follow a similar pattern, which relates to the form and maturity of the host company. This pattern reflects phases in industrial growth and illustrates how, with expansion, the desire to capitalise upon purchase power leads to progressive centralisation. This continues up to the point at which the alleged remoteness of central purchase and, indeed, legitimate questions of logistics produce a call for greater powers to be vested in units (**Table. 2.3**). This may be termed mixed mode organisation and is reflected in the different levels at which contracts are negotiated or call offs made. The National Coal Board in 1960 (**Fig. 2.4**) was an early example of this successfully implemented in practice. Others were however less successful.

## ● Leverage and flexibility

This may be illustrated by reference to the aero engine industry where the acquisition by Rolls Royce of Bristol which in the 1960s was not followed by a determined effort to assimilate and integrate. As a result, almost 20 years later, purchase at Rolls Royce was essentially site-based, with purchase being found at Derby, Bristol, Leavesden, Barnoldswick

• **Table 2.3**
Developments in purchase organisation

| Stage | Type | Purchase organisation | Focus of purchase decision | Purchase role |
|---|---|---|---|---|
| I | Single Units | Diffused | Owner/managing director | Clerical: progressing: invoice payments |
| II | Multiple Units | Diffused but moving to centralisation | Board for key production items/property/promotional expenditure. Purchase department/manufacturing for other | Clerical with commercial overlay |
| III | Coherent Unit | Centralised | Purchasing in collaboration with users | Commercial |
| IV | Coherent Unit | Centralised | Move towards functional integration | Strategic: make or buy |
| | *or* | | Local control of some logistics | |
| | SBUs | Decentralised | Board | Commercial: clerical |

and Glasgow. There was relatively little corporate presence and it required major reforms to bring about the necessary structural changes with the organisational theme changing to a commodity focus and a much strengthened central focus.

At almost the same time, the question of devolution to factory units was gripping purchase at Boots, the manufacturing chemists and retailers. Pharmaceutical purchase in Boots was strong in its commercial orientation with internally-set cost targets providing the benchmarks for achievement. The requisition and order scheme produced what was perceived by internal customers as a heavy administrative burden. Departmental lead times were of the order of 14 days, and to shorten this and to give greater flexibility and lower inventories, a two-tier system was introduced in 1989. Local control over quantities, delivery and expediting was vested in user factories, which enabled pharmaceutical purchasing to concentrate more on price. In an industry where substantial price elasticity of demand exists in the end market, this refocusing represented a recognition of the fact that purchase must concentrate on its prime tasks, i.e. those most directly impinging upon competitive advantage, devolving as appropriate in otter to achieve this end.

## Purchasing and logistics

The second issue, that of *purchase and logistics*, is frequently related to size and has many of the superficial characteristics displayed in the centralisation question. As long ago as the late 1950s the then National Coal Board (see **Table 2.4**) evolved a flexible response to the question, with differing levels of contract negotiation affording greater responsiveness through local call-off. Purchasing, logistics and the physical storage and transportation of goods all fell under the same authority and this remains a widespread pattern. However, the sheer volumes of transactions may prove to be a burdensome distraction from more proactive buying, and one can see a move towards greater freedom to manage the purchase portfolio, based upon freeing the function from the great weight of day-to-day call-off and progressing activity.

*The case for separation*

At a meeting of the 1989 MCE Advisory Comittee on Purchasing, Jeremy Handley, purchasing manager for Procter & Gamble (Europe), remarked that the purchasing department in his organisation was now only about one sixth of the size that it had been at the beginning of the

- **Table 2.4**
  National Coal Board: 1960

|          | Contracting level                                                                      | Call-off                                                                                             |
| -------- | -------------------------------------------------------------------------------------- | --------------------------------------------------------------------------------------------------- |
| National | Mandatory contracts (PCNS), usually variable quantities at fixed price from specified sources |                                                                                                     |
| Division | Mandatory contracts with fixed or variable quantities at fixed prices                   |                                                                                                     |
| Area     | Local orders                                                                            | Call off to area central stores against national and divisional contracts                           |
| Colliery |                                                                                        | Call off against national and divisional contracts<br>Receipts against area orders on central store |

The normal duration of divisional and national contracts was one year although, in some cases, six months was preferred

1980s. One of the ways in which this had come about was to reduce volume purchases by the use, for example, of frame contracts. It had also been brought about by getting out of order placing and expediting, and introducing systems of call-off. In other words, an attempt had been made to segregate the truly commercial aspects of purchasing from those concerned with the provision of supply of services or logistics.

It would not, however, be true to suggest that the movement towards separate purchase logistics is solely due to a desire to reduce volume impact on the purchase function. The logistics movement itself, although perhaps at times apparently uncertain as to its direction or method of development, has become a very powerful force, and has been recognised in many ways. For example, bodies such as the Institute of Purchasing and Supply, have set up logistics committees, and, recognising a perceived need for this aspect of the function, have sought to create a new and discrete identity.

In some major organisations, a movement has therefore developed, which sees purchasing logistics as separated from purchasing marketing. In the traditional organisation of a purchase department, grouped by commodities, a purchasing manager or buyer has responsibility for both commercial and logistics aspects. Amongst the advantages of this method is that accountability for the provision of goods or services to the customer clearly rests with one individual or one section. Where a department has horizontal divisions, and the stores function has a separate identity, then in many ways the purchase function's impact upon the customer is coloured by the way in which that customer perceives service over the counter. This is certainly true, for example, in companies as renowned for their operations as ICI, and can, in some circumstances, act to the detriment of the purchase function. Therefore there is a good deal to be said for placing the full accountability for locating the needs of customer satisfaction with one individual. In this way, a section of the supply chain is integrated through an individual with expertise not just in the formation of supply relationships, but also in the negotiation of viable contracts, and in call-off and expediting. The individual therefore has responsibility through stock control for such matters as working capital.

Superficially, there are great attractions to this method, and over the years the approach has found widespread favour, not least because of the way in which it develops managerial responsibility. The Jeremy Handley argument, however, is that there are different forms of expertise needed for these differing aspects of supply, and that the purchasing professional's true role is in the location of appropriate suppliers and in the formation of business relationships, which will extract from the supplier the maximum of benefit.

Increasingly, volume and logistical complexity have meant that in many organisations this is the path that is now being systematically followed. The divison of purchasing into logistics and marketing has effectively reshaped the form of the purchase function. Purchase logistics has four major elements:

1. *Database management*, which has information regarding the whole of the supplier portfolio and the basis of purchase.
2. *Materials management.* Beginning with a material requirement plan, this covers, through ABC analysis, all aspects of inventory control including data links to operational management and including the need to manage not simply an active stock but also to dispose of rejected material. Delivery updates also fall within this area.
3. *The mechanics of the purchasing process.* This is order placing and the processing of order confirmation and discrepancy, the control of purchase delivery variances and the monitoring of prices.
4. Finally, under the heading 'special task', the *logistic connections to suppliers,* and where appropriate, *just-in-time* production programmes, *ship-to-line* programmes, and the establishment of *data links*. In addition the sales of *inactive inventory* fall within this area.

These are all elements that call for a high degree of systemisation but that have high volumes and are inevitably time intensive where rectification of failure becomes necessary. By in effect hiving off, space is generated for creative tasks within the commercial orbit.

Purchase marketing has three main aspects:

1. *research*;
2. the *reduction of cost*; and
3. the *management of essential interfaces*.

In the first place, market research is primarily concerned with the establishment of the availability of new items, and with the selection of new suppliers. Market situations must be evaluated and attempts made to establish the viability of individual suppliers. Where appropriate, requests for quotations or bids must be processed and the system of placing business carried through. The specific identification of these operations as a discrete area is a hallmark of sophistication in purchase, not least because of its budget implications. In Ford, for example, the work of this team has gained an enviable reputation which transcends the company's own boundaries.

The reduction of cost, the second major area, implies the negotiation of agreements and contracts and, where appropriate, the forecasting of material prices. Price negotiations and the measurement of purchase performance, one of the most difficult tasks, falls to this section. Finally, the management of interfaces should be considered. These involve analysis of competitive products and approval procedures for the purchase of new commodities and the development of new product lines. In these cases material costs must be estimated and quality management fully exercised. Building upon market research, the work of this section complements that of material cost reduction and impacts directly upon the perceptions of purchase's customers.

Whether or not it is appropriate to go down the road of segregating purchasing logistics and purchasing marketing depends upon the degree to which purchase focus is appropriate to corporate need. Departments that have or should have a strategic profile need to have the ability to squeeze benefit from more sophisticated supplier links. It is in order to achieve this that the logistic and commercial elements are defined. The order to delivery process typically accounts for at least 60–70% of total time available.

As T. Kowalski revealed at the Frankfurt Purchasing Conference (1988), Siemens in Germany had a total of 70,000 suppliers handled by 118 purchasing departments. An analysis carried out at three plants into the time devoted to the marketing as opposed to the logistics aspect of purchase produced the figures:

|         | Purchasing marketing | Purchasing logistics |
|---------|---------------------|---------------------|
| Plant 1 | 42%                 | 58%                 |
| Plant 2 | 27%                 | 73%                 |
| Plant 3 | 35%                 | 65%                 |

Purchasing marketing embraces supplier selection and evaluation, material cost reduction, quality management and material aspects of new products. Purchasing logistics included data-base management, order processing and materials management. It also covered special

● **Table 2.5**

Purchasing logistics and marketing

| Purchasing logistics | Purchasing marketing |
|---------------------|---------------------|
| Database management | Market research |
| Database | Selection of new suppliers |
| Supplier data | Trade show visits |
|  | Evaluation of market situation |
| Materials management | EIS (commodity code system) |
| Inventory control | Supplier evaluation |
| Material requirement plan | Processing of RFQ/bid |
| Disposition inactive stock |  |
| Disposition rejected material | Material cost reduction |
| ABC–analysis | Determination of purchasing success |
| Data link to operations management | (PPC) |
| Delinquent material | Organisation of purchasing committees |
| Daily delivery updates | Corporate agreements/contracts |
|  | Price negotiations |
| Order processing | ABC–analysis |
| Order placing/processing | Use of purchasing methods and tools |
| Purchase delivery variance control | Material price forecast |
| Processing of order confirmations, |  |
| discrepancy | Purchasing interface with accounting, |
| Monitoring prices | manufacturing, QA and R&D |
|  | Analysis of competitors' products |
| Special tasks | Quality management |
| Sales of inactive inventory stock | Approval procedures for new |
| Logistical connection to suppliers | commodities |
| Just-in-time production | Responsibilities for new product lines |
| Ship to line programs | Estimate of material costs for new |
| Data link to suppliers | product lines |
| Reduce no line items |  |

Source: Siemens, T Kowalski

projects, such as ship-to-line, the establishment of data links, and just-in-time.

The change from a purchase department organised by commodities with purchasing agents responsible for both purchase marketing and logistics, to one where these functions are divorced, is illustrated in **Table 2.5** and **Figs. 2.10** and **2.11**. It represents a major change in orientation, which is to be found in many other organisations, but which, in Siemens, is compounded by the sheer size of the purchase problem and the resultant volume of transactions.

*The case for integration*

So far the purchasing/logistics situation has been considered primarily from the point of view of achieving greater focus. In some industries, however, the emphasis would appear to be almost exactly the opposite, with a clearer supplier–manufacturer–distributor–consumer chain creating different demands. Rowntrees, the UK confectionery company, developed, during the late 1980s, a major impetus towards supply chain integration, which featured close linkage between purchasing and logistics. The case for doing this was argued by the purchasing director, Tom McCuffog, in the following terms:

> 'In the first place, companies fail to bring these two functions together in part because of the wide range of different interpretations of logistics. To too many people logistics is seen simply as goods out, whilst goods inward is purely a purchasing function. This is a very narrow interpretation, which fails to recognise that the whole of the supply chain, if more effectively integrated, can be managed with substantially greater added value. The integration of the supply chain is a logistics function, and purchasing should be an ally concerned primarily with effectively managing relationships with suppliers.
>
> The reasons why this becomes important is that in recent years customers have become more powerful, competitors more aggressive, and consumers more perceptive. An organisation that is multi-site, multi-product, multi-customer, with an operation supplying hundreds of different packs, using thousands of materials to seasonal markets both at home and abroad, has significant operating problems. It is always important to try and be right first time and to reduce lead times, but in this situation and in this environment, purchasing and logistics can add so very much more value. The logistics operation in this company was created in 1986 and combined with an existing purchasing operation.'

In Rowntree, objectives of the purchase function were defined as the development and management of the relationship between users and suppliers. Success was judged through the assessment of the quality of supply and the overall cost. Measurement focused on service levels, security of supply and the capital invested in stockholding. Satisfactory performance was perceived as being closely related to relationships with suppliers that were both secure and profitable. This implies the development of the logistics area and its new systems, so buyers could be relieved of volume problems and allowed to specialise in market analysis and concentrate through negotiation, upon a better understanding with suppliers.

'Pure' purchasing has three main aspects:

1. *Raw materials buying*. The essential characteristic of this area is the need to match with great skill, clearly defined specifications of what ingredients are needed to manufacture, with those that are actually available. The reason why this presents a major problem is that natural products vary from crop to crop and they can be sourced in a wide variety of current and future markets.
2. *Packaging purchasing*. Buying packaging is always a major area of operation, with those companies that interface directly with the consumer in the end market-place being a key element in competitive success. Confectionery requires packaging not simply in terms of product protection but also in promotional terms. The speed of change both in specification and design is very rapid indeed. It is normal to change at least once a year, and frequently the lead time available is very short. Rowntree saw the effective procurement of packaging items as one of the most critical activities in the company's supply chain. Quality, time and price are all important, with margins for error very small.
3. *Support stock*, both technical and clerical. These range from major purchases of plant and equipment to office supplies and other small value items. A characteristic of such areas is usually the wide variety of items and the size of the supply base. Frequently purchase can experience resistance from those users who consider themselves to be experts, perhaps even the sole experts, in determining what should be bought. Good internal customer relations here are all important.

In terms of logistics at Rowntree, this function was understood to be 'the development of a systematic understanding of the operation of the total business'. To achieve this it is necessary to work closely with other functions and improve overall operation by better integration. Logistics embraces the management of the total supply chain from initial suppliers to end customers, balancing supply and demand, and, at the same time, optimising all costs including working capital.

Like purchase, logistics falls into three principal areas. The first, *logistics development*, relates to the activities of the supply chain; for example, the development and implementation of systems and procedures. Good systems improve supply chain resource productivity whilst optimising customer service. They bring together all functions and encourage inter-functional co-operation, using information technology as a primary tool. The wide availability of common data with underlying assumptions fully exposed, is a cohesive force of great power. It is a characteristic of all organisations that·view supply chain management as a major competitive weapon.

The second area of logistics is *operational research*, a descriptive term largely bereft of the aura which surrounded it in the 1950s and 1960s. Supply chains and logistic trade-offs lend themselves to the development of models, for purposes of simulation.

The Rowntree model is based upon the sales and despatch plan examined for feasibility, and identifies any area of conflict that could produce a reduction in overall productivity or customer service. It is then translated into a production and a purchasing plan for each product and for type of material. Operational plans are generated for each link in the supply chain. This specifically includes the control and administration of the pack development process. New packs are a product of a rapidly changing market environment. This places demands for increasing numbers of specially designed packs with lead times that are getting much shorter. Development demands flexibility and speed in order to give trade customers exactly what they require. All consumer areas share this requirement; a requirement exacerbated by the increasing importance of special promotions in marketing terms. Hence the availability of special materials for packs is described as *the* critical element in the manufacturers' supply chain. If such packaging is late, then production efficiency is diminished and the market-place suffers. There must be speed and flexibility, in spite of a world-wide trend towards increasingly complex labelling legislation. In Europe, the increasing flow of directives and regulations means that the systems that were used in the 1960s, 1970s and 1980s for developing new packaging, no longer work effectively. This can adversely affect customer services and lead to loss of sales. Logistics in consumables is therefore increasingly concerned with generating pack specifications, using computer aided design technology to enhance the creative process and speed up the production of artwork. Once this process has been completed, and the revised design meets the original pack specification, purchasing must obtain the materials required. All these activities require a system, documentation and a means of tracking progress. Good logistics eliminates the late delivery of new material, reduces pack development cost, and significantly impacts upon the lead time between requirement and delivery.

The third area of logistics is *storage*. Together with stock in transit, this is where the heaviest demands upon working capital are made. Logistics determines requirements and movements, and can, through good planning, scheduling and tracking, reduce selling costs by anything up to 20%

This then represents the alternative puchase/logistic scenario. The two key factors are the extent to which integration of the supply chain is a major competitive factor and the way in which organisational development can best be facilitated. Customer demand requires a total view of service. Equally, as purchasing moves away from the transactions mode into the commercial and strategic modes, so the demands upon purchase time and the skills needed, change. The greater the emphasis upon supplier selection and upon negotiation, the greater the need to create space by systematising logistics. It is clear that both elements need to be satisfied and that what may appear at first sight to be divergent paths are, in fact, complementary. In the first instance, volume and time intensive elements are filtered out. As purchase enters the strategic mode, supply chain management demands integration rather than being seen as a series of discontinuities. Developed separately, purchase and logistics then re-emerge to form a coherent whole.

*Functional integration: procurement engineering in operation*

It is paradoxical that in the smallest firms, the very absence of specialists leads to the very integration of functions that has only, in recent years, become a feature of large sophisticated organisations. In the latter, the bringing together of teams comprising design, manufacture, marketing and purchase has become a standard response to increasing competition. Frequently called procurement engineering teams, they have as their *raison d'être* the need to ensure that new products are produced with all dimensions – operational and commercial as well as design – adequately covered. This reduces lead time from concept to product launch, and is a key competitive factor. Additionally, from a narrower purchase viewpoint, the shortening of product life cycles so reduces the window for the delivery of materials that sourcing decisions must be taken as early as possible in the design stage.

### Developing new products

The traditional approach in the west towards new product development has sometimes been typified as a relay race. A clear pattern, whereby functional specialists each perform particular aspects of the task and then pass the baton on to the next group, has frequently been the norm. Indeed, this sequential approach has for many years been virtually enshrined within the international motor industry as a standard method of attacking the problem.

Among the consequences of this method of working has been extended development cycles. For example, in Detroit at the present time, it is difficult for a new model to be taken up to the stage of manufacture in much less than five years. The comparable Japanese figure might be three and a half years. If we look at earth moving equipment, western companies might typically find that a new piece of equipment will require three and a half years to bring to product launch whereas major competitors in Japan, such as Kawasaki, would address the same problem in a little more than two years. The overriding need is for speed and flexibility in development. Often in western companies, the various functional areas suffer from a very formalised relationship and at worst there can be both mutual incomprehension and mistrust. Delays in the passage of items along the chain can frequently occur and any major problem can mean a recycling to an earlier part of that process.

The methods pioneered in Japan and used in different forms now by many western companies, are to adopt an approach based upon a hand picked and multi-disciplinary team. The members of the team work together from start to finish of the development process and often enjoy a high degree of autonomy, which gives an extreme flexibility. Different stages can be overlapped or even combined and, as appropriate, suppliers are brought into the process. Project teams of this type include marketing, industrial engineers and manufacturing, and purchasing, together with the outside representatives. In recent years this area has attracted more attention in the project field than any other. Companies as diverse as Nutricia in the food market, Dun and Bradstreet in information, Schlumberger in services to oil, Apple in computers and Dantek in scanning equipment, have all focused upon the project team approach as a better answer to development problems than previous methods based upon co-ordinators or departmental leadership. Ever

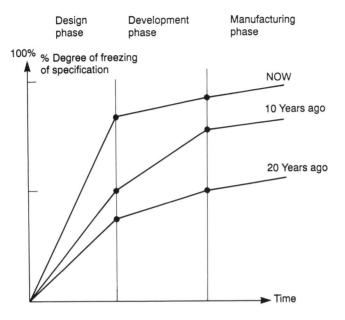

**Figure 2.7** Purchase freedom: influence on design

present has been the example of Far Eastern rivals, like Epson, who claim that their success has been due to the adoption of the so-called rugby tactic of 'scrum and scramble'.

In purchase terms, the first implication of procurement engineering is that it becomes possible to place the opinions of manufacturing, design and marketing in a commercial context. In terms of the influence on design, there have been, over the last 20 years, marked changes in the percentage degree of freezing of specification (see **Fig. 2.7**). In the electronics industry, for example, whereas in 1970 barely 40% of product design was frozen at the end of the concept stage, today that figure is something like 80%, and by the time the development phase is finished, less than 10% of all purchase decisions will remain to be taken. If purchasing is not involved at this stage then a number of dangers arise. The first is that design may easily be tempted to lock into a particular supplier, for technical reasons, without sufficient regard to the commercial implications. Purchase must evaluate the commercial result of adopting any one particular supplier or course of action.

To do this purchasing must have an indepth knowledge of the supply market. It must be able to identify the number of suppliers who are available at any given level of technology and to assess the competitive intensity of the market (see **Fig. 2.8**). Purchase must be aware of the activities of the competitors in their market and of the specific

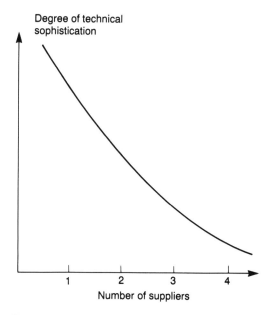

**Figure 2.8**  Purchase freedom: number of suppliers

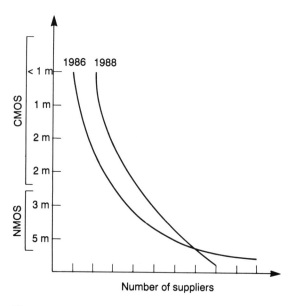

**Figure 2.9**  Purchase freedom: competition
Source: Bell Alcatel

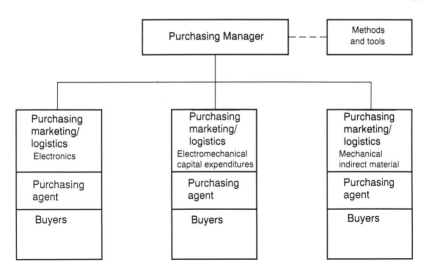

**Figure 2.10** Organisation of a purchasing department grouped by commodities

competences of the suppliers concerned (see **Fig. 2.9**). An evaluation of the number of suppliers at different levels of technology made by Bell Telephone in 1986 was projected forward two years. Upon the basis of this projection a further attempt can be made to identify the cost implications of different approaches. Time margins illustrate the impact of the development of new technologies (see **Fig. 2.12**). At the time of design

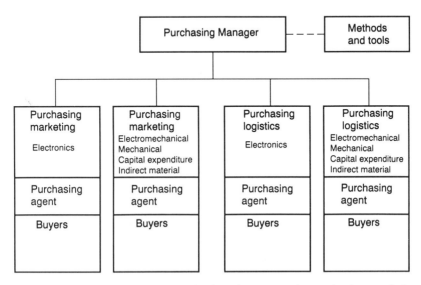

**Figure 2.11** Organisation of a purchasing department in purchasing marketing and purchasing logistics

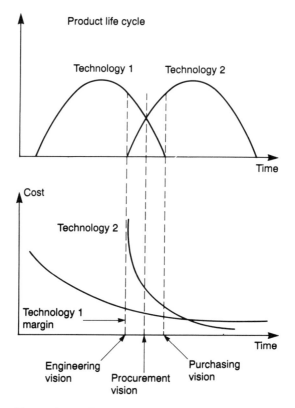

**Figure 2.12** Time margin

– the engineering vision stage – the new technology, through its innovation, offers major market advantages but is significantly more expensive than the existing approach. The essential feature is the relationship
of product life cycles, technologies 1 and 2, with the learning curve or
experience curve attributable to each product. At the time of placing
business, the second technology remains more expensive but the gap
between the two is closing, with the result that soon after orders are
placed the two technologies are equal in cost but offering significantly
different levels of advantage. The key element is the accuracy with
which future cost levels may be predicted. The precise relationship of
two cost curves is clearly crucial and if it should be that a wrong assessment is made by purchase, extremely serious consquences could result.
It is well known that in the development of the RB211 engine by
Rolls Royce in the 1960s, the fixing of a selling price to the Lockheed
Corporation made assumptions regarding not only technology in
respect of carbon fibre blades but with regard to the cost component in
the engine. A combination of major error in cost prediction and a fixed

end market price can be a devastating mixture. In areas of supply or price volatility – DRAMS for example – risk factors are self-evidently high. The importance of good market intelligence cannot be overemphasised. Visits to suppliers, meetings with representatives and discussions with buyers from other firms, all offer opportunities for soft data collection. This should be systematically sifted to give an edge to forecasting that cannot be gained simply from more widely available data.

To enter upon procurement engineering is to make new demands upon purchase. New questions arise, which call for a more rounded approach, questions such as: will the commercial benefits of innovatory design be sufficient in the customer's view to offset the extra costs involved?; at what point should one make decisions in terms of the design cycle?; is it better to wait until development has occurred and there has been progress on the cost learning curve, or are the dangers of losing competitive advantage too great?

The purchase contribution is to add market knowledge to the technical dimension, ensuring that new concepts or innovations are not compromised through ignorance of the commercial scene.

● The centralisation issue: an illustrative case

The centralisation issue in purchase is rarely what it seems. Even more rarely is it a simple question of commercial advantage being balanced against user service and flexibility. Extraneous factors such as territoriality and fashion almost always impinge. The latter should, incidentally, not be dismissed lightly as a formative influence, nor the former disregarded as an irrelevance. Centralisation is indeed frequently only the symptom and the symbol of wider issues, and when it surfaces it is often because of the existence of deeper tensions within the organisation.

In commercial terms the case for uplifting purchase has varied little in the last 20 years. External competitive pressures may be stronger but the forceful power of quantity buying, with its corollaries of standardisation and rationalisation, remains.

It is for these questions of purchase organisation that outside consultants can often be of major assistance. The ability to compare different companies through experience, and to have a more detached view, are important advantages. Typically it is the relationship between the demands of local manufacturing units, regional or product groupings and central purchasing that is the cardinal issue. Such a situation arose in the late 1980s in one of Western Europe's major packaging companies, partially as a result of plans for corporate reorientation and partly because of a view amongst senior managers that development in purchase was lagging behind changes both in the market-place and in manufacturing.

The group had acquired some 30 manufacturing sites, and role confusion between these and central purchasing was growing. The principal factors bearing upon the role of purchase were seen to be:

- The environments in which the business operates.
- The company's strategic objectives.
- The appropriateness of the structure to the objectives and environment.
- Relationships, means for resolving conflict, and integrating mechanisms, rewards and motivation.

An initial assessment showed that both buyers and internal customers saw the main elements constraining overall company buying performance as:

- Role confusion between centre and local buying.
- Insufficient co-ordination when dealing with suppliers.
- Fragmented pattern of professional buying skill and experience.
- No clear objectives or performance measures for buying department.
- A need for improved communications between user and central buying.
- Not enough time spent on purchasing research.
- A lack of co-ordinated computer systems.

Whilst no priorities are indicated within this listing, all are found to a degree in major companies, particularly those that are well established in mature sectors of manufacturing.

As a second stage in the evaluation, workloads were assessed, a common step in this type of approach. Detailed analysis of the outputs of the existing central buyers organisation revealed the following breakdown of tasks:

| | |
|---|---|
| Routine and clerical tasks | 55% |
| Non-routine and creative | 33% |
| Other work | 12% |

This breakdown may be related to the focus of purchase effort that, in general terms, should be commercial for this type of company. There was a clear indication here of a lack of organisational development, and at first sight a review of systems with a view to reducing the proportion of time spent on routine or clerical work seemed necessary.

Alternatively, devolution of the routine and clerical tasks such as material scheduling, order placing and progressing to the divisions would have been feasible since, including the 30 staff involved in the central buying function, the company has about 140 staff covering the purchasing functions (excluding stores) in the UK. Considerable scope for improvement in local purchasing procedures was indicated by a wide variation in the costs per order placed, and the fact that 47% of the invoices processed had a face value of less than £100.

A range of options in terms of purchase levels was considered. These were assessed in the context of the company's strategic objectives and operating environment and ranked in preference order, based upon 'best fit'. The possibilities appeared to be:

- Decentralisation linked with a corporate buying co-ordination role.
- Complete decentralisation to business.
- Retain existing core buying tasks, but with a wider coverage of key purchase spend, devolve all routine and clerical tasks.
- Retain existing core buying tasks, devolve all routine and clerical tasks.
- Existing central buying organisations.

A prime objective of the review was to inform management in order to facilitate choice in this area.


## A profile of the purchase department

In order to give some perspective to this review, the principal characteristics of the department as then existing may be considered.

Purchases of raw materials and consumables, and external charges for services, accounted for 70% of net operating costs of over £1 billion. With an additional £50 million of capital spend, the department's financial contribution in percentage terms was higher than would normally be found in this type of company and was not reflected either in focus or in terms of apparent professionalism.

The geographical locus of purchasing control resulted from evolution over time rather than from conscious decisions.

The broad split of:

| | |
|---|---:|
| Central buying | 46 |
| Local (UK) | 13 |
| Local (overseas) | 12 |
| Independent buyers | 29 |
| Total | 100 |

disguised the fact that:

- Four packaging suppliers accounted for 79% of the purchase value and central buying only negotiated with two of these.
- 64.5% of suppliers (6,580) accounted for 1.1% of purchase value, most served one user factory and a dual accounting system was used for control of invoices. Both these factors were revealed by a straightforward pareto analysis, at one and the same time the most frequently used order/invoice assessment technique and in many cases the most useful.
- There was a fragmented understanding of corporate and buying function objectives; an aspect common to the majority of buying organisations, even in some major corporations.

Over eight years the buying function organisation structure had gone through a range of changes from corporate to group type, then divisional, and arrived back (albeit with far fewer people) at a corporate style of structure located within a division.

Computerisation had been introduced in purchase to a limited degree and no great scope existed for expansion within the department, but benefits could accrue if other computer applications were better co-ordinated.

## Relating purchase to the business environment

Each of the manufacturing divisions that the central buying department served had different products, markets, operational profiles and buying needs.

1. In the highly automated volume division, there was strong competition and overcapacity across Europe. Raw materials were key purchases with a need to buy more cheaply than the competition, to use volume to gain advantage and get protection on foreign exchange purchases.

2. The second division, based upon food products, enjoyed a strong market position in the home industry. A wide range of products, made at 11 factories, was produced in small batches, albeit with a high degree of automation. As a major main user of tinplate, this division had a direct interest in negotiations for this commodity in a difficult, virtually monopolistic, supply market.

3. The division that was concerned with non-specific products served a highly fragmented market, with overcapacity and aggressive pricing in many sectors. Factories at 15 locations served different market sectors making in small batches, with a much higher labour content than the other divisions. Although a significant user of all of the key raw materials, the number of locations, different specifications and relatively small batch sizes placed demands on central buying for considerable co-ordination to get the best deal from suppliers on a company-wide basis.

4. The international division covered activities outside Europe. Central buying acted as procurement agents for key materials, but with African markets prone to economic problems, it was necessary in the interests of being competitive to obtain raw materials at prices at least 20% below the developed countries average producer prices.

On a company-wide basis, a number of other factors in the operating environment needed to be considered. These elements would find reflection across many other firms and included:

- Raw materials, consumables and external charges for services accounted for approximately 70% of the total operating costs.
- Some key materials such as tinplate and aluminium were provided by one or two powerful suppliers, posing a fundamental question regarding leverage best addressed, not through the powerful yet relatively unsophisticated pareto approach, but by the use of purchase portfolio analysis.
- Suppliers took advantage of being able to make contact at factory level, division level and centrally.
- Over a period of six years, the workforce had been dramatically reduced at all levels and in all parts of the company, including buying.

## Strategic objectives as a yardstick

A major yardstick against which the appropriateness of a purchase organisation needs to be measured is the company's strategic obectives. Ideally the organisation should be a good 'fit' with these objectives.

Generally, five items have direct relevance to buying. In this particular case, these were:

1. *Profitability*, expressed as growth in earnings per share.
2. *Market position*, having four key aspects expressed as an intention to:
   - continue to raise the level of product quality and service;
   - concentrate on strengthening the core businesses;
   - increase relative market share in areas of profitable future growth; and
   - rebalance the international portfolio of activities by means of further expansion in Europe and the USA.
3. *Innovation*, through investment in R & D programmes to ensure that the company was in the forefront of innovation and engineering in its chosen fields.
4. *Productivity*, continually seek to improve production use of physical, material and financial resources.
5. *Human resource, organisation and motivation*, to develop, motivate and retain the people needed to achieve the company's long-term objectives and to develop a more market oriented organisation structure.

*Central buying outputs*

The examination of the environment and the relationship of purchase to corporate strategic objectives provided the basic yardsticks against which comparisons could be made. Buying outputs were the next step. With the assistance of the key staff in the buying department, principal outputs were defined for each of the sections within central buying, and the man years and costs allocated against each output. The key staff then made an evaluation of the value of each output; whether it was fundamental to the business or discretionary, how long it would be before damage would be suffered if the output were stopped, who was the principal user of the output, and whether they had identified any improvement potential related to the outputs.

A summary was made of the efforts related to the main outputs in central buying as shown in **Table 2.6**.

The non-routine and creative tasks that had a major influence on total purchase expenditure accounted for 32.55% of the man years, while 55.36% of the time was spent on routine and clerical tasks. For the type of industry in question and, more specifically, having regard to the company's strategic objectives, these proportions raised the issue of whether central buying should concentrate on the more influential tasks and devolve the routine and clerical tasks to the divisions or factories.

- **Table 2.6**

  Main outputs in central buying

  | Routine and clerical tasks | % Total |
  | --- | --- |
  | − Material scheduling and inventory work | 4.95 |
  | − Order placing and progressing | 21.63 |
  | − Invoice checking and administration leasing service | 5.73 |
  | − Recording and filing | 2.16 |
  | − Preparation of statistics (vendor rating) | 7.53 |
  | − Shipping and transport | 12.36 |
  | − Disposal and scrap | 1.00 |
  | Sub-total | 55.36 |
  | − Strategic planning | 2.81 |
  | − Supplier selection | 3.40 |
  | − Purchase research | 7.60 |
  | − Negotiation of contracts, price, claims, funding | 18.57 |
  | − Disposal of surplus machinery | 0.17 |
  | Sub-total | 32.55 |
  | Other work | % Total |
  | − Management control | 2.09 |
  | − Secretarial | 10.00 |
  | Sub-total | 12.09 |

This is the kind of problem that is frequently highlighted by organisational analysis and reflects the change in purchase to being a more strategic and proactive function.

*User survey*

Post Crosby, user perceptions have become much more important as a barometer. The managing directors were asked to assess the outputs for central buying from the following aspects:

- Those outputs that they considered would be most appropriate to continue to be provided centrally.
- Those outputs that they considered should clearly be devolved to the divisions.
- Those outputs that did not fall clearly into either of the two categories above.

A wide variety of views were held about the central versus development issue, although it would be unusual in this type of case to find unqualified or even substantial support for central purchasing. However, there was some common ground between all of the user executives. They all considered that the material scheduling, placement of orders and progressing, invoice checking and recording outputs related to major raw materials should be devolved to the divisions.

On the other hand it was felt that non-routine and creative tasks, which had a major influence on total purchasing, expenditure (such as purchase research) negotiations of contracts, and strategic planning related to purchasing, should be retained at the centre.

This view was by no means universally accepted, with at least one powerful voice arguing that, with only a few exceptions, all the central buying outputs should be devolved to the divisions or contracted out. It was alleged that this would provide a closer match with the corporate objectives of achieving clear delegation of accountability and authority for achieving results to each managing director. This argument for local enhancement was coupled with a call for a much tougher line with suppliers on quality and for a simpler complaints procedure. This contains more than a hint of paradox, since here is an issue where one central channel embodying full leverage would have a clear advantage.

*Factory buying survey*

Calls for devolution inevitably posed the question 'devolution to what?'. This highlighted the need to examine more closely the numbers of people involved in the purchasing functions in the factories, to enable an assessment to be made of the balance of workload between the centre and the factories and of factory capabilities. In addition, the possibility of further devolvement from the centre created a need for more information about the factory purchasing functions. This included the purchasing systems in use, the numbers of personnel in the buying and stores areas, the value of purchases, the numbers of orders placed, the invoices processed and the activities undertaken.

Needless to say, the location and level of the buying function within each factory varied considerably. In some cases a designated buying post existed, in others it did not. In most cases, the person directly involved in the purchasing functions operated at two to three levels below the factory manager.

It was estimated that in addition to the 85 designated buying function posts, a further 25 man years of purchasing work were carried out by other posts such as stores, accounts, etc.

In all, 140 staff covered the purchasing functions. Much of their actual work was routine, calling for knowledge of basic procedures but not necessarily the buying expertise associated with supply.

## Market knowledge and negotiation skills

Much of the buying function work consisted of placing and progressing orders and checking invoices. As a measure of operating efficiency, the

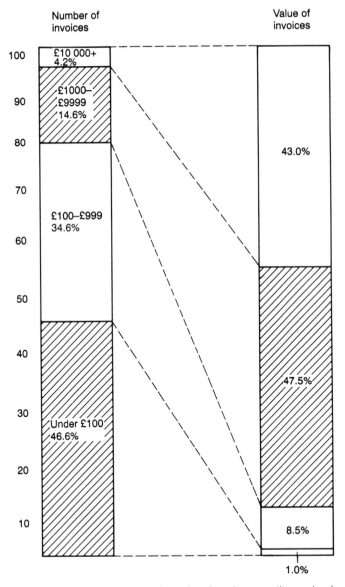

**Figure 2.13** Analysis of purchase invoices by quantity and value

cost of orders placed using a value of £12,000 per head was on average £6.32, but there was a range between factories from £1.19 up to £17.14.

The pareto distribution of invoices was skewed. A breakdown was made of 28,000 invoices processed, valued at £47 million (see **Fig. 2.13**). The outstanding feature of this analysis was that 47% of the invoices were for values of less than £100 and that in total they only accounted for 1% of the value of invoices. Even more significant was the fact that 5,400 of the invoices (or 19% of the total) were for values of less than £25. This clearly indicated the dangers of moving away from well-established centralisation to factory buying without first making a detailed review of the factories buying operational efficiency. Hence the clear conclusion was that the operational policy in a number of areas needed to be reviewed. These areas included setting guidelines on economic order quantities, use of local monthly accounts for areas such as engineering suppliers, and greater delegation for payment of invoices. In total it reinforced the view, identified by users in the initial broad reviews, of a fragmented pattern of professional buying skills and experience.

Where visits to factories were made, the following features emerged:

- That the routine work of placement of orders, progressing, invoice checking, and maintenance of records accounted for about 70% of the factories' purchasing workload in comparison with 29% at the centre. The conclusion to be drawn was that the numbers of orders processed was closely linked with the workload at the factories.
- That even where there was a clear designation of buying posts, the amount of time spent on purchasing functions was often less, due to other work being carried out.
- That the output analysis enabled standard data to be compiled as a basis for auditing workloads. For example, placement of orders and progressing averaged 11.4 minutes per order.

## Preliminary conclusions

The combination of the detailed analysis of central buying outputs, discussions with internal customers and review of the factory buying, led to certain conclusions by the buying organisation:

- That there should be a greater devolvement from the centre of its routine and clerical tasks such as material scheduling, order placing and progressing.

- That, in view of the users' growing dissatisfaction with both the cost and level of service from maintenance, a detailed review was needed on the spares and tooling buying output.
- That (and this is a major, albeit frequently found, conclusion) there was evidence that the 110 man years of purchasing effort located in the factories might not be as effectively used as they could be and required a thorough professional appraisal of both operational policy and effectiveness.

Arising from these views, two extreme options present themselves. These are to retain the central buying department, or to dissolve it, transfer all the activities to the appropriate divisions and nominate lead buyers for key supplies. This latter pattern is one frequently found in organisations with major units that are separated geographically. It is, for example, found in Britain's National Health Service and in the Polymers Division of Exxon Chemicals. Intermediate organisational possibilities exist, but initially the two extreme options may be set against criteria previously defined.

In terms of the central buying organisation in this example, what emerged as key advantages were:

- Effective co-ordination of total negotiations with key suppliers on price, supplies, claims and supplier funding.
- A central source of specialist professional advice on purchasing different key raw materials, general materials and shipping services, and on supplier quality assurance.

The key disadvantages of the existing organisation structure as revealed particularly by the user surveys were:

- It was a poor 'fit' with the corporate objectives of achieving a more market orientated organisation structure and greater autonomy and independence of the divisions, particularly when an average 68% of divisional operating costs related to purchases of goods and services.
- That there was a lack of direct involvement and understanding of local division buying needs.
- That more than half of the central buying outputs were concerned with routine and clerical tasks not linked with the vital buying negotiations role.

In reviewing how well the organisation matched the environmental circumstances, it was clear that each division had very different buying service needs due to the nature of its products, markets and operational profiles. Central buying co-ordination and communications of both divisional and factory buying needs in these circumstances was not assisted by the fact that there was no intermediate layer of buying at divisional level, between the centre and the 28 different factory locations. Location of central buying, though economically sound due to the costs of moving people, was inefficient in terms of communication and co-ordination. From these aspects it would be better based near headquarters of the two main divisions that accounted for over two-thirds of the UK packaging spend.

On a positive note, a strong central control is always advantageous in an environment where many of the suppliers are large, powerful and persistent, and are not above playing off factories, divisions and the centre to achieve their own ends.

## Complete decentralisation of the central buying organisation

Complete decentralisation of buying would imply the winding up of the central buying department and the transfer to appropriate divisions of all of the activities with the nomination of lead buyers for key suppliers to facilitate company-wide co-ordination.

Each divisional buyer would be accountable to the managing director for strategic plans for profit improvement, supplier selection, purchase research and negotiations of contracts, price, claims and supplier funding.

They would have a monitoring and auditing responsibility for the factory-based purchase functions within their division, and would also be made directly accountable for co-ordinating the company-wide negotiations for particular key goods on services where the bigger 'clout' is advantageous. Lead buyers would be required for key commodities or services.

The routine and clerical tasks, such as material scheduling, placement of orders, progressing and invoice checking, would be devolved to factories or divisional operational material control.

The split of staff between divisions would be done so as to give a reasonable spread of skills, and the overall staffing would probably be reduced. The role of buying director would be eliminated, and if major differences arose they would be resolved at executive board level.

The decentralised model, when matched against the company's strategic objectives, appeared to show substantial benefits.

Divisional buying was seen to provide a good organisational match with many of the corporate strategic objectives, including greater autonomy and independence of divisions, more market orientation, concentrating on strengthening core business, co-ordination of R&D programmes and improving productive use of resources. It provided a good vehicle for extending coverage on key suppliers to give a total of 60% cover on purchasing spend and it was thought would facilitate negotiations with suppliers related to discounts.

The key disadvantages of the fully decentralised structure were identified as follows:

- That divisional priorities and objectives might not always be in the best interest of the total company, and in the absence of any formal corporate buying co-ordination, this would not be readily identifiable.
- That advantages depend to a large extent on calibre, experience and status of the buying team within the division and their ability to wear a corporate hat when operating as a lead buyer.
- That the company might be more vulnerable to the coordinated approaches of large, powerful and persistent key suppliers.

Intermediate options might offer some of the advantages of both centralisation and decentralisation, with disadvantages minimised. Organisational change could be reduced. The intermediate options represent more sophisticated and more widely applicable approaches than either of the polarised structures. Possibilities include:

1. The retention of central buying but with the devolution of all routine and clerical tasks, such as scheduling, procurement, preparation of statistics, shipping and transport to the divisions. The centre would retain the non-routine and creative tasks of strategic planning, supplier selection, purchase research, negotiation of contracts in relation to prices, claims, funding for the present commodities and services covered.
2. As option 1. above, but with the extension of the centre's buying role to cover the bulk of the top 2% of the suppliers who account for 80% of purpose spend.
3. Overcome the disadvantages of the complete decentralisation option by retaining a buying director post, directly accountable to a member of the executive board for co-ordination of total purchase strategy, supplier development, purchase research and lead buyer negotiations. The tasks would include assisting in resolving any interdivisional conflict related to buying and developing with all the division managing directors, appropriate co-ordination meetings and

management controls to meet total needs. The purchasing account-ability would be world-wide. To ensure only key issues were dealt with the buying director would have one permanent assistant and a secretary. (This might prove to be optimistic!)

### Conclusions

In the context of the company upon whom the case was based, the board was advised that if one was to rank the various organisation options in order of the closeness of the 'fit' with the company's strategic objectives and the environment on which it operates then the outcome would be:

1. Decentralisation linked with a corporate buying co-ordination role.
2. Decentralisation to divisions.
3. Retain existing core buying tasks, but with a wider coverage of key purchase spend, devolve all routine and clerical tasks.
4. Retain existing core buying tasks, devolve all routine and clerical tasks.
5. Existing central buying organisations.

External views can frequently be used as a means of overcoming difficul-ties arising from the politics of organisations. The board, reviewing the possibilities, declined to sacrifice existing leverage benefits. Option 3. was the preferred outcome but with the appointment of a new pur-chasing director charged with devising and implementing a programme designed to give a sharper purchase focus and, longer term, a proactive role.

There is nothing intrinsically difficult about revising purchase organi-sation. The essential issues are few in number and easily articulated. Politics and personality present the problems: this is why the outside view so often provides the key.

### ● Centralisation or decentralisation: an assessment

This issue perennially occupies purchase management and is likely to continue to do so, particularly as *electronic data interchange* (EDI) impacts more and more. Against strategic criteria there are eight broad lines of assessment:

- **Table 2.7**

  Key statistics that illustrate the case

| Supplier profile | |
|---|---|
| *Purchase value* | *No. of suppliers* |
| 1.1% | 64.5% |
| 19.6% | 33.4% |
| 79.3% | 2.1% |

| Invoice analysis | | | | |
|---|---|---|---|---|
| | *Number* | | *Value* | |
| £10,000 + | 4.2% | | 43.0% | |
| £1,000 – | | | | |
| £9,999 | 14.6% | | 47.5% | |
| | | 18.8% | | 90.5% |
| £100 – | | | | |
| £999 | 34.6% | | 8.5% | |
| £100 – | 46.6% | | 1.0% | |
| | | 81.2% | | 9.5% |

| Cost breakdown | |
|---|---|
| Material purchases | 50.9% |
| Service purchases | 12.6% |
| Personnel | 28.9% |
| Other | 7.6% |

| Levels of purchase commitment | |
|---|---|
| Central buying | 46% |
| Divisions | 29% |
| Local | 25% |

## Criterion 1: to achieve a sustained growth in earnings per share

Centralisation provides greater leverage, although it is often the case that a smaller percentage of the total annual spend than might be expected is actually handled centrally. Remoteness from the scene of operations leads to rigidity and can result in local management being insufficiently involved.

Decentralisation can lead to co-ordination problems and a loss of effectiveness where suppliers have dealings with more than one division. A lead buyer approach can be used, but at times this can, through lack of perceived authority, produce less than optimal results.

## Criterion 2: to continue to raise the level of product quality and service

Centrally, it is possible to bring maximum pressure to bear upon suppliers in the case of quality assurance claims. Quality effort, however, is focused at plant level and this detracts from the efficiency of a central operation.

Decentralisation puts responsibility in the hands of the divisions or factories themselves. Hence there is no detraction from local accountability for profits but it is necessary to ensure that the quality ethic fully permeates all parts of the organisation.

## Criterion 3: to concentrate on strengthening core businesses

Where good divisional interfaces exist centralisation affords good results with economical operation. No direct local involvement can affect motivation, however.

With decentralisation, local buyers can develop purchase plans explicitly geared to the needs of their own division and giving appropriate priorities to local needs.

## Criterion 4: to increase market share in growth areas

This can be seen as a key area, particularly to the extent that purchase moves towards the strategic mode and is in essence calling for better quality people. Centralisation is more likely to attract high calibre purchase resources. However, market share essentially relates to divisions, and dedicated divisional buyers can therefore have higher personal motivation. Only if products cross divisional boundaries is this constrained.

## Criterion 5: innovation – to maintain an R&D programme to ensure that the company is a leader in its chosen fields

Centrally, it is possible to devote resources to purchase research. Suppliers of innovative products and ideas not specifically tied to division, separate businesses or factories, can be identified. If sufficient resources are, for whatever reason, not available, then central buying becomes less effective. Decentralisation can imply a procurement engineering team bringing purchase into the design or planning stage and into very close contact with manufacturing. This can eliminate delay due to sequential activity and lead to a shortening of product development times by an application of a team approach.

### Criterion 6: continually to seek to improve the productive use of physical, material and financial resources

Centralisation leads to effective oversight of the deployment of working capital, to the creation of a proactive mode and to the cost-effective development of systems. Since operating costs occur at the units and divisions, however, close user contact would imply a decentralised mode. Personal involvement is more important than abstractions regarding proactivity.

### Criterion 7: to recruit, develop, retain and motivate key staff who are essential to the achievement of the company's long-term objectives

Centralised departments may attract a higher calibre recruit. A recognisable career progression becomes more feasible. However, this approach is not readily compatible with the creation of countable business units.

Although, conversely, recruitment and career prospects may be damaged by decentralisation, there is the potential for achieving harmonisation between individual achievement and profit performance in the divisions.

### Criterion 8: to develop a more market oriented organisation structure

Central buying is not compatible with this objective unless it too is conceived as a profit centre selling its services and products in competition with outside sources.

Divisional buyers can be much more aware of particular market needs and form a part of the profit-focused team. It is easy to relate their remuneration or compensation to local profit achievement.

## ● Summary

It can be seen that organisational arguments are both comprehensive and complex. In the organisational case, the best fit of options against company strategic objectives ranked decentralisation first and the retention of the existing central buying last. A decision of this type, however, rarely rests upon objective criteria. It depends upon historical, political and personal factors. Frequently the latter, perhaps in the form of a highly career motivated individual identifying self with purchase proactivity, can exercise a decisive influence. In the case of Rolls Royce plc, a clearer corporate presence replacing minimal central staffing was the precursor to a wider ranging purchase reform. In the Metal Box Company, prior to the Carnaud merger, mixed mode operation was clearly retained. In Courtaulds plc, Sir Christopher Hogg's predilection for the Strategic Business Unit approach led virtually to complete decentralisation and, in some people's view, to the dissipation of purchase power. Ultimately, leverage and flexibility must be harmonised. Mixed mode with a central overview of staffing, and of systems development combined with frame contracts, would appear to have many advantages. What can be so easily lacking is customer focus and ongoing knowledge of customer needs. The management of logistics calls for flexibility and speedy response and it is this issue that must be addressed.

# 3

# Managing the supply chain

## ● Introduction

In his seminal works upon the topic of managing for profit, Peter Drucker observed that organisations make profits where they meet the outside world. Internally they only generate costs. Hence the profit frontier is where organisations interface not simply with the end market for their goods, but also where they obtain labour, capital and production materials. From this approach it is but a short step to seeing these profit frontiers as zones of conflict (see **Fig. 3.1**). In particular, suppliers are antagonists to be defeated, always inherently hostile, with trust a remote and usually inapplicable concept.

For many years competition has been seen as the buyer's principal weapon in this environment, with the classical situation one in which a number of suppliers offer through tender action to meet the organisation's needs. Uniformity and an appropriate quality level was, it was assumed, guaranteed by a tight specification. These assumptions led over the years to a classical view of the supply chain as a series of discontinuities with fragmentation rather than integration the keynote.

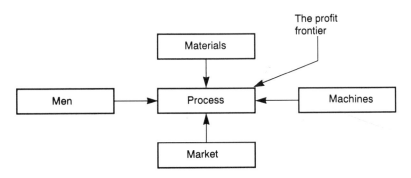

**Figure 3.1**  Profit generation

## ● The supply chain concept

The Supply Chain (see **Fig. 3.2**) is increasingly recognised as a distinctive challenge to Purchase Management. The principal characteristics of the conflict dominated traditional supply chain were, and indeed still are, the presence of well-defined organisational boundaries with inconsistent policies being pursued in each area and with independent control systems. The problems caused by the lack of harmony between the differing areas and by the assumption of conflict as a natural state were concealed rather than resolved by the creation of inventories along the chain. The size of the investment in stock reflected the extent of the uncertainties that existed, and in turn had a major effect upon profitability and the ability to compete.

### Organisational divisions

A typical supply chain is under varying ownerships. Some ownerships represent legal entities with the transfer of goods between them giving rise to payment. Others are functional within the same organisation.

Each division of the chain depends for its effectiveness upon forecasts produced by others, frequently seeking for greater accuracy through second guessing. The usual outcome of this approach is that each successive forecast is adjusted by its recipient to achieve either greater security or flexibility. Lead times can become artificially lengthened

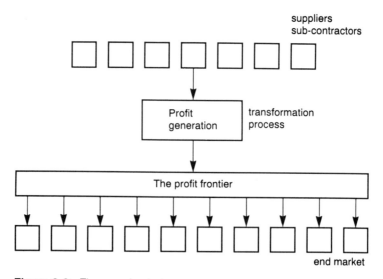

**Figure 3.2** The supply chain

in response to higher forecast call-offs producing in turn increased quantities demanded in order to cover the lead time extension. Small wonder that forecasting has generated millions of words of print! The real problems are, however, not those of technique but of perception and judgement.

## Inconsistent policies

Each separate stage in the supply chain jealously guards its own independence. Policies and objectives locally developed are frequently not simply out of harmony with those elsewhere along the chain, but may actually conflict. The classic dilemma of materials management torn between customer, i.e. manufacturing, demand for 100% service and finance's requirement for reduced inventory is well known. In the traditional context it may not be possible to resolve such a problem; inventory is the battleground where conflict is managed at an operational level. It is therefore scarcely surprising that logistically this classical model of the supply chain is inefficient and uncompetitive.

## Independent control systems

Manual systems of control, in so far as they possessed common features, did so only in broad outline or in response to legal requirements. The adoption of Electronic Data Processing brought with it the possibility of harmonisation leading eventually to integration. This exciting prospect was initially dampened by divergency exacerbated by the competing claims of a whole breed of new software houses. In 1986 the consultants Booz Allen and Hamilton, pioneers in supply chain management, claimed that world-wide computer installations and systems with a capital cost of more than £2 million had at best a 15% chance of success. As traditionally perceived, the supply chain did not need detailed information linkage, and frequent changes in its structure rendered them superfluous in any event.

## Staged inventories

Given such a varied scenario, it has not been surprising to see the sub-optimisation of purchase inventories, work in progress and stocks of finished goods as being of the highest priority. Indeed, the basic underlying assumption of materials requirements planning and of distribution requirements planning is that the fundamental imbalances between marketing and manufacture are irreconcilable and hence must be planned for and managed through inventory.

## Today's approach to supply chain management

The modern approach to supply chain management differs from the classic pattern in four respects:

1. It departs from fragmented responsibility for the supply chain, viewing it as a single entity, integrated at different levels of management, strategic planning and operational.
2. It depends upon a strategic decision to move supply centre stage, making it a shared objective of all functions on the chain, and highlighting its impact upon market share and overall costs. The effect upon supply policy of characteristics of demand, lead time, reliability of service and quality of data, is evaluated and possible trade-offs assessed.
3. Inventories are seen as a last resort in balancing activities and not as a natural outcome. This new role stems from reducing structural imbalance along the chain, from demanding not 'how much stock is where?' but from 'why is it there?' Inventory control systems move from status reporting into the areas of simulation and goal setting.
4. Systems must be integrated and not simply interfaced. The interface approach is expensive in terms of manpower, particularly as a result of involvement in meetings, and additionally frequently produces distorted information. Systems modules reflect segmentation, which becomes intolerable as industries become typically more international. Along an international chain, data must flow across boundaries without delay or distortion; there must be linkage for purposes of purchasing, manufacture, inventory and distribution. Above all, however, ownership of information must be shared with high visibility in terms of orders, inventories and despatches.

## ● The river of supply

The supply chain is analogous to the flow of a river from mountains to sea (see **Fig. 3.3**). The external frontiers and internal barriers through which the river must pass may be perceived as dams, both delaying the flow of water and causing lakes to form. These two parameters are of major importance in assessing the effectiveness of supply chain management equating lead time and capital employed.

The lead time element reflects not merely the geographical length of the river, but also the number of points at which different barriers are encountered. Both external frontiers and internal barriers imply delay

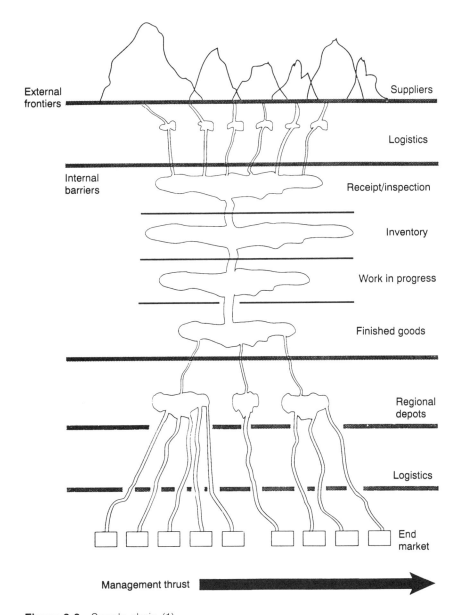

**Figure 3.3** Supply chain (1)

and each of these delays will lead of itself to the formation of lakes tying up capital. In practice, the internal barriers are often as significant as the external frontiers, and indeed the power to facilitate crossing them may be weaker internally than externally. In every case, the principle of territoriality applies and this is compounded by the other factors (previously referred to) of inconsistency of policy and independence of control systems.

Stock levels, as represented by the size of the lakes, reflect these features. Their size will depend, upon service levels, upon the accuracy of forecasts of demand, and upon policy decisions regarding that portion of stocks held for safety or buffer reasons.

Upstream, we are looking towards the supply base. Reliability of lead time rather than its length is the first important factor. The longer the lead time, the greater the risk of fundamental changes in the end market demand, but variability itself inevitably leads to additional investment in safety stock. The other major factor is, of course, the quality dimension. The nearer we approach to zero defect, the smaller the proportion of stock that must be held for any given service level to ensure against variation in quality of the incoming product. In practice, once more, management confidence plays a major role in determining policy. Recent studies appear to show that it is policy regarding stocks that is the main cause of instability along the supply chain, and that it is in harmonising policy changes that the biggest contribution can be made to reduced overall investment.

In this traditional model, minimal linkage is all that is required between the various stages in the supply chain. The existence of these discontinuities is wholly compatible with adversarial negotiation or with a dealing mode. It does not of itself require any significant attempt at integration and for this reason alone it is unresponsive to change in the end market.

When we look at Supply Chain (2) (see **Fig. 3.4**), the essential difference is that management thrust now extends along the vertical axis. The supply base has been rationalised and the absence of barriers impacts directly upon capital employed. Overall lead time is much shorter and less investment is needed to sustain any particular level of activity or service function.

This implies that there must exist not only a strategic overview of the entire chain, but also operational control of the different segments and the ability to make trade-offs in one part of the chain in order to maximise benefits elsewhere.

In terms of customer satisfaction, Supply Chain (2) offers a much more rapid response to need and at the same time, through lower inventory

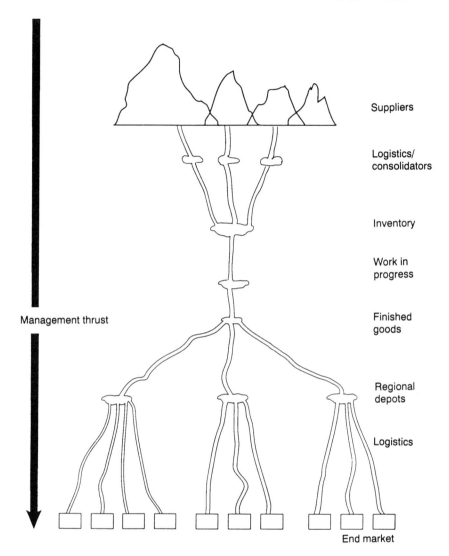

**Figure 3.4** Supply chain (2)

and shorter lead times, a significant reduction in overall costs. Each of the different levels focuses on the end market and not upon its immediate neighbour.

The essential prerequisite for this approach to be successful is that principal players must see mutual advantage in working together to achieve competitive advantage in the end market. Partnership is the watchword, but it should not be imagined that this needs in any way to be equal. The classical Marks and Spencer chain preceded theoretical investigation of supply chain management and is completely dominated by the purchase organisation. Its most remarkable testament is how it has endured for so long and how participating companies have sought to increase their sales to Marks and Spencer to 100%. The result is akin to vertical integration, which, being without common ownership, preserves the advantages of independence whilst gaining the benefits of real co-operation.

## ● The development of thinking upon supply chain management

Consideration of the advantages to be gained by a more integrated approach to the supply chain has occupied those concerned with the purchase function for over 20 years. A major player in this development was the firm of Booz, Allen and Hamilton, with J B S Houlihan being a leading advocate. The Houlihan message was based on the observation that whilst logistics was essentially a question of balancing inventory, between production capacity and the demands of the customer, many hidden costs were bound to creep into the system. Too easily, these were seen as a fact of life and something that just had to be carried. It was changes in the perception of logistics that led to a view that this type of approach in sum added up to a no-win material management policy. The traditional approach sought to trade off the various conflicting objectives of the main function of the supply chain, manufacturing, distribution, sales and purchasing. These functions tend to exhibit a degree of possessiveness and, in Houlihan's striking phrase, 'as a result inventories accumulate like snow drifts at organisational fences'. It was the inability of organisations to cope with changes in the supply market, which led to a natural tendency to build in safety margins – an approach increasingly incompatible with the greater competition that was building up through the late 1970s and the 1980s.

The Booz Allen investigation of inventory turnover and facility utilisation, completed in mid-1980, showed for the first time the extent to which the position of European companies had been undermined, with regard to both the Japanese and the Americans. It reached the conclusion that those European and American companies that were competing with reasonable success with Japanese companies had certain identifiable characteristics. Supply and demand were seen by them as a strategic issue and the balance between them was based upon a company-wide approach and overall, rather than purely functional, objectives. Information was transferred quickly and was widely accessible. The fact that it was shared encouraged the development of a broader view on supply chain management, and led to decision-making that reflected the overall objectives of the business rather than local or parochial views. It is interesting to compare this view with the sentiments of David Fanthorpe of Black and Decker some eight years later. In Amsterdam, David Fanthorpe said that in the context of total customer service, the task of purchasing was to establish a supply base – a supply base that had a different form of relationship with the company. In particular, he said, that

> 'Crucially the willingness and ability to give suppliers real time access to the supply chain programme as it flexes against the volatile consumer demand, that is one critical test of the new partnership relationships with suppliers and a prime task for purchasing. To establish the trust and confidence on this particular supply chain interface is to make it happen.
>
> Speed and accuracy of information flow through the supply chain. A precondition of meeting the new customer service objectives is dependent on suppliers' access to the changing demand.'

At Black and Decker this meant that it was imperative to develop and implement sophisticated computer systems, which suppliers could have free access to, if necessary on a real time basis by electronic data interchange, the manufacturing planning and control data of the company. This may well be regarded as the acid test of *co-makership*, the major breakthrough that determines when supply chain partnership is a reality.

When Booz Allen Hamilton introduced their concept of supply chain management, it differed from the classical pattern in four main ways. In the first place, it departed from the perception that the supply chain must always be a series of separate relationships to one which viewed it as a single entity. Integration was to be achieved at different levels of management – strategic, planning and operational. The second feature was derived from the first. It was that supply should move supply centre stage, making it a shared objective of all the elements of the chain and highlighting its impact upon market share and overall costs. The effect upon supply policy of the characteristics of demand, lead time, reliability of service and quality of data were to be evaluated for the first time in a systematic way with a view to establishing where trade-offs might prove advantageous. Simply by holding inventory higher up the supply chain in a raw or semi-finished state with less value added could both increase flexibility and speed of response, and at the same time reduce capital employed.

Third, inventories were seen as a last resort in balancing activities and not a normal first step. This new role stemmed from reducing structural imbalance along the chain and from posing the question not 'how much stock is where?' but 'why is it there?'. Inventory control systems therefore move from simple reporting of status into the areas of simulation and goal setting.

Finally, supply chain management required a new approach to systems. Integration, and not simply interface, was to be the key. The interface approach was deemed to be excessively expensive in terms of manpower and frequently produced distorted information. Segmentation became increasingly intolerable as industries typically became more international. Along an international chain, data must flow across boundaries without delay and distortion. There must be linkage for the purposes of purchasing, manufacture, industry distribution, but, above all, ownership of information must be shared appropriately with high visibility in terms of orders, inventories and despatches. Today this last characteristic is no longer revolutionary. Brussels-based Cerestar, Europe's largest manufacturer of starches and derivatives, operates 14 plants in eight countries, through tightly integrated logistics.

Houlihan forecast that all of these changes in approach, when coupled with the challenges of the changing business environment, would make it necessary for top management to be involved in the supply chain. He alleged that only they could ensure that conflicting interfunctional objectives were reconciled and balanced, and that inventories were relegated to a proper place, i.e. simply as a mechanism for dealing with inevitable residual balances. This called for an integrated system strategy to reduce the level of business vulnerability.

It is a natural feature of business life that functional objectives are frequently in conflict. One outcome is that inventory can be seen as a means by which the consequences of different priorities can be contained. Rather than this, one should look for trade-offs between the key elements of those strategies that have significant multi-functional or cross functional implications. Any marketing strategy, for example, produces particular requirements for demand, lead time, reliability and responsiveness. Manufacturing is similarly concerned with lead time but also with flexibility, and increasingly with the implications of the batch of one. Product strategy may call for variety, which must be considered in the context either of making for stock or of flexible manufacturing systems. The outcome is that it is necessary to challenge basic assumptions, for example that lead time is an ally, and that the longer the lead time the greater the safety of the organisation.

In terms of stocks, the allegation that for the future these were simply the mechanism by which an inevitable residual imbalance was bridged, rather than being the primary tool of management, represents a quite revolutionary change. The performance of Japanese industry, with its much higher stock turns, and the movement to buy rather than make, creating significant assembly companies, make it necessary to reassess the role of inventory and to look at policies for sourcing, which analyse customer service and match it with delivery performance.

Once a strategic framework is in place, mechanisms and control systems need to be produced. The key word in the case of systems is integration; integration rather than interface or interaction. In order to achieve this, the whole strategic process of the organisation needs a stronger logistics impetus. It is the competitive environment that has made this necessary rather than simply desirable.

● Buyer–seller relationships

**The traditional view**

Based upon competition as the key to good buying, the relationship between buyer and seller has been seen as an arm's length relationship. It was necessary to keep at a distance, neither becoming too dependent upon a supplier nor allowing a supplier to become too dependent upon any one customer. It was even possible to suggest that it was unethical to get too close to a supplier.

This view led naturally to multiple sourcing as the norm; sole sourcing effectively placed too much power in the hands of the supplier. Allied to this concept of choice as a vital feature of the purchase portfolio is that of periodic re-tendering. A consequence of annual contracts is that the supplier must legislate for the contingency that he could lose any particular contract. This might be in spite of excellent quality and service, and be due simply to the action of competitors. Hence each term contract needs to be financially profitable on a stand alone basis. This can affect prices when plant or equipment investment needs to be recovered over a short as opposed to a long term.

It also diverts creative talents into a continual search for possible replacement business and at the same time raises for buyers the need to readjust at regular intervals to the costs involved in supplier change.

**Supply chain relationships: the need for long-term relationships**

Inherent in the concept of managing the supply chain, is the notion that there should exist mutual dependence between supplier and customer.

This is totally at variance with the traditional approach. In the mainstream activity, the survival of each party is correctly perceived as being dependent on the other. This implies a long-term commitment not simply to do business with each other but also to find new business for each other. Suppliers support their customers even at the cost of short-term difficulties for themselves. Benefits in terms of profitability or of quality improvement are there to be shared. They are not to be negotiated one from the other but shared, based upon an open relationship. This is therefore the notion of partnership based upon a perception of mutual advantage.

Supply chain relationships of this type are of the essence of the purchase components of just-in-time. Although they do exist outside of this concept they are not commonly found. One example that is frequently cited is that of the British retailer Marks and Spencer. In 1985, of a portfolio of approximately 700 suppliers, continuous relations had existed for 100 for between 25 and 45 years, and for over 45 years in the case of a further 50. This example is, however, one of partnership based not upon equality but upon the sheer attractiveness to suppliers of one particular customer. The longer-term advantages of association with such a formidably profitable retailer led even major suppliers into a position of dependency more usually found in adversarial relationships. Profit margins were essentially determined by the customer in a way reminiscent of those Japanese companies classified as dependent supplier firms.

Within the European version of this Japanese form of vertical integration without ownership, the basic philosophy is one of steady, long-term growth. For this, profit is, of course, essential but the element of continuity of business takes much pressure off a supplier. Return on investment can be seen in a different time perspective over the whole life of plant or equipment. In addition, since the supplier feels that he has greater security of business, less creative time need be spent searching for new customers. Professional strength is therefore directed primarily at improving productivity and seeking continual improvement.

**Case study: the Japanese approach to buyer–seller relationships translated into European environment**

This view is based upon a presentation, one of a series, made by Terence Hogg, of Nissan Manufacturing (UK) Ltd, to the International Purchasing Conferences of Management Centre Europe.

*Japanese approach in Europe*

Nissan Motor Manufacturing (UK) Ltd (NML) was established as a wholly owned subsidiary of Nissan Motor Company of Japan in 1984. In February of that year NML signed an agreement with the British Government to build a new car plant in Sunderland, Tyne & Wear.

Our first employee was hired in October 1984, he was the personnel director, a fairly logical decision since he had the responsibility for pulling together, from scratch, a whole new organisation on a greenfield site. The plant was built in 62 weeks and handed over at the end of 1985. During that year we sent the first 160 or so of our new employees to Japan for training. The original reason for this was straightforward; we didn't have a plant in which to train them and the part of the world where we are based has no motor industry tradition – it is historically shipbuilding, mining and heavy engineering.

*The customer–supplier relationship*

*Japan*  In Japan's history of supply, there is a concept of mutual dependence that the customer is as dependent on the supplier as the supplier is on the customer. They see it not as a totally dependent business, more of an integrated business; they see the business as a whole. The supplier and the assembler or customer planning together so that one cannot survive without the other; they tend to see the business as a whole in terms of who makes investments and who makes the benefits thereof.

This leads to the fundamental part – the long-term commitment. Both the supplier and the customer have this, not necessarily contract specific, but clear understanding of a long-term commitment to do business with each other. If you are a customer you will go and find further business for your suppliers. If you have a supplier who makes one type of component and you are about to eliminate that component, you will normally try to find him some other business. For example, if certain parts of the wiring have been substituted by something else, you will normally try to encourage your supplier to provide that substitute so that he will keep a business relationship going. You are committed to keeping him in business. Similarly, a supplier is committed to keep a customer in good business; that means a supplier will do things in a way that they won't normally in Europe. They will do things that might, in the short term, be extremely difficult for their business, in order to support their customer. They will undertake responsibilities for their customer that would not normally be considered here in Europe.

A third part of the Japanese system is this concept of shared benefits. This means they see the total profitability, quality improvement, whatever aspect of the business, as something to be shared by both, not negotiated one from the other or obtained mainly by one or the other, but a very open relationship about what is involved in both parties and a willingness to share it.

**95**

The sharing may well be different at any given time, for whatever benefit it is, but over time it is seen as a very equal partnership without any particular power on one side or the other. If you compare that with the UK, the historical pattern is completely different.

*United Kingdom*   First of all, supplier and customer must keep at a distance; you must never become too dependent on the supplier and you do not want the supplier to become too dependent on you. As an example, I was recently talking to the UK purchasing director of a very large organisation who insisted that his company would not allow any supplier to be more than 20% dependent upon him, irrespective of how beneficial it would be to both parties.

With that goes an approach to multiple sourcing. It is common practice not to have just one supplier for one component, but maybe two, sometimes even three. By and large, this is an approach that says you cannot afford to give any other business that much power over your own business; you cannot afford to put a supplier in a position where he is your monopoly supplier for a type of component. This is now changing, not necessarily across the board, but it is worthwhile saying that these Japanese aspects are gradually being adopted certainly by the more progressive companies in British industry, and to an extent the European ones as well, because of the visible benefits. Our claim at present, not made with great gusto, but our position at present is that we are further down that road already than any other European business because we started that way and do not have the encumbrances to shake off.

One other big difference is re-tendering, and to explain that a little let us take an example of a supplier supplying one of your plastic mouldings for a car. He has been supplying you with that part for a particular model for three years. You introduce either a change to that part or you have a new car coming in or you just have some significant economic change, for example, more sales less sales. You go back to this supplier and his competitors and you ask them to re-tender. You give them specification documents and drawings and you say to them 'please tender against that specification for that part'. That is completely different coming out of the Japanese view of long-term relationships. If you are asking the supplier and his competitors to re-tender, you are automatically suggesting to him that from that point on, the relationship you had is over, until it is restarted. Even if he does get the business, you have weakened the business relationship you had with him because you told him on the day you requested him to re-tender, that he might not have the business any more. We are talking about principle, and if you look at the Japanese industry and the UK industry these are fundamental differences.

What that leads to in the UK is what I call contract return review. Because the supplier knows he might lose the business – and he might lose the business not because of something he has done but because of something you do as a customer, or his competitors do – then he is forced as a businessman to look at each contract on an individual basis. Each time you approach him for a component he has got to look at that piece of business and say 'can I make that business, on its own, pay. If I am going to produce this part, is it going to be good for three years, is that going to be a paying business? How much do I need to charge to do that?'. It is a detailed review he must go through each time he is asked to make a business proposition. As an example, I recently talked to a supplier of injection mouldings who, in discussing this general issue, made a point to me that in the preceding year he had been out seeking new business and on an existing £18 million business base he had acquired an extra £6 million worth of new business. But when he actually came to look back a year later, his turnover had gone to £20 million not £24 million, and that is because he had lost £4 million worth of his established business. It had gone to somebody else, therefore he had put a lot of time, effort and resource into trying to grow his business, and instead of growing it the 33% he had expected, he had grown it by about 10%. All that effort going in, essentially for no gain. If you look at that more globally, if you step back for a minute from that single-picture, you only have a limited number of suppliers of certain types of component and you only have a limited number of customers. What that reflects is people going around a roundabout. It is customer A saying this year I am doing business with supplier C and D, next year I will do business with D and F and the year after F and G, and then I will be back to C and E again, and I will have finished the circle. And you have other customers doing the same and there is a lot of effort by both business parties to no real positive gain. All they are doing is chasing round a circle; that effort is not directly gaining anything, it is just moving stuff around, wasting management resources.

*Supplier objectives – UK*

Take that philosophy and say what does that mean for a UK supplier. (Forget the customer for a minute.) It means he has to put a lot of time in searching for new business, even if he is not after substantial growth. If his objective is gradual growth, he still has to put enormous resources in because he has to be prepared to lose some of his business by the nature of this process.

Secondly, already mentioned but worth dwelling on, he has to put a lot of effort into a single contract review. He has to look at his investment and try and maintain that at a minimum, because he might only need that investment for three or four years maximum.

He has then to look at his pricing and make sure that his pricing recovers his investment within that period, and that brings UK businesses to the concept of a satisfactory rate of return for investment. It is worthwhile to note that if you talk to most UK motor industry suppliers about what they expect as return on investment, it is considerably higher than most Japanese business for a particular industry.

What comes with that is a philosophical difference that is harder to see but does exist. UK businesses, when they present themselves to you for initial discussions, will tell you that they are actively managed on the financial front and will have a clear idea of what a satisfactory rate of return is for their business. Most Japanese suppliers would find it very difficult to answer that question.

### Supplier objectives – Japan

Japanese suppliers do not even have this concept in the traditional way; they want to be profitable and to grow, but this is usually expressed the other way round. They will usually say we want steady growth, and for that we need profitability. They do not have the same concept of return on investment, the concept is not as critical to them. That isn't because they are bad businessmen, it is because their view of the business is different. They are looking over a totally different time-scale.

A Japanese supplier will see the growth of his business over a long time frame. This may be from obtaining new customers but will be primarily either through development of a new product so that he has something new to offer, or that he can use more of, or that has higher added value, or alternatively through growth of his customers' business.

Therefore a supplier to the motor industry will do his best to support the growth of the assembler's business, because that is his way to growth. He will do this by assuming a wide range of responsibilities. The supplier in the UK – in the west generally – will tend much more to think about business growth by new contracts with new customers. They tend to see the way to grow business differently. Again that is a reflection of this concept of long-term relationship and shared business, compared with arm's length, stand alone business. Because the UK supplier operates within that environment, he has to look that way, when a Japanese supplier operates within that different environment he is able to see things differently, and in a way all those things take pressure off a supplier, but in return for that removal of pressure there are certain responsibilities that the supplier must accept.

Because of a long-term relationship, the Japanese supplier can concentrate on increasing his investment – he is looking over a long term, he is not looking at a three-year contract. He is notionally looking at as long as the equipment will last, because if he does not produce this part, he will produce the next one and he knows that he will have the business for that next part, so he will be prepared to invest in better facilities. Facilities in this context is actual production facility rather than tooling. In addition to this, because he has security of business and he knows he does not have to put together packages and go in search of new business and to make proposals and evaluate new drawings, he is able to better utilise his manufacturing engineering professional strength by directing his attention to improving productivity instead of searching for new business. These are two positive things that can come out of a long-term relationship with a Japanese supplier, resulting in a focusing of attention on cost reduction. British suppliers, on the other hand, direct their attention to minimising investment because they have got to be prepared not to need that investment after the life of a particular part, and secondly to finding new business to replace the business they might lose and also to evaluating ways to sell to a new customer. The attention is being directed a different way.

*Supplier responsibilities*

The first of these responsibilities is to maintain a consistent and acceptable quality level. We are not talking quality in the sense of a Rolls Royce compared with a Mini, we are talking quality in the sense of making the right component to the right production quality, of achieving the required standards, making sure the component is produced to specification and it is produced with a zero defect rate.

It is clearly a supplier responsibility to achieve that, to improve it and to police it. It is never a customer responsibility. Customers should not have large inspection departments; they should not have incoming inspection reports; they should work to the principle that they have delegated this responsibility to suppliers who know the standard and are prepared to accept responsibility for consistently achieving it: regular routine achievement of quality targets means not having rejections. It also means quality through the warranty stage because we believe a supplier has to be responsible for the warranty of his components right through the life of our vehicle, so he has to have enough control of his process to be happy to warrant that part for 100,000 miles or three years, because that is our vehicle warranty.

Most Nissan suppliers in Japan are now operating to rejection rates – defect rates – measured in parts per million. We are still talking in the west of percentage points; if we are lucky, we might achieve less than 1%. By contrast the Japanese are orders of magnitude ahead in terms of their ability to control production quality.

In addition to the responsibility for quality, it is the ongoing responsibility of the supplier for continuous improvement. Because we are not going out for re-quote every year does not mean we abdicate responsibility, nor do we expect our suppliers to abdicate responsibility for trying to improve productivity and cost; so they have to be looking at continuous improvement in their product. The supplier feels responsible for making improvements to his product, to his process, to his material usage, to show up in terms of quality and cost. That is not forced on him by contract review, it is his bringing to the table what he brings for that long-term relationship – continuous improvement.

Another aspect of supplier relationship is a very strong requirement on the supplier to undertake development and testing work. Again it stems from the basic relationship. If you are saying to your supplier, long term you are going to make my door trim pads, I do not want to buy these from anybody else, then as a customer you are also saying to yourself that means I do not have to commit myself to producing lots of drawings of these things to send out every three years to get people to quote. On the same basis, I can trust my supplier to do that; he is the expert. So suppliers are given much more responsibility to develop their part of the product and therefore for testing it in its early stages. I am not talking about production testing, I am talking about new product testing. You find in Japan, for example, big vehicle assemblers have far less component testing facility than in Europe, and that is because *they* do not do it – suppliers do it and each supplier has the equipment required to do new product testing on his component, not the assembler. It is a very different pattern here in Europe.

Finally, one of the supplier's responsibilities is continuous improvement. Japanese suppliers expect, and are expected, to improve productivity year over year on any component. They are expected to share the benefits of that improved productivity with their customers. They have at times startlingly high targets for that.

We are aware of Japanese supplier improvement rates consistently in the high single figures per annum, for example 9%. Sometimes, for example over a period of 18 months, we can experience 15–30% per annum improvements in productivity. Sometimes, some years, on some components, these improvements are not startling. What is true is that they are consistent; there is always improvement. We know because we buy from Japan and we do get component prices going down year over year. What tends to happen in Japan is that the customer and the supplier talk each year about how much the price can go down, whereas in Europe the supplier is generally talking to the customer about how much the price is to go up. That is what we mean by commitment to productivity improvement. My belief is that it is not because they are better individuals, it is because in knowing that they have a long-term business, they have the ability to concentrate over time in improving investment and improving productivity, instead of minimising investment and maximising the search for new business.

### Nissan Motor Manufacturing (UK) approach

Having covered some of the basic differences we, as a company, have identified between Japanese and European suppliers, I would like to move on and explain the specific approach Nissan UK has taken in establishing a wholly new supply base; one that will take us to 80% local content. To do this I would like to review three specific areas, first, principles of supply relationships; second, supplier selection; and third, review what we term the 'Nissan way'.

### Principles of NMUK/supplier relationship

First let us look at the principles of the supplier relationship. You will see we have adopted many of the Japanese ones, modifying them as appropriate to suit our particular requirements. We go for the long-term relationship. We tell our suppliers up front, right at the start, of any business with us, which we expect to stay doing business with them. What we say to a supplier is you will not have to re-quote, we will not put your part out to tender on the next model or in three years' time; if you are making that part for us you can expect always to be making that part for us. All you have to do, supplier, is to stick to our way of doing business. That means adopting the supplier responsibilities we talked about earlier. If your quality is right, if you improve your productivity, as long as you do those things you get to keep the business.

We add to that single sourcing for the very reasons we spoke about earlier. We do not believe that we can say to a supplier, and ask him to believe us, that you have that long-term relationship, without us demonstrating that, by putting our money where our mouth is and saying you are the sole supplier for the part.

We believe in the concepts of shared benefits. We expect our suppliers to have profitable businesses. We do not expect people to do business with us for the sake of it, we also expect to share our benefits with them and vice versa. Therefore when they come up with cost reduction ideas, which we expect them to, we won't expect to acquire all those cost reductions ourselves, but neither do we expect any secrets – we expect to sit down openly and talk about how we share those improvements.

It is true that Europe is going the way we are, but they are not going as far as us now or as fast as us yet, because although people are talking long-term relationship and less sourcing, I cannot think of anybody who talks long-term full stop, in single sourcing the way we do. Many suppliers are not conceptually happy with the idea. They are not yet, in many cases, fully convinced that it is the truth. They are not totally sure they believe us; however, they are all prepared to go along with us in principle, and we have actually started to turn some of these notions into practice. We have achieved agreement with suppliers about what they are going to do on productivity, what it is going to do for their price, where it is going to go. We have convinced those suppliers that once they have a part, we are only going to talk to them about it. We have convinced them in practice that if they come up with ideas to improve the part we will listen to them and make that change and you will be surprised how often that does not happen in the industry where the assembler tends to say 'look I told you what part to make you just get on and make it, I do not want to improve it now'.

We now have suppliers coming along to us with ideas for improvement. We are agreeing to many of these and are prepared to consider much smaller improvements than most motor companies would be interested in. Not because they, in themselves, are of enormous benefit but because we have a belief that over time all those little things add up and do make them more significant, and also because it is a necessary gesture of faith on our part to demonstrate that we are prepared to do it. It is part of building that credibility with our suppliers, creating the mutual dependence. At this stage we are still a small enough customer for that to be making relatively minor impact on suppliers, especially the big suppliers so there is not an enormous wind of change blowing through the supplier. However, as our business grows and our volume grows, then to most suppliers we will become a very significant customer.

We have, for example, one supplier who, because they have obtained our business and because they wanted to do it our way, have effectively roped off a part of the inside of their plant and said this is for Nissan.

Within this clearly defined area, they have been able to make significant changes in employee attitudes, in plant and equipment, and they have obtained agreements about flexibility and ways of working, which they have not been able to obtain elsewhere in the plant. Now clearly, they will hope to expand that opportunity once they have shown people it is worthwhile, once they have shown people it is nothing to be afraid of, then they will adopt these working practices through the remainder of their plant so in that sense some of the benefits we bring will spin off to their customers, because it will make that supplier more efficient.

What is proving more difficult at this stage, if we are very honest, is getting suppliers to the point where they are able to undertake the product development and testing role. Many are simply not geared up for it and we are the only customer presently that asks them to do it. In many of those cases we have sometimes had to fund directly from Nissan the investment in developing and testing facility from them. What is true is that this task is easier in Japan because in Japan there is usually some form of link between major supplier and major customer. Sometimes there is a shareholding by the supplier in the customer and vice versa. Also very often, there is a common major shareholder, for example, one or other of the Japanese banks will be a major shareholder in both businesses and that leads to a much greater understanding.

What is much less common in Japan than here is a supplier supplying more than one customer. You tend to get suppliers who supply to Nissan or to Honda or to Toyota, but rarely to all three. It is only the big, really big, majors that are suppliers to all three. People like Hitachi. We believe that the approach can still work when the supplier works for more than one customer, and we are quite happy with our suppliers also being suppliers to others.

*Supplier selection factors*

Supplier selection is probably the single most important part of the purchasing procurement role. Because once you said you are going to stay with somebody and work to improve them, the important bit is to have chosen the right partner. Quality first – this should be relatively straightforward – does he produce to specification? However, to have confidence in a supplier's capabilities, it is necessary to go somewhat deeper:

1. He should have a quality philosophy that he can explain to you. Not because we just like to see them as good things but because if he has not

already thought of those it is reflective of his approach to quality improvement.

2. Is he able to develop objectives that give over year improvement? I do not want somebody who says 'my objective on quality is to do this'. He should already have sight of where that is going to lead him in the future, how to keep the quality trend improving.

3. Because it is fashionable in the motor industry, does he understand statistical process control? Is he approaching his production process in an analytical engineering fashion, or is he still back in the days of throw more people at it?

4. Does he have an improvement programme? I do not mean a suggestions programme, I mean an improvement programme for housekeeping, for safety, for productivity, for quality. He does not have to have all of those, but has he got that approach to his business? How well developed is his supplier involvement programme? It is important to remember that we do not deal with anybody who does not, in turn, have some suppliers. Has he thought of working with them to improve their delivery quality to him. Because if he does not, he will undoubtedly have problems in fulfilling both his and our objectives.

5. Is he a person who really sees he has got to get to zero reject? It is a commonly used phrase nowadays. I think I mentioned earlier in talking to you that there are now Japanese suppliers that genuinely deliver parts per million of failures and they are still trying to improve. We are not interested in somebody who just says I want zero rejects; we want to see somebody who appears to be turning his organisation towards it. It will take a few years; that is fine – it will take us a few years.

We want somebody with development and testing capabilities on component because they are going to have responsibility for developing them. We look hard at somebody's production process, we look at how suitable it is. At his present components, for other customers, at his controls on production, and that is not just process controls, it is production control type controls. How does he schedule it? Does he know how he schedules it? Does he realise when he is running a batch how to organise material flow in and out? Is he somebody who is looking at ways to improve his production process, is that feasible and is it reflected in his plan? Is he talking about further improvements he can make? These may not always be major; we are not looking for people who say 'I am about to throw this process away and start again'. We are looking for somebody who is considering minor ways of improvement, because that shows an attitude of continually refining the production process.

*Supplier selection factors – product development*

We look at the supplier's ability for further development – what investment have they got in facility, what investment have they got in the expertise and people?

Do they already do design on components, or do they buy their design of components and tooling? Are they used to working from absolute detail or can they be asked to provide something, a component or an assembly, to do a job rather than provide something from a drawing on a piece of paper?

I call this 'systems effect'. I do not think there is a proper name. But if we consider a supplier of a certain component, there is often another single or related group of components, which together with that major one make up a system. We like to look at a supplier and to say 'does he understand the system?'. We talk to him about the whole system instead of about the component within a system because that makes our life easier and in the end makes his life easier. It makes for better management because you are managing fewer things.

The top example of that is brakes. You can buy brakes where the only people who see a braking system are the motor vehicle assemblers. There are calipers here and tubes there and something else there and something else there and none of the separate suppliers has any concept of the total brake system. You can also buy brakes by going to one of the big companies because a few of them do have the expertise to manufacture a complete system, and saying we need brake systems for this motor car. Now there are all sorts of stages in between that.

*Supplier selection factors – production capability*

When looking at production it is important to look at engineering capability. It is surprising how many British companies do not have real production engineers, but it is fundamental to a manufacturing business.

We look at their level of automation, but do not insist on it. However, we are aware that well-chosen automation is important for consistent quality achievement and it is important for maintaining productivity levels.

We always show a healthy interest in inventories, especially WIP. Many motor industry suppliers carry a week's stock of finished product, not necessarily because they want to but because it has been a requirement in the past from their customers. Our particular interest is how much is within the production process. If it is work in progress, unfinished stock part way through the manufacturing process, why is it there, what is that telling us about the ability of the supplier to manage his business adequately?

And lastly we are interested in a supplier who genuinely believes his role in life is to improve productivity faster than economics; if he sees an inflation rate of 3% on labour then he should be aiming for an improvement of 4% on labour productivity as a minimum.

*Supplier selection factors – pricing*

In order to maintain minimum pricing we look at the way suppliers manage their business, especially the way they manage in production control terms.

The first task is to find people who recognise that their job is to produce what they have to and no more. Whenever you are walking through a production plant and you see somebody who wants to pour things into a black hole at the end of it just to maintain a stock of goods, then his production management system has got some fundamental flaws in it.

Second, we want people to understand the concept of pulls scheduling. Ideally we want to move to the position of having a part produced as you get the order for it, not in terms of anticipation of that order. Cascading this down the production system ensures that WIP inventory is kept to an absolute minimum, which in turn minimises the amount of material movement and handling.

It is still true that if you compare the average British company, or European component plant with a number of the better Japanese ones, you would see effectively no inventory at all in a Japanese plant because a part is always in motion somewhere; it is hardly ever waiting. And the degree to which handling has been refined so that handling is an integral part of the process rather than an actual operation.

### The Nissan way

When we talk to suppliers as part of our supplier selection process, one of the slides that has the most impact concerns quality. Originally it was developed for our own internal use and is a visual representation of how we perceive total quality control and how the fundamental actions of teamwork, flexibility, quality consciousness and commitment to the project are integral parts in the process of giving complete customer satisfaction.

The most telling part of this slide is the top portion, which states that 80% of problems are attributable to management. This is something that we believe and that we preach to suppliers. We believe it is important for them to believe it also, if they delude themselves that their problems are the result of unions, supplier problems, delinquent operators or whatever then they will never solve problems or make improvements.

### Role of purchasing

The approach I have outlined in dealing with suppliers has a major impact in the way the purchasing department goes about its role in the organisation and the way we have traditionally perceived it in the west.

The first and most important task of the purchasing department is supplier selection. If we are honest, the traditional method of supplier selection is to write to a number of known potential suppliers, then bargain with the most likely ones to get the lowest price or best package deal. Normally however, our selection process is much more stringent than this and based on clearly identified parameters that are designed to establish successful, long-term relationships.

The next two points deal with supporting the supplier. Practical support is only possible if you are close to your supplier; not close in a geographic sense but aware of his needs on an ongoing basis. This is a continuous process and large customers can frequently provide invaluable support to their suppliers in many guises, further developing the dependency aspect of their relationship.

Long-term support is equally important if somewhat different. Both supplier and customer require to be creative if a good supplier is to be encouraged to grow into other fields. This may be necessary for a number of reasons, for example, due to technology change. Even good suppliers will not necessarily do the same job or the same amount of business over an extended time frame; it is the responsibility of purchasing to recognise this and identify other work opportunities, ensuring that over time, whilst relative workloads may change, suppliers can continue a successful and beneficial relationship.

Finally, purchasing have responsibility for pursuing a policy of negative pricing – they are responsible for teaching the concept of negative pricing and working with suppliers to achieve a continuous cost reduction effort. The concept of purchasing being proactive in discussing price reviews well in advance of implementation is somewhat different to the traditional adversarial negotiations that traditionally take place. This process works well in Japan. We currently buy a number of parts from Japan and benefit from their continuous cost reduction achievements; a number of parts show price reductions year on year.

### The differences summarised

Finally, to summarise what we see as the differences. The western approach is based on one adversarial relationship requiring re-tendering and multiple sources, with the customer always protecting his ability to be independent of his supplier.

The Japanese approach is fundamentally different, with the customer taking the view that he and his supplier need each other equally and that they must have a long-term business relationship together.

## ● Supplier relationships in a consumer product environment

This discussion of supplier relationships in a consumer product environment is based upon the experience of Toshiba Consumer Parts UK Ltd.

Toshiba Consumer Products UK Ltd was established in Plymouth in 1981 to manufacture colour television receivers for sale in the United Kingdom. Subsequently, another factory was built in order to manufacture microwave ovens. In the United Kingdom all production is sold through a sister sales department, Toshiba (UK) Ltd, located in Surrey. Distributors were appointed to market in other countries of Western Europe.

The consumer durable market is one of the keenest in Europe and there is great pressure on a continuing basis to reduce prices and to provide a very high degree of service to customers. It is deemed by the manufacturers of the utmost importance that a high quality product is available at the right time and price. Demand for the product is cyclic, with a high proportion of production required in the last three months of the year. This requires a degree of smoothing of production and a policy of stock holding during the summer months. There is great attention to detail planning, and a monthly planning cycle has been devised. The degree of change requested by the sales company is virtually nil and this has been a great asset, which meant in fact that it is possible to work with very short lead times.

Toshiba established a set of fundamental principles in terms of supplier relationship. In particular, they insisted that there be no change in orders, that payment be on time as long as parts were delivered on time and that payment would be in full provided that parts were of good quality. These fundamental planks and this philosophy were maintained even as volume and complexity developed.

In line with Toshiba's own philosophy, a number of reciprocal attitudes were expected from suppliers. In the first place, Toshiba did not expect to have to progress. Once an order was placed and accepted, it was expected that the delivered goods would come on the specified day. In the second place, on receipt there was neither inspection nor count. Exact quantities and a quality product were required at all times. Toshiba felt that in terms of many traditional Western European attitudes, some of these aspects were very difficult to achieve in the early part of the 1980s. Indeed at that time, an analysis of the supply base showed that Far Eastern suppliers were far more accurate than local suppliers, and if there was any tendency to supply incorrect quantities then in the Far East, error would be on the high side, whereas local suppliers had an equal spread about the required quantity. Toshiba prepared a league table of vendor performance and without giving away confidential information, used this as the beginnings of a supplier enhancement or development programme. For example, one company that was near the bottom of the table responded very positively in a short space of time and made a considerable improvement. This had been achieved, it was said, by looking at internal procedures and disciplines, and making a number of radical changes to bring philosophies into line with those of Toshiba. This had led to an improved performance not only to Toshiba but to the entire customer base. It enabled them to take on more business as all customers saw a rapid improvement in performance and hence were prepared to order more.

In terms of sourcing, there were two major areas from which components were obtained, the Far East and local. In the Far East supplies were obtained from Toshiba and from direct suppliers, the latter being located in Japan, Singapore, Malaysia, Taiwan and Korea. As, and this is a paradox really, as in so many under-developed countries, in the United Kingdom, Toshiba operated a localisation programme. This was designed continually to seek out new sources of components consistent with price quality and delivery. The perceived benefits were that this localisation programme would offer a measure of protection against a fluctuating exchange rate, would cut out up to 40 days of shipping and customs clearing time, would make for flexible response if problems should occur and would lead to the avoidance of freight and duty. In terms of the possibility of achieving complete localisation, the main obstacles were that Toshiba's design capability was locked solely into Japan. This meant that in the first instance most designs embraced Japanese components. Second, if any local component was sought, then it took time and resources to obtain approval by the Japanese design, and lastly, at certain times, Japanese and Far Eastern countries were considerably cheaper than local equivalents.

In terms of cost, it was expected that the component cost would be negotiated in line with a number of factors, which were to a degree interdependent. These included the behaviour of the finished product market, the need to be competitive with other suppliers, the volumes to be obtained and transport questions. All these were determinants of the price that Toshiba was prepared to pay. It was observed that in many cases, Japanese companies would give, upon the basis of internally generated costings, a price that the supplier had to meet. In addition the word inflation virtually did not exist in the company's vocabulary. Toshiba expected, in common with other Japanese manufacturers, to receive a cost reduction at least once and if possible twice per year; indeed the nature of the end market made this essential. Whereas when Toshiba began their operation the average price of a colour television set was approximately £320, and the average wage in the United Kingdom about £30 per week, by the end of the decade the comparable prices were £230 against an average weekly wage approaching the £200 mark. In other words, the real price or the real cost, had fallen by practically a factor of ten. This meant that, in common with many other Japanese companies, Toshiba perceived themselves as being aggressive as regards price and were prepared to change their organisation in order to achieve their objectives.

In essence, the procurement section of the department is responsible for day-to-day activities and for scheduling, and also for ensuring that parts are delivered on time. This allows the purchase aspect to devote much more time to the commercial function, in particular to price negotiation and to the introduction of the new parts. Major reduction exercises such as that that was called SCORE – *successful cost operating reduction exercise* – were introduced to look at all aspects of the business that impacted on cost. This project involved not only Toshiba UK but also the parent company in Japan and two suppliers.

In terms of vendor–customer relationship, Toshiba took the view that whilst they could be hard, tough and uncompromising it was necessary, as appropriate, to be supportive of suppliers. It was necessary to recognise that from time to time problems could occur and that these should be immediately communicated to Toshiba. Only if the problems were ventilated was it possible to identify how assistance could be given to resolve the matter.

In broad terms, Toshiba aimed at long-term relationships. It was believed that in so doing, far greater understanding would be achieved between customer and supplier. This understanding had to be at all levels, managing director to managing director, production controller to production controller, sales representative to buyer. As a result of the long-term commitment, suppliers were not changed lightly. Very few suppliers were altered and then only after a long period of much effort to try and make the relationship work. As Peter Bayliss of Toshiba observed, 'it is only after it is apparent that there is no future in the relationship that we would take the final step of terminating it'. As with so many other companies, the aim was to make suppliers feel part of the Toshiba family, and although in the UK much progress had to be made to compare with Japan, a great deal of work has been done to foster this idea. Supplier conferences were held to bring together vendors and let them see the Toshiba factory, to reinforce with them fundamental principles and to give an insight into the future. There was a social dimension to these conferences, and it was not uncommon for suppliers who were in competition with each other for Toshiba business to discuss the position together as well as with Toshiba themselves. The Japanese parent company holds supplier conferences twice a year and, in conjunction with the suppliers, form the Toshiba suppliers co-operation group. This group, meeting three or four times a year on a regular basis, discusses mutual problems and every two years organises a foreign tour.

**109**

In the United Kingdom, Toshiba has considered the possibilities of extending the supply chain relationship into *just-in-time*. The potential is perhaps limited. In respect of Far Eastern supply, whilst what is ordered exactly corresponds to that which is required on the monthly basis, just-in-time becomes impractical because of shipping schedules. With local small parts, policy is to order exactly what is required on a monthly basis, but with two parts per month. Again, with these parts the true just-in-time approach is not practicable. With large parts, Toshiba order by batch with a lead time of one to five days before production and consider that their position here begins to approach the just-in-time mode. And finally, packing. Ordering is by batch with delivery on the day of production, or the day before that – two deliveries per day. This is very close to, in fact virtually is, just-in-time.

Toshiba consider that much of this is conditioned by the question of vehicle load sizes. It is clearly practical and most economic to deliver full loads, and as far as possible this is the case. This does mean, in a number of instances, just-in-time cannot be operated although lead times can be reduced.

## ● Just-in-time

One specific form of supply chain management that self-evidently demands harmony as between marketing manufacture, purchasing and logistics, is *just-in-time*. That just-in-time is now a major, indeed almost a common, theme throughout Western Europe, cannot be denied. It has many attractions to senior management, not simply in terms of reduction in inventories and better control of stock, but also in achieving greater company focus on profitability.

Just-in-time first came to prominence with the visit to Japan by major American and European companies and with articles such as that in *Fortune*, which made claims that so-called just-in-time systems could operate with only 20% of normal stock levels. The early visits to Japan were in fact dominated by those of a manufacturing persuasion and this is the reason why a great deal was made of performance improvement in this dimension. The belief became established that just-in-time was essentially a low inventory manufacturing system, which could be applied in certain restricted cases particularly in automobiles and electronics.

### The impact of Japanese thinking

Just-in-time was initially perceived as a competitive weapon devised by the Japanese, which could be matched only by competing in kind. Although this perception was quickly obscured by misconceptions, many of which still persist, just-in-time does reflect an innovatory approach to the management of the supply chain as well as a philosophical shift in the approach to long-standing and fundamental problems. It embraces not just purchasing but also marketing, manufacture and logistics. It is underpinned by total quality and at its head lies technological capability best expressed by the phrase 'batch of one'. Just-in-time rests upon seven fundamental elements – *the seven keys to just-in-time* – and its full potential rests not just upon each as a separate unit but also upon the synergy that comes from their combination (see **Fig. 3.5**).

## Innovatory elements of just-in-time

The just-in-time approach challenges two basic premises of western management. First, it exposes the view that the supply chain must, of necessity, be conflict dominated with resulting imbalances concealed by the creation of inventories. The size of such inventories reflects the degree of uncertainty generated and has a detrimental effect both upon the ability to compete and upon profitability. Organisational boundaries producing a horizontal compartmentalisation along the supply chain are a reflection of varying ownerships.

Such ownerships are not confined to those having legal prescription but exist with equal clarity within organisations. The intentions of what we may describe as these sovereign or semi-autonomous bodies are conveyed to others who depend upon them with varying degrees of precision or integrity. The forecast is a message of dubious worth giving rise to the art of second guessing. Perception and judgement are more important than technique in the search for security with flexibility.

Inconsistent views upon inventory tend to be reflected in oscillation or stability as the respective advocates of service or cost control wax and wane in power. Broad brush factors in the economic environments, or

1. Management will
2. Informed and committed workforce
3. Flexible manufacturing
4. Right first time quality
5. Electronic data interchange
6. A commitment to innovation
7. Choosing the right partners and establishing long-term links

**Figure 3.5** The seven keys to Just-in-Time

fluctuations in the size of the value added margin, colour the views of higher management who are frequently at a remove from the hurly-burly of the day-to-day struggle. It is well known that the factor that is potentially most disruptive to the smooth operation of the supply chain – partner change apart – is a change in inventory policy at a particular point. It potentially destabilises lead times, other inventories and manu-facturing programmes, and in true cyclical fashion does so with a gearing that exaggerates the movements generated.

Naturally each of the discrete elements along the supply chain would be likely to favour its own particular brand of control systems. Where these were manually operated, linkage with other parts of the chain were minimal but in fairness a chain of the traditional type could operate with reasonable success without detailed interchanges of information. Indeed, frequent changes in the structure or in the components of the chain made them virtually superfluous in the first place.

The final characteristic of this conflict dominated model was of course the proliferation of staged inventories. Sub-optimisation was the order of the day. Each looked to his own without regard to end market impact, not least because the concept of joint effort to meet consumer need did not really exist in the majority of cases. The basic assumption, which Japanese example was to undermine, was that fundamental imbalances were in fact simply not reconcilable and that only by inventory could they be legislated for and managed.

The second challenge to traditional western thinking lay in the way in which stock was viewed. This affected both the approach to batch size and also to so-called safety stocks.

The notion of an economic batch size can certainly be traced back to work at Babcock & Willcock in 1917 and indeed conceptually to a much earlier date. Although based upon simplifying assumptions regarding consumption rates and demand patterns, which should in the over-whelming majority of cases have rendered the formula of but academic interest, the EOQ/EBQ approach did turn out to be of significant value. Whatever errors might be present in the input factors – set up or pro-curement cost, stock holding cost, and above all forecast demand – the square root nature of the formula significantly reduced their impact upon the resulting batch size. EOQ/EBQ proved an efficient diminisher of mistake or misfortune and herein lay its true value. What was over-looked, however, was that set up costs need not necessarily be immutable and that it was this element that effectively led to higher rather than lower batch sizes and in consequence to more inventory than might otherwise have been the case.

The significant contribution to management thinking of the Japanese may, in the long run, turn out to be of an iconoclastic nature. By attacking the root of the problem through, for example, SMED (*single minute exchange of dies*), an example was set that many have subsequently followed. Of course it would be both foolish and inaccurate, not to say insulting, to imply that set up time reduction had not been practised in the past. It is simply that it had not been subject to such a continuous and determined assault and had not been pursued beyond what was perceived as a reasonable point. Obsessed with the notion of waste, the Japanese so extended the frontiers of what was possible as to make the 'unreasonable' just a normal aspiration. On any given set of assumptions, a reduction in batch size will reduce stock, since it cuts into that portion not kept for reasons of safety or as buffer stocks.

A second line of attack was also developed. That element of stock held against the unpredictable safety stock is always a source of difficulty for inventory controllers. Those for whom this safety stock is held have always looked askance at any moves for its reduction or elimination. This is the area where 100% service levels have long been demanded and where the worst case scenario dominates management's thinking.

By its nature, this component of the inventory shows movement only when disturbances occur in the rate of demand, or in lead time, in product quality, or, of course, when stock policy changes. To produce or eventually eliminate demand and lead time variation calls for the highest standards of product quality and the ability to guarantee delivery. By a happy coincidence, the total quality concept fits well alongside the partnership concept with proven vendors and with an ability to ship to schedule. Of course other factors – electronic data communication, stability of manufacturing programme and a consistently followed inventory policy – should be present, but the overriding need is for quality in its widest sense.

Buffer stocks, designed to adjust processes of different volume performance and facilitate balanced lines, also called for attention. Work in progress had long been the bane both of the manufacturing engineer, in the context of shop floor loading and good housekeeping, and also of the financial controller concerned with the effective use of limited working capital. UK calculations that in the engineering industry as much as 95% of manufacturing lead time lay in waiting or queuing, simply reinforce the perception that this problem was no mere inconvenience. Rationalising and modernising production methods could do much to improve the situation, but the adoption in Japan of the Kanban system of production control did much more. By its nature, the pull approach (each stage manufacturing only to the prescribed need of the next stage and no more) had a dramatic effect upon work in progress

**113**

and in particular upon buffer stocks. For Kanban to be successfully introduced, a number of factors must be present. The one that presents the greatest conceptual difficulty in the west, however, is that machine utilisation dates may well tend to fall. The notion that an idle line is not 'paying its way' dies hard and there remain those who, in the face of all logic, persist in the making of unwanted materials simply to satisfy outdated dogma.

## Just-in-time and culture

In the early 1980s there was a tendency to identify stock turn as the most important or at least the most distinctive change as a result of the introduction of just-in-time. Some of the figures that were produced and publicised did indeed show stock turns of truly magnificent dimensions. The visits that took place did much to popularise a view of Japanese management that verged almost upon the mystical. The Japanese contention that just-in-time was about the elimination of waste and respect for people was frequently quoted and it therefore became a matter of importance to consider to what extent it was possible to translate the particular elements of just-in-time to the west in the face of major cultural divergence.

Since 1945, the Japanese had pursued one fundamental economic goal – full employment through industrialisation. Of recent years, however, this has been translated into a much more proactive approach to domination of world markets. The Japanese carefully chose industries where they believed they could achieve significant dominance and, where appropriate, based their efforts on imported technology. The entire Japanese semi-conductor industry was, in the first instance, built around a $25,000 purchase from TI for the rights to the basic semi-conductor process. The Japanese avoided major R&D expenditure whilst negotiating licence agreements. They focused upon the factory in order to achieve high productivity and low unit cost. The best of their engineering talent became diverted to the shop floor in the form of production engineers. Together with this they embarked upon a drive that took product quality reliability to levels that were previously unheard of in western organisations.

One of the expressions quoted earlier, which could easily become little more than a cliché, is 'the elimination of waste'. To the Japanese, waste has a very specific meaning. In the industrial context it means the absolute minimum either of equipment or materials or people, which are absolutely essential to achieve production. The absolute minimum implies that the notion of surplus or safety stock does not exist. Stock does not become, as in the western world, any form of asset. The Japanese believe that if something is not required now then it should not be made at all. Hence the key concept is the adding of value. Value is only added when actual work is performed upon a product: assembling and packaging add value to a product; but moving or holding and sorting do not add value – they only add cost.

Let us now consider some of those elements that are perceived as helping to eliminate waste. The first of these is the focused family network. The Japanese prefer to build small plants, which are highly specialised. To an extent this is a reflection of space limitations but it also simplifies the process of management and eliminates to a large degree the dangers of bureaucracy. Japanese management styles do not lend themselves easily to large plants. Additionally, when a plant is specifically designed to do one particular thing, it can be constructed and operated more effectively than the larger plant. The bulk of the Japanese plants have between 30 and 1,000 employees. Very few employ over that number. Within the plant, group technology and cellular manufacture are employed. Even now, at the beginning of the 1990s, this concept is only beginning to permeate to much of our western manufacturing scene. Rolls Royce is currently engaged in the introduction of this approach. The object of cellular manufacture includes the reduction of waiting and moving time. This can easily occupy between 90 and 95% of the total process time. It is a natural consequence of organising the manufacturing area into departments that specialise. With cellular manufacture, equipment is allocated or semi-dedicated to a particular group or family of parts. In physical terms, the arrangement facilitates a sequence in which operations are performed on that family, with machines being placed very close to each other and in essence forming a line very similar to an assembly line as devised by Henry Ford. This type of arrangement helps to achieve balance. One-at-a-time flow along the machine line significantly reduces internal lead times and virtually eliminates work in progress in inventory between operations. It reduces the direct labour element and makes it possible to introduce other aspects of just-in-time, such as greater schedule stability and flexible crew sizes. Flexibility is indeed important. One operator may run more than one machine. This will greatly increase his utility and eliminates move and queue time of the operations in a given cluster. In order to achieve this, however, it is necessary for the worker to identify with the company and have a high degree of job security; something much eroded in recent times.

Quality at source is the third aspect that we must consider. There is no way that just-in-time can be operated with the old fashioned approach to quality control of inspection after the event. With just-in-time, everything has to be done correctly the first time since without this it is not possible for the line to function. Total quality control or quality on the line requires a major attitude change. It is necessary that everyone understands that defect free output is more important than the quantity of output (see **Fig. 3.6**). This, for practical purposes, rules out incentive systems and bonus payments. In the second place, defect error can be prevented. It is possible to take the view that we learn from errors, because we believe that inevitably they will happen again. We become reactive rather than preventive. The just-in-time approach requires that ways be found of preventing errors. Every defect can be prevented. Indeed, prevention costs much less than doing things more than once. It is only a few years ago that one could conventionally state that there was a point at which quality began to cost more than it was worth, and this was based upon the idea that quality was some kind of unspecified perfection. The modern approach departs from this view.

**Figure 3.6** Good Japanese supplies practices

## Uniform plant loading

On the shop floor it is necessary for production to flow as smoothly as possible. Uniform plant loading must be achieved. The objective of this is to even out the cycles that normally occur in response to schedule variations. The Japanese view is that this problem can be attacked by ensuring that in the end the movement of customer demand is as near level as possible. Consequently, ripples will go through the shop floor and not shock waves. This is accomplished by setting production plans for, say, a month in which the output rate is frozen, and with the same mix of product everyday, even if the total quantities are themselves small. The Japanese concept of cycle time is that production rate must equal sales rate. It should be pointed out, however, that in some organisations (Toshiba in the United Kingdom is one example) the existence of a wholly owned sales company facilitates this. The production will be the minimum necessary units that, under normal circumstances, would be sold. Customer networking as practised, for example, in 3M is a western attempt to make this more feasible. A paper by Steven Burns and Fred Seggelink of the 3M organisation addressed the issue. Customer networking seeks actively to manage the demand through the plant rather than simply passively forecasting it. The study in question involves the 3M Imaging Systems Division and one of the Division's largest customers. Irregular delivery performance was, in the customer's view, attributable to 3M's poor delivery performance. From the 3M side, the problem was identified as a highly erratic demand from the customer to be met by building inventory and by working overtime. Meanwhile the customer alternated between inventory levels that were too high and poor customer service. A review of the detailed statistical pattern showed that, in fact, the customer's demand history was relatively flat. The problem was that the demand was not being passed in a clean manner to the 3M organisation. Four primary problems were identified:

1. The lines of communication were long and there were stages in it that had little or no added value. All communication took place by telephone and in consequence, data problems occurred when information got changed as it was passed along.
2. The order policy was a second cause of difficulty. The customer normally entered a six-month blanket order. The result of such a long order period was not, as had been supposed, to give clear visibility to 3M but simply to provide an opportunity for the customer to begin, normally less than one month after the placing of the order,

to make frequent changes to the shipments. This inevitably led to a loss of control over production.

3. The third key aspect, concerns the inventory policy of the customer. The safety stock element of the policy was that a quantity would be held, which could be as much as six weeks, or as low as two weeks. It is a basic tenet that the more inventory the customer has the greater are the effects on the supplier of inventory policy changes. One conclusion that can be drawn from this is that from the supplier point of view, the most advantageous situation is where the stock held by the customer is as low as possible. In an article by J W Forrester as long ago as 1958 in the *Harvard Business Review*, the allegation was made that a 10% increase in final customer demand could produce a 40% increase in shop floor demand. This is a good example of the leverage effect of changes in the end market.

4. Finally, as a result of these three factors, the customer simply did not believe that 3M had a commitment to customer service. Credibility disappeared. The manufacturing plant could not believe, when large orders were received from the customer, that they were in fact going to be required. Hence the plant was very much exposed as a result of factors that appeared to be beyond its control.

The agreement developed in order to try and achieve some form of equalisation demand, was that the customer would in future order within a negotiated quality range. The lead time to shipment would be reduced and 3M would commit themselves to having stock available to ship up to the maximum of the range on a weekly basis. So the customer ordered within minimum and maximum limits, these sizes being largely based on demand history as well as on such factors as lot size and product configuration. The basic rules that governed the range were that no changes would be allowed for the next week's shipment but that temporary deviation from maximum or minimum could be allowed for the second week. New ranges could be renegotiated at any time and would become effective within three weeks. Communications were improved with direct contact from user to manufacturer. This eliminated the intermediary steps. 3M provided terminals at no charge in order to facilitate this process. They also guaranteed that they would give immediate notification to the customer of any anticipated changes in requested shipments.

This notion of customer networking clearly rests upon a joint approach to the problem and is a classical win/win situation that limits the extent of its applicability. Guidelines for consideration of such an approach include not only this particular relationship but also short lead times, small batch sizes and distance to travel being within one day of the supplier's factory.

This, then, is the concept of uniform plant load. We must now consider cycle time, which is the period of time between two identical units coming off the production line. In Japan this figure is used to adust the resources to producing *precisely* the quantity that was needed – neither excess nor deficit. It is an indicator of how to assemble resources to meet a given month's production. If the rate for the next month was changed, the resource required would be revised accordingly.

The Kanban or card system of production control gives very good management visibility. It is simple and self-regulating, using dedicated containers and recycling the various travelling cards. It is a pull type of re-order system in which the authority to manufacture comes from downstream operations. The whole system depends on everyone doing precisely what is authorised. It is necessary that procedures be exactly followed. In consequence, on the shop floor, there is no need for production coordinators, but co-operative work attitudes are essential to success. In many ways the appropriate analogy is that used in Japan – that of a supermarket. Whereas in the west, manufacturing companies using Materials Requirement Planning tend to schedule the assembly, explode this into its components and issue shop orders, everyone having a schedule and being ordered to do things by a certain date, the Japanese follow the supermarket example. There the customer comes in and asks for small quantities of whatever is needed. The customer knows they will be on the shelf. Soon after the customer has picked what is required, the shelf is restocked. If the item has not been taken by a customer, then there is no need for replenishment. The customer, by action or lack of it, has decided what shall be done and when. The units are small and replenishment speedily. In the factory, with this system, it is the assembly department that controls the feeding departments. For this reason assembly is controlled extremely carefully and activities are carried out smoothly in a predictable and repetitive manner.

At the heart of just-in-time is batch size. The batch of one is of fundamental significance. For virtually two centuries, manufacture has been dominated by Adam Smith's doctrine of specialisation. The division of labour and benefits of the learning curve were extended into machines designed and built for specific purposes. As a consequence, the underlying tenet was that economies of scale dependent upon large-scale manufacture brought volume related competitive advantage. The long production run thus acquired a major significance, constrained only by resulting inventory costs, which precipitated the development of the EOQ/EBQ formula.

The economic order quantity approach is attractive in that the total cost of procurement or manufacture comes close to being minimised. This is achieved by balancing the set up cost and the costs of holding resulting inventory. The principal reason why this method has dominated Western European industry for so long, is that the resultant formula is tolerant of significant error in the forecasting of demand. Notwithstanding the fact that the underlying assumptions of the ideal inventory pattern and constant rates of demand can actually be shown to be rarely applicable, this formula has remained attractive. It produces a flat bottomed total cost curve, demonstrating that a significant error in the input factors has, proportionately, relatively little effect. It is virtually impossible to stray far from the point of minimum cost and this means that that great difficulty – the problem of forecasting consumption – becomes of much less significance in terms of its practical effect. In its operation and within classifications, set up cost or the value of procurement and the stockholding cost can be deemed to be constant. Hence the formula reduces to a constant multiplied by the square root of the annual forecast consumption.

Where the Japanese have revolutionised this approach is by attacking the assumption that set up time is virtually unchangeable. The successful challenge to this notion has so reduced the costs involved that it becomes possible to produce or purchase quantities as small as one within the same overall cost parameters that previously applied to large-scale manufacture. The Japanese have achieved this reduction either by the introduction of flexible manufacturing systems, by investment in reserved capacity, or, in the majority of cases, by straightforward technical efficiency. In this latter context, the Japanese have separated the set up time into two principal components. Internal – the part that must be done while the machine is stopped; and external – the part that can be done while the machine is operating. Typically the Japanese have been able to reduce set up times by up to 90%, and it is quite clear that any organisation going down the just-in-time road needs to address these technical issues at a very early stage.

The consequences of the reduction in set up time are that there is an increase in the number of lots produced. There may also be an increase in the amount of time the machines are not actually operating. This has long been an area of major concern, and in terms of justification for investment many Western European engineers have difficulty in handling the concept that low utilisation of machines may in fact be beneficial rather than detrimental.

These, then, are the principal technical factors that were diagnosed in the very early stages as underlying the just-in-time approach. There were also preoccupations, however, with those social factors that came under the general heading of respect for people. An attempt was made to identify the extent to which cultural factors, indigenous to Japan, were prerequisites to the just-in-time approach. At different stages, lifetime employment, company unions and different attitudes towards workers came under the microscope. The phrase 'it won't work at Longbridge', with reference to the then strike-troubled British Leyland plant, was coined to cover the many doubts that were raised; doubts compounded by misunderstandings regarding the true nature of just-in-time and unfortunately by its misapplication in circumstances clearly inappropriate to its use.

It is now clear that just-in-time is by no means universally applicable across the whole range of manufacturing. In fact, it must be applied selectively, to appropriate mainstream activities. We must also be careful to distinguish between two forms – pure just-in-time and just-in-time delivery.

### Pure just-in-time

In its pure and near Japanese form, just-in-time reflects the model that was developed by Toyota in Japan (see **Figs 3.7** and **3.8**). It is a business strategy calling for the close integration of the supply chain through tightly coupled logistics and for a clear perception of the true value of the partnership approach to satisfying the needs of the end market. Sustainable competitive advantage is to be gained through customisation and innovation, to shorten product life cycles. Quality is axiomatic and costs are reduced by the replacement of the competitive adversarial approach with co-operation along the supply chain. This is based not upon some vague form of idealism but upon a mutual perception of the compatibility of self-interest. If it is anything, the pure form of just-in-time, as practised say by IBM, under the term continuous flow manufacturing, or by DAF, is a corporate approach based upon consumer focus.

```
Corporate strategy based on:
● Market differentiation
● Short product life cycles
● Tight logistics
● Supply chain partnership
● Quality axiomatic:
● Flexible manufacture essential
```

**Figure 3.7**   Just-in-Time

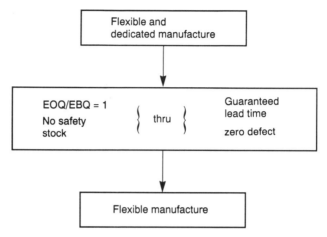

**Figure 3.8**  Pure Just-in-Time

It may well demand radical changes to procurement or investment in a flexible manufacturing system, but it is, in essence, a marketing oriented response to what is, at the end of the day, a marketing problem. The attempt to be more competitive on a sustainable basis in the end user market, means that pure just-in-time is not about redistributing costs, but about eliminating costs along the whole of the supply chain.

A manufacturer employing a pure just-in-time approach must, at the heart of the entire manufacturing process, have the ability to make a batch of one. This is essential if quick customer response is to be obtained without the need to invest in heavy inventory. Looking up the supply chain, the feeding of such a line demands in turn guaranteed quality, zero defect and frequent deliveries with again, a guaranteed lead time. In the pure approach, this must be achieved by pushing the batch of one capability up the supply chain to suppliers. A failure to do this means that the supplier in turn would rely on high inventories to give guaranteed service of guaranteed quality items. When one bears in mind the essential fact that the just-in-time competitive approach pre-supposes short product life cycle, and stresses innovation as a means of competition, then it will be seen that the traditional manufacturer, relying on old technology, is invariably going to incur a high risk of obsolescence. In this situation, who is to bear these costs? Clearly there are only three possibilities: either they are passed on to the customer, our manufacturing unit; or they are absorbed by the supplier; or the supplier has the facility to load other customers' prices without destroying his competitive advantage. None of these three approaches represents a satisfactory outcome, nor is the situation much helped by the fact that the need to achieve schedule stability implies a very restricted customer base to the supplier. Indeed it may be said that dedication is the only way of assuring the kind of response that just-in-time demands.

*Just-in-time delivery*

In contrast, just-in-time delivery (see **Figs 3.9** and **3.10**) is neither a philosophy nor a strategy. It is a system of low inventory manufacture working within very narrow parameters. Elimination of waste, as understood by the Japanese, may not be practised and cost may, in fact, simply be redistributed along the supply chain. It is, however, simple to apply and does not call for involvement by and the commitment of top management to the same degree. Structural imbalances do remain, and to the extent that the reduced manufacturing lead times are accompanied by shorter product life cycles, the continued existence of costs will naturally exacerbate the high obsolescence cost problem. The supply chain is not perceived as a single entity integrated at different levels of management and facilitating logistic trade-offs, but is seen

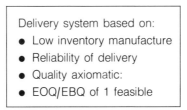

Delivery system based on:
- Low inventory manufacture
- Reliability of delivery
- Quality axiomatic:
- EOQ/EBQ of 1 feasible

**Figure 3.9**  Just-in-time: delivery

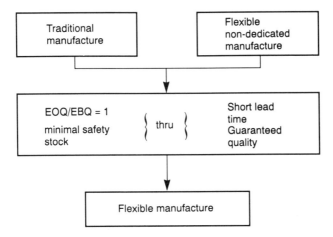

**Figure 3.10**  Just-in-time delivery system

**123**

as a series of discontinuities to be smoothed rather than confronted directly.

## The role of purchasing materials management

The part to be played by the purchasing function will reflect the degree to which the total organisation is committed to just-in-time as a business strategy. For the comprehensive form to be adopted, the necessary corollary is the strategic decision to move the purchase function centre stage. Logistics becomes a preoccupation along a supply chain that shares a common vision of the market and cost. To achieve this requires a reappraisal of the role of purchase and there is ample evidence that this is a preoccupation of virtually all successful major companies.

A recognition in recent years of the essential difference between the concepts of efficiency and effectiveness, has merged with clearer perceptions of industry life cycles to bring about this reassessment. Given the differing impact upon purchase policy of seeking a competitive edge by product differentiation, by sheer marketing effort or professionalism, or by simply being the lowest cost producer in the industry, the importance of the appropriate focus of purchase becomes obvious.

In its pure form, just-in-time requires a positioning that reflects purchasing's strategic role with an emphasis upon effectiveness. This implies proactivity with purchase involvement with product development at the design stage, and a climate in which senior management is sympathetic to such concepts as sole sourcing and long-term contract, recognising that both these courses of action bring their own particular risks.

Just-in-time delivery, on the other hand, requiring a positive but perhaps less central role for the function, may permit an approach that is commercial as opposed to strategic. There is a need for less integration, both functionally in the firm and also in external logistics.

In both kinds of just-in-time, however, purchase must move inevitably through vendor base reduction towards sole source, producing in turn a need for the adoption of long contracting horizons. Terry Hogg's perceptive comments upon the implications of short-term contracts with regard to Nissan, both in terms of pricing and supply commitment, are relevant in this regard. At any significant level of contract, set up costs for tooling means that a supplier constrained by say a 12-month contract term must be expected to seek a higher rate of return per unit sold than would be the case over a long period of time. Additionally, where short-term contracts are the norm, a significant part of the time and creative energies of the supplier's management team must be devoted to a search for new business to replace what will be inevitably lost as a result of repeated forays by buyers into the competitive market. By seeking growth from new businesses, suppliers can be diverted from existing contracts to the detriment of both themselves and their customers.

A powerful case can therefore be made for long-term sole sourcing whenever appropriate suppliers exist, but two major problems still remain to be overcome. In the first instance, sole sourcing calls for much higher standards of supplier selection. Top class suppliers with requisite quality standards and levels of commitment are at a premium. They will certainly not be discovered by sampling the market through orthodox competitive tender action. It is in this context that the purchase portfolio matrix analysis is of particular value. The buyer, in conjunction with representatives from other functions acting as a unified project team, must seek out process capability of an appropriate level allied to systems such as statistical process control and a clear management commitment to a joint venture. The just-in-time supplier must share a common perception of the needs of the end market and of the implications of closely linking logistic systems to meet that need. The requirement for data along the supply chain to be made visible and indeed to be in common ownership, for commercial knowledge to be shared mutually and not be the exclusive preserve of one party, must be understood and agreed. As pointed out by David Fanthorpe of Black and Decker, it is this sharing of knowledge, this access to master production schedules, which in many ways is the acid test of the nature of the supplier relationship. Appropriate partners of this type can in fact be rare, and a supplier development programme may be needed. Hence the buyer will face heavy new demands upon his time and it is appropriate once more to reflect on Terry Hogg's view that the most important of all buying tasks is to ensure that first class suppliers alone are selected as partners in a joint venture.

Needless to say, faced by this challenge, buyers with heavy burdens of day-to-day activity, may have difficulty in adapting to their new role in order to satisfy their internal customers. This leads to the second major problem, in the context of this form of sourcing. As a generalisation, and notwithstanding the sentiments of purchase directors, many European buyers are temperamentally and emotionally opposed to long-term sole source. Educated to the enormous competitive tendering, there is a deep rooted suspicion about the ability of suppliers to maintain their edge once the competitive pressures are removed. There appears to be a belief that power is being transferred to the supplier in a manner that is undesirable. The notion that the buyer may have to go more than half way to meet the supplier, that from a position that may be one of strength based upon leverage you have to make concessions rather than demands, is very difficult to accept. The deep rooted nature of this attitude is recognised, even in organisations with significant experience of the new mode. Mike Bowes of Ford, for example, has written that single source long-term contracts are the manifestation of a policy that is directional rather than mandatory. As such a policy is fundamental to just-in-time, it is understandable that the concept is viewed with misgivings in some purchasing circles.

## Purchasing and just-in-time – essential requirements

What then is needed from the purchase function if just-in-time is to be successful? First, the corporate view of just-in-time, fundamental business strategy or manufacturing system, must be known. Purchasing must be in a position to respond by choosing logistic systems as appropriate. It must adapt strategies tailored to meet needs and guide senior management about the implications for supply of their policies. To do this, high calibre people with clear focus are needed.

- **Table 3.1**
  Just-in-time: key elements in the process

| Purchase/ sub-contract | Logistics | Manufacture | Logistics | Market |
|---|---|---|---|---|
| Just-in-time | Consolidators | Small batches | Specialised transport | Customisation |
| Rationalised vendor base | Electronic data | Low set up time | | |
| Supplier quality assurance | Interchange/ integration | Line change | Electronic data | Short product life cycle |
| Innovation | | Short manufacturing Lead time | Interchange/ integration | |
| | | | | Electronic point of sale |
| | | Rationalised processes | | |
| | | Automation | | Data generation |
| | | Product friendly design | | |
| | | Kanban | | |
| | | Manual control | | |
| | | Worker participation | | |
| | | No storage | | |
| | | Integrated function | | |

Secondly, the purchase portfolio must be analysed with care to identify suppliers with the capability to offer just-in-time partnership who
have a clear desire to gain from it. Even such a committed organisation
as DAF has, after some ten years, barely half their suppliers by value in
a just-in-time mode. This is because just-in-time relates to the mainstream and calls for a partnership view of the supply chain based upon
negotiations in the co-operative mode.

In particular, there are three major areas that need attention. These
relate to the reliability of the supplier, to the identification of goodwill
and to the integration of both buyer and seller in terms of design, market
strategies and logistics.

## Reliability

The essence of just-in-time is that gains can be obtained through
enhanced reliability. As a minimum, these pertain to the ability to
guarantee delivery within an agreed lead time, which may have implications both for allocation and for the supplier's own processes of operational management. They also relate to total quality. It is essential that
the performance of the supplier be in parts per million mode and that
in terms of manufacturing processes and of the involvement of people,
there is an understanding that this dimension be raised as near as possible to the standard of zero defect. The supplier must have demonstrable quality systems such as Statistical Process Control. There must
be a commitment to the strategy of just-in-time, and a programme
whereby this approach can be comprehensively extended up the supply
chain. It is simply not enough to push stock into areas of lower added
value. Cost must be reduced overall, not simply redistributed. Inherent
in this notion of reliability is the desire to eliminate waste, which finds
a concrete expression in the ability to reduce real prices. By joint effort,
buyer and seller must seek economies and improvements by endeavouring to create new business opportunities for each other and expand
one another's affairs.

## Goodwill

The element of goodwill is a reflection of the fact that there must be
something over and above normal business relationships. Just-in-time is
not a temporary arrangement but a true partnership based upon mutual
advantage. Buyers frequently find the word 'trust' difficult to apply
across the whole range of commercial transactions, but there must be a
sufficient degree of commitment to make worthwhile tangible aid from

buyer to seller in the form of capital, equipment and know-how, and to make it appropriate to share with the supplier key information regarding market strategies and investment decisions.

## Buyer/seller integration

The third element of the buyer/seller relationship is integration. Amongst the forms that this may take are the bringing together of information through *electronic data interchange* (EDI), and an approach to integrated logistics that requires an overview of the supply chain and a mechanism to make trade-offs in terms of inventory and lead time. Given that just-in-time, in its widest sense, is based upon a common interest in the end user market, the ability to change or enhance the designs is important. Innovative capability is a highly prized commodity and it is essential for the supplier to be able to integrate within the design process, those elements that can be contributed with a view to difference in the final market. This degree of integration will, ultimately, lead to an ability to make joint long-term plans in the firm knowledge of continuing business relationships. Almost inevitably, long-term contractual arrangements or understandings that it implied, lead to a restructure of the portfolio and probably to sole sourcing. From the buyer's point of view, the two principal problems that this presents at the moment are: (i) that too few suppliers can readily fulfil the criteria performances that are needed; and (ii) that buyers in the western world find great difficulty in accepting this perceived loss of power.

By its nature, just-in-time cannot be a temporary arrangement. Continuity is inherent in it and, as CADCAM (Computer Aided Design Computer Aided Manufacture) and CIM (Computer Integrated Maintenance) extend their range and more processes acquire low set-up costs, just-in-time will increasingly become the norm. This will not happen, let it be stressed, in its pure form except in clearly defined circumstances. Elsewhere, just-in-time will be adopted in a modified form, tailored to meet individual needs.

It is not difficult to list the ideal characteristics of just-in-time suppliers. Some of these can be specified in objective or quantifiable terms, for example process capability. Others are perceptions that are more subjective and much more variable. A commitment to customer needs, an eye to innovation and a willingness to provide exceptional service particularly in times of difficulty may all be less tangible, but in the just-in-time context they are none the less of great importance. In all cases, just-in-time will be in the mainstream of the supply chain with advanced technology or flexible manufacturing giving small batch capability. A willingness to hold stock may meet just-in-time's service needs, but exposure to frequent design change negates its value as a longer-term factor in viable just-in-time.

The supplier who moves into a just-in-time framework does so to gain commercial advantage, not least through continuity of business. At one time it was suggested in some circles that just-in-time must lead to higher prices because of the quality standards demanded and because of more stringent lead time demands. This is certainly not the case today with competitive pressure once more forcing price to the fore, and the just-in-time supplier must now regard real price reductions as an almost inevitable consequence of the environment within which he operates. Of course the continued health of the supplier demands an adequate return on investment and for both the effective handling of basic factors such as scheduling as well as technical and logistical support. Issues that must, in addition, be faced are warranty costs and the control of sub-contractors. Many large organisations expect their suppliers to undertake to meet a share of the former and this may well extend into the subcontractor network. At one time some degree of responsibility for the suppliers' own sources might have been retained by the purchaser, particularly where quality was concerned. At one time, for example, Marks and Spencer did this. Today, however, this is much less acceptable, with suppliers expected to be responsible for all aspects of their products.

Small quantities, let alone variations in lead time, present significant delivery problems and could easily play havoc with the economics associated therewith. The specialist carrier can thus have a major role to play in just-in-time and, particularly where significant distances are involved, the consolidator can be a key element in the just-in-time chain. An early example was the Xerox European pipeline, where European supplies were routed via Vento or Schipol to the Rochester plant. The drawbacks of long lines of communication are, as in the military sense, apparent and they can easily nullify much of the flexibility associated with just-in-time.

Finally, there is the question of the legal form to be adopted and the way in which it should be expressed. There is some discussion as to whether the just-in-time agreement should be a simple declaration of intent, whether it should be a comprehensive, all-embracing contract, or whether it should be a three-stage contract, each within different envelopes. It is probably true to say that the declaration of intent is increasingly finding favour. It is to be found in use by organisations as diverse as IBM, Digital Equipment and Rolls Royce. Comprehensive agreements are frequently favoured by companies with a tradition of legalistic and formal arrangement. At one stage, Schlumberger, for example, fell into this category. Finally, envelope contracts will be found, for example, at DAF Trucks in Holland, where the different forms of the just-in-time arrangement are each encompassed, one within another.

\* The End \*

WAY-HEY!

# 4

# Quality

● Introduction

It has sometimes been suggested that the first move in launching a quality initiative is to decide which guru to follow, and, indeed, there is today a range of offers. The principal differences lie between approaches with substantial statistical or mathematical implications such as Deming and Taguchi and those that emphasise customer relationships – the Crosby methodology. To a degree, choice depends upon the industry concerned and the issues to be addressed, and new developments continually occur. One approach that is currently gaining ground for example – *quality functional deployment* – synthesises much previous thinking, bringing together customer perceptions, operational implications and competitor response. All, however, are ultimately based upon four key elements: (i) prevention as opposed to cure; (ii) focus upon the customer; (iii) universal participation; and (iv) continuous improvement.

## The nature of quality

Quality is about giving total satisfaction to a customer. This means that manufacturers must be able to achieve complete consistency in all those aspects that give appeal to a product – function, appearance and features. Novelty or excellence in only one area is no longer enough: total quality equates with total consistency.

In view of the apparently obvious nature of quality, it is perhaps surprising that views about it have changed as dramatically as they have in recent years. Notwithstanding the work of Deming and Duran, conventional wisdom on quality, until relatively recently, was that there was a clear limit to the cost that could be justified in order to give appropriate satisfaction to a customer. The sharply rising curve shown in **Fig. 4.2** was seen as being the only cost curve relevant to this problem.

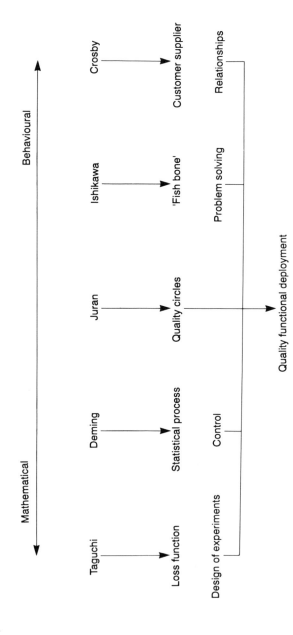

**Figure 4.1** Quality gurus – their relationship and significance

**Figure 4.2** Quantity/cost relationship: a 1970s view based upon inspection costs

It was perceived that a single dimension – a dimension of inspection – was relevant. The exponential nature of the cost curve made it possible to allege that at some point it was no longer worthwhile to invest in further improvement. Sampling techniques could be used at the lower levels of the cost curve as a means of ensuring customer satisfaction by extrapolating the results of testing or examining in order to ensure that the acceptable quality of the whole consignment fell within previously defined boundaries. In this approach, a failure rate of 2 or 3% could easily be perceived as being quite acceptable, and it was hoped that if rectification costs were incurred they could be held within reasonable bounds. It was only the successful penetration of western markets by Japanese firms, which led to the perception that good quality could be a factor of major competitive importance. This awakened the United States and other western countries to the need to raise standards, and in one way the 1980s may be characterised as the decade of quality. During these years, faced by the threats of competition from the Pacific Rim, the management of western companies became alive to the need to make quality not just a concern but a positive obsession. They became aware that it was now necessary to identify customer requirements with much greater clarity, and to meet them in a way and to a degree that had previously been regarded as unobtainable. In Crosby's words, quality had moved to the top of every agenda to be pursued with persistence and with what is referred to as emotional attachment. It was therefore possible by 1984 for David Garvin to claim with accuracy that most major North American companies ranked as their principal current concern 'production to high quality standards'. At this time there was a question regarding the precise nature of quality, and certainly a lack of consensus as to how it might best be addressed. In part this could be attributed to the fact that the issue was being approached from a number of different directions, the most obvious example of this being the conflict between marketing and operational management. There were undoubtedly a number of common concerns. Was quality, for example, an objective or a subjective concept? Was it autonomous in its nature or was it socially determined? Did it co-relate with price, cost or market share?

## The economist's view of quality

One of the main difficulties arose from the fact that different backgrounds generated very different approaches to these questions. If it were to be accepted that it was important to go beyond the view that quality was some form of innate excellence that could not accurately be defined, then it had to be decided precisely what attributes should be measured and assessed in order to determine appropriate quality levels.

The economist offered possible solutions. In the first case quality was related to the nature of the product. It was something that could be costed and measured. For example, French jam will typically contain some 55 g of fruit per 100 g of product, compared with 45 g or more commonly 35 g in the United Kingdom. In this context, quality therefore is perceived as having a hierarchical dimension. This may be reflected in variable price. Such a concept can be difficult to come to grips with unless virtually all buyers agree on the precise attributes. Two corollaries do arise, however. In the first place, since attributes can be ranked, higher quality can be related to the higher costs thereby incurred. In the second place, quality is both objective and measurable. To this extent, therefore, quality enters the domain of the exact, and subjective elements are relegated to a minor aspect of the question. Closely allied to this view in its origins was the notion of quality as a user based concept. Individual consumers have different scales for wants and for needs, and those goods that best satisfy preferences were perceived as having a higher quality. This was both subjective and to a degree idiosyncratic. It posed the problem of how individual preferences might be aggregated in order to establish a meaningful definition, and also how the different elements might be weighted. In addition, the question arose of whether or not quality really could be equated with the satisfaction derived. Is it really true, for example, that if a product meets more rather than fewer needs, that it is necessarily better than another? There is also a historical perspective. User perceptions do depend, to a significant degree, upon social viewpoints and upon changes in the economic environment.

Today, durability is once more an important aspect of quality and long life goods are frequently preferred to those that wear out. Automobile testing in Sweden, for example, has led to the conclusion that the long life of the Volvo invests it with a desirability not found in other cars less well structured to the demands of the Scandinavian winter. Swedish industry has, in general, seen in durability a very important source of competitive advantage. White goods in the kitchen – dishwasher, washing machine, dryer – all these are products where a typical Swedish approach will be to engineer to higher standards in the quality and durability dimension than those derived from other sources. This has made it possible to command a selective market niche consisting of those impatient of built-in deterioration or built-in obsolescence. By contrast, in the nineteenth century, durable goods were seen primarily as possessions of the poor and the assumption was therefore made that there was some correlation between durability and inferiority. This is no longer the case today.

## An operational management perspective

A very different view stemmed from the quarter of operations management. There, quality was seen either from the point of view of the manufacturing function or in terms of intrinsic value. A focus on the supply side based upon engineering practice leads to the notion that quality is 'conformed to requirement'. Once a specification or design has been agreed, a natural conclusion was that any deviation implied a reduction in quality. Excellence therefore became synonymous with meeting specification or with 'making it right first time'. This could be achieved by focusing upon different elements of quality at different stages of the manufacturing process. In the design stage, emphasis is placed upon reliability. It was good practice to weed out deviations at the earliest possible stage. This element was then supported in the manufacturing by the use of SPC, which, it was believed, was the key to discovering when a process itself was moving outside the acceptable limits. This particular avenue of approach has been significantly developed in recent years and, particularly in Japanese industry, the view has gained ground that variation is the key to customer satisfaction and that variability within a process must be reduced by the use of experimental techniques. It is perhaps true to say that it is in this dimension that the conveyance of requirements to suppliers has now reached its most precise form.

## The value approach

An alternative, operationally based approach is to define quality in terms of cost and price. Termed a value base definition, this has a quality product as one that is offered at an acceptable price or alternatively gives *conformance* at an acceptable level of cost. For example, if a pair of shoes were to cost £1,000 it js unlikely that it would be considered to be a quality product since at that price no matter how well it was made, it would find only a few buyers. Whilst this may have significance, a difficulty remains with this particular avenue of attack that quality as a measure of excellence is being equated with value, which is a measure of worth. The two are not necessarily synonymous and the hybrid view of affordable excellence is, in practice, difficult to apply. One implication of the fact that there were so many roads apparently leading to Rome is that it helps to explain the difficulty of conveying to suppliers precisely what the purchaser sought in the way of quality. Marketing and manufacturing were approaching the issue from very different viewpoints. To marketing, better performance and enhanced features were hallmarks of high quality. Inevitably these implied extra cost. The customer, the arbiter and the field were more important than the factory. Manufacturing engineering, on the other hand, seizing upon conformance and upon doing it right first time, increasingly equated poor quality with greater scrap or rework. Any improvement in quality was necessarily defined as a clear reflection in cost reduction.

It might therefore be appropriate that, perhaps at different stages in manufacture, different aspects of quality assume a greater importance. There becomes a need to move the approach to quality as a product passes from the design to the development stage to market. In the first instance it might be that market research would identify the users' perceived requirements. These might then be translated into product based attributes, which could be guaranteed by ensuring the performance of the manufacturing process. Ultimately marketing could then present the consumer with a product that met the varying requirements of different functions and that was effectively a synthesis of all those elements that might be seen as pertaining to the quality issues.

## Changes in attitude

Today it can be said, without fear of contradiction, that it is simply not true that at some point quality costs more than it is worth. The current multi-cost approach to the question is demonstrated in **Fig. 4.3**. This places into context the relationship between the costs of appraisal and failure and the costs of prevention. As can be seen, a modest increase in the prevention cost element can impact very significantly upon total quality costs because of savings in the appraisal/failure dimension. Indeed for a small increase, a major reduction is easily achieved. **Fig. 4.4** derived from a major European electronic manufacturer, charts over three years the actual cost in quality relating this to the three specific dimensions. As will be seen, a change of approximately 1.5% in prevention costs has been accompanied by a total reduction of the order of 8%. Such experience has been typical of manufacturing industry and has led to the clear recognition that prevention is better than cure. The real problems therefore arise which proactive measures warrant adoption. Indeed, of the three major principles that have come to be accepted in recent years, prevention not cure might be seen as the first. The second is the need to build in quality at the design stage, to avoid unnecessary complication, unrealistic tolerances and to ensure above all

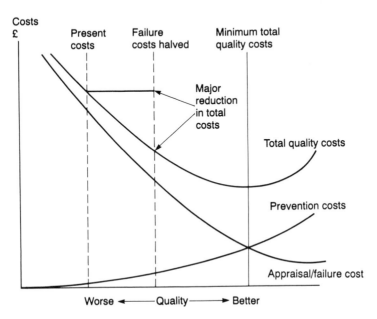

**Figure 4.3** Quality/cost relationships

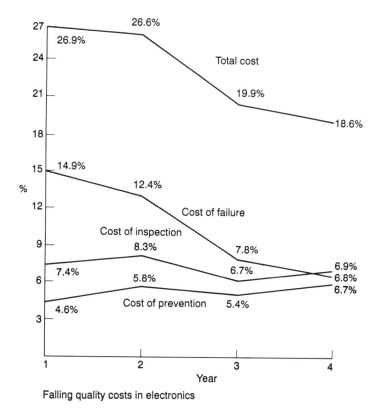

Falling quality costs in electronics

**Figure 4.4** Trend of cost of quality

that processes are appropriate to need. The third principle, owing a great deal to perceptions arising in Japan of the need for total employee participation, is to see a change in the nature of operator responsibility. As soon as there are no financial penalties for revealing the existence of poor quality, the operator can assume the role of inspector. The operator can be trained in appropriate quality techniques and become a very effective part of the prevention force.

In the early 1980s, the Peugeot Motor Company was wont to advertise the fact that one in seven of all its workforce were inspectors. At that time the cynical might have made the jibe that quality must have been poor if as many as one person in seven was assigned to the job of inspection. This was, of course, not the message that Peugeot had hoped to put over. Today one might similarly criticise this approach but from a different viewpoint. It might be asked what are the other six doing, since all seven should be quality inspectors? Quality is not the preserve of a specialist force; it is the concern of all those engaged in the organisation.

Psychology is also important. Historically, quality has been seen too much in defensive terms. Strategies, such as extending lead times, increasing order quantities and raising safety stocks, were designed to conceal amongst other things the effects of poor quality. In essence the approach of cost reduction was to see quality in terms of less scrap, of less rework or disruption, in terms of fewer warranties, fewer concessions – to see quality essentially as an inward matter; a matter of monitoring and control. Henry Ford laid down a text for consumer focus when he remarked that 'if customers are truly satisfied, profits will follow'. It is therefore possible to perceive quality in terms of an offensive strategy. The PIMS (Profit Improvement Marketing Strategy) approach made it abundantly clear that as quality goes from low to high, so do productivity, market share, profit on sales and return on investment. Quality is the cause of change; the other factors are the results. Better quality products mean higher sales and quality is therefore not a cost but an asset. Quality can be increased in value without restriction, since it is investment that brings returns in the form of direct gains on the bottom line.

## ● Some dimensions of quality

Communication of quality needs to others (and in particular suppliers) makes it necessary to consider the different features that quality description might possess. In the first place, the primary attributes relate to fundamental performance. In the case of a television set the picture clarity, colour and sound would fall within this category. Such core characteristics would then be enhanced by features. These are embellishments, such as free drinks on an aeroplane, which add to the total customer perception but are ancillary to the primary performance. This is not to say that they cannot, by clever presentation, be manifested to the customer as having an importance out of all proportion to the cost of provision.

Then there is reliability. The mean time to first failure, the mean time between failures and failure rate per unit time are all capable of objective measurement. They are more relevant to durable goods than to services or products that are consumed instantly. Once, the primary performance has been satisfied, however, and ancillary features taken for granted, reliability can be of fundamental importance because it is with the consumer throughout the whole life of the product. Reliability has certain affinities with conformance. Conformance is the need to match pre-established standards. It can cover incidence of service calls or the frequency of repairs under warranty. For the most part, therefore, this can be objectively assessed.

Durability is the fifth characteristic. In technical terms this is the use that may be obtained from a product such as a light bulb before it physically deteriorates. Alternatively, where repair is possible it is the use before a product breaks down and replacement becomes preferable to continued repair. This will clearly vary with changing economic conditions since these will have a bearing upon the perception of product life. Product life reflects repair cost, loss due to down time, quality of components and personal evaluations of time or inconvenience. The implication therefore is that durability, reliability and quality perceptions are closely linked. Durability can be due not simply to technical improvement or use of longer life material, but to changes in the underlying economic environment. In North America, for example, the life of an automobile has been extended by rising petrol costs, which have led to less use and to legislation that sets out more restrictive parameters governing their operation on the road.

Serviceability is the next facet of quality. The speed, courtesy and competence of service organisations also lives with the consumer during the entire time of product use. Technical competence can be measured by the speed of reply to the customer and by the incidence of service calls to correct a single problem. Some customers call for more repeated repair and reduce down time with high quality and some organisations – for example, J C Bamford in the field of excavation – owe a great deal of their market pre-eminence to the well-established strength of their service function.

Finally, there are two characteristics that are much less tangible. Aesthetics – views regarding feel or sound or taste or smell – are a matter of personal judgement; whilst perceived quality – one of the main determinants of price – is impaired as a workable concept by the fact that customers do not always have complete information about product attributes. In such circumstances customers tend to rely on an indirect measure, such as reputation or affiliation, both of which are capable of manipulation without reference to the underlying characteristics of the product or the service.

The statistical implications are that quality cannot be segmented into specific dimensions. Different niches can be targeted; different niches that require different producer characteristics or attributes. The Japanese have shown great skill in disaggregating the aspect of quality. For many years Japanese cars were typified as being of poor design and indifferent appearance but available at low cost. Subsequently came the development of durability as a primary operating characteristic, followed by enhancement of features, and finally the adoption of high price design characteristics has been demonstrated. The policy emphasises different parts of the quality function in order to achieve progressive market penetration.

To conclude, there is a quality cost relationship. Any expenditure on manufacturing or service that is in excess of what would have been incurred had the product been completed exactly right first time, constitutes waste in the Japanese sense of that term. Hence it must be eliminated in order to achieve an overall objective, which is to match high quality in the eyes of the customer with low cost on the part of the producer.

● Tackling variability

**The loss function**

It was William Scollard, vice president of engineering and manufacturing at Ford who said 'Our new quality thinking should be reduced process variability around the nominal'. In manufacturing, the impact of Taguchi and Shainin has been primarily to identify the extent to which a concentration upon variation in the process can reduce the losses sustained by the consumer as a result of product failure in any form. Taguchi defined quality as 'the loss imparted to society from the time a product is shipped'. Value for the customer was to be ensured by design processes that minimised loss. The Taguchi loss function could be measured by relating the variation of the process to a loss constant.

**Figs. 4.5** and **4.6** illustrate the need for variation reduction in a striking way. In the first, which is a typical western view provided that the product falls between the lower and upper specification limit, there is a presumption of complete customer satisfaction. Such a view makes for ease of production and for loss assumptions based upon a transition from total satisfaction to total dissatisfaction. On reflection, the lack of realism in this view is apparent. The Japanese view, as characterised by the Taguchi loss function, is based upon the cardinal principle that regardless of the nature of the specification, any departure from target value represents a cost (see **Fig. 4.5**). At the target value, dissatisfaction is zero but it increases exponentially as the product moves away from that central target. The essential and overriding need is to recognise that

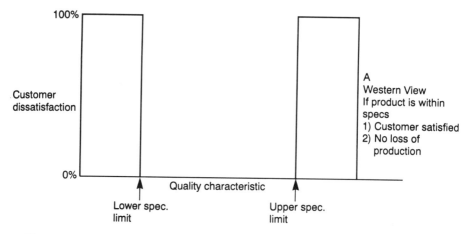

**Figure 4.5** The American view of quality characteristic

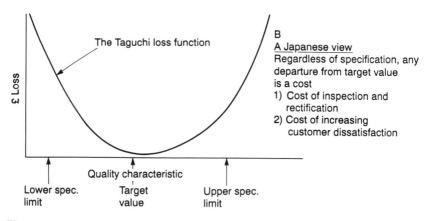

**Figure 4.6** The Taguchi view of quality characteristic

above all customers want uniformity of product and consistency. Failure to achieve these gives rise to increasing customer dissatisfaction and also potentially to increased costs of rework and possibly of inspection. The Taguchi focus upon variation reduction is therefore designed to bring units close to the target value through better design both of product and of process. Better process capability would ensure that uniformity and consistency are achieved rather than a large number of products being generated, which although meeting the specification in practice vary very widely.

## Sources of variation

Bhote has identified six principal sources of variation (see **Table 4.1**). The first of these is concerned with management. Duran has long pointed out that it is poor management that gives rise to the overwhelming bulk of manufacturing problems. Many managers have little knowledge of or any policy on variety reduction. Not enough time, money, effort or training are devoted in most companies in order to ensure that what is to be done has been properly thought through and appropriately designed. The design of experiments (DOE) is the major field in which gains might be made here, and with management training and involvement, DOE is a way in which organisations can begin to impact upon variation. All too frequently, however, this aspect is neglected and less appropriate means of problem-solving are adopted. Included amongst these are quality circles and problem-solving techniques such as that ascribe to Ishikawa, which do not address the real issue.

In the second place, the human factor in the form of operator error comes to bear elsewhere in the process. Badly trained operators – with poor instructions working with inadequately designed processes, relying on external inspection and not seen as essential members of the team – are recipes for disaster. In no other area will there be more attractive returns to scale than here; through investment in training, through the perceived involvement of management, through means of sharing gains that are made, and the adoption of foolproofing techniques. A third source of failure is the absence of a comprehensive quality system. Notwithstanding some of the criticisms made, the systemisation inherent in BS 5750 or in ISO 9000 (see p. 165) can be seen as providing the beginnings of an appropriate quality system infrastructure. These standards put in place foundations for the systematic reduction of variation.

In respect of materials, poor specification of components has long been a major problem. This is particularly true in areas where product innovation has made it necessary to seek technologically attractive solutions, beyond the bounds of that which has been well tried. Linked with this have been broadly based specifications and the all too ready adoption of supplier published specifications. In the nature of things, components are linked elements and it is important to establish the extent to which variables arise from such linkage or interaction effects. Design of experiment techniques at the first run or pilot run stage can be used to separate important variables from those of less significance and to begin the process of determining which variables give rise to the most important consequences.

• **Table 4.1**

Sources, causes and reduction of variation

| Source | Causes of variation | Variation reduction |
|---|---|---|
| Poor management | – No knowledge of or policy on variation reduction<br>– No resources allocated to DOE<br>– No championship or involvement in DOE<br>– No DOE training or its implementation<br><br>– SPC and control charts – especially for problem solving | – Top management training in DOE overview<br>– Management steering committee for DOE<br>– DOE training and workshops for tech population<br>– Monitoring the DOE 'process' rather than just goals and results |
| Poor product/process specs. | – Selling over marketing<br>– Pushing state of art designs<br>– Wide tolerance V target values<br>– Reliability not a specification<br>– No DOE in systems testing | – Value research and multi-attribute competitive analysis tools<br>– Evolutionary V revolutionary designs<br>– Target values and use of loss function<br>– Optimising old equipment not junking it<br>– Multiple environments over-stress tests for reliability<br>– Extension of DOE in customer application |
| Poor Component Specs. | – Fascination with technology<br>– Indiscriminate and tight tolerances<br>– Boiler plate specs: supplier published specs<br>– Monte Carlo and worst case analysis<br>– Formulas linking variables non-existent, wrong or unable to determine interaction effects | – DOE techniques at pilot run stage to separate important variables from unimportant ones. (Part B for detailed techniques) |

● **Table 4.1**
*(Continued)*

| Source | Causes of variation | Variation reduction |
|---|---|---|
| Inadequate Quality System | – Comprehensive quality system not developed<br>– Quality peripherals overlooked | – Infrastructure of a quality system<br>– Positrol:process certification:pre-control |
| Poor Supplier Materials | – Too many suppliers<br>– Control and negotiations and table pounding<br>– AQL, incoming inspection | – 'Best in class' partnership supplier<br>– Physical proximity, continuous help<br>– DOE training<br>– CPK of 2.0 as a minimum |
| 'Operator' Errors | – Poor instructions, training<br>– Poor processes, materials, equipment<br>– Design for non-manufacturability<br>– External inspection<br>– 'Pair of hands' syndrome | – Training in 7 QC tools and DOE<br>– Encouragement, support, management involvement<br>– Self-inspection and poka yoke (foolproofing)<br>– Gain sharing |

Frequently, components are supplier generated and historically, many organisations have had an excessively wide supplier base. Incoming inspection and Acceptable Quality Level approaches have proved to be damaging concepts, both in terms of result and in terms of attitude. Of course it is true that there are areas where incoming inspection is a necessary prescription, either by regulatory body or by government agency, but elsewhere the current trend is towards requiring that suppliers become self-certifying agents. The first well publicised group to visit Japan in order to investigate its economic success was the Harbour Committee, and their prescription of 'getting closer to fewer' must be qualified by the addition of the statement 'but better'. There is a need for the best of breed or best in class approach, for the adoption of partnership with suppliers based upon the mutual perception of benefit in the end market, but above all, for continuous help and training. It has been advocated that a corrected process capability of two might now be regarded as a necessary minimum, and this approach does indeed begin to turn the question of supplier process capability into something capable of more objective assessment.

Sixth, but by no means least in importance of the causes of variation, has been poor specification of product or process. There is a need to avoid excessive indulgence in wide tolerances or in advocating untried state of art designs, and it is here that much of the Taguchi effort can be seen to bear fruit in terms of emphasising the importance of process capability.

● Process capability

Of the many key elements in current quality thinking, *process capability* in the appropriate circumstance is clearly the most powerful. Process capability is a measure of spread and it may be defined as specification width divided by process width. In broad terms, higher process capability reduces cost.

The diagrams in **Fig. 4.7** relate the width of specification of a product with the process width. In order to achieve higher levels of performance it is necessary that the process width be sufficiently tightly defined as to make it impossible for that particular process to produce items that are not to specification. If we define our product as falling within a lower specification limit of let us say 20 and an upper specification limit of 40, then the following comments will apply. Given process width defined as plus or minus 3 sigma limits in A there is only a two-thirds chance that items produced will meet the requirements of the

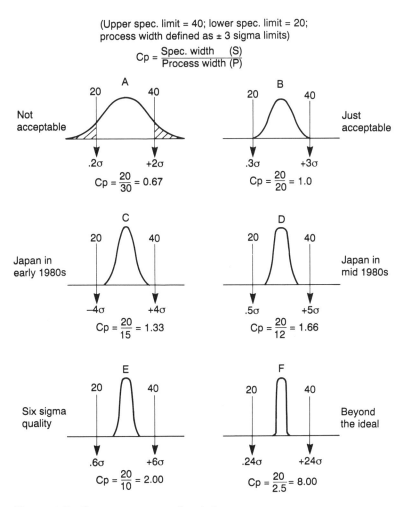

(Upper spec. limit = 40; lower spec. limit = 20;
process width defined as ± 3 sigma limits)

$$Cp = \frac{\text{Spec. width} \quad (S)}{\text{Process width} \quad (P)}$$

**A**

20    40

Not acceptable

.2σ    +2σ

$$Cp = \frac{20}{30} = 0.67$$

**B**

20    40

Just acceptable

.3σ    +3σ

$$Cp = \frac{20}{20} = 1.0$$

**C**

20    40

Japan in early 1980s

−4σ    +4σ

$$Cp = \frac{20}{15} = 1.33$$

**D**

20    40

Japan in mid 1980s

.5σ    +5σ

$$Cp = \frac{20}{12} = 1.66$$

**E**

20    40

Six sigma quality

.6σ    +6σ

$$Cp = \frac{20}{10} = 2.00$$

**F**

20    40

Beyond the ideal

.24σ    +24σ

$$Cp = \frac{20}{2.5} = 8.00$$

**Figure 4.7** Cp – a measure of variation

product specification. This was a characteristic of American industry in the 1970s. Turning to B, some ten years of advance in the area brought many American processes more into a situation where there was an exact match between specification width and process width. This too is almost out of control because any slight change or drift in the process will cause rejects to arise. This is in spite of the widespread use of statistical process control. As we move to C, representative of Japanese industries in the early 1980s, for the first time we can see that there is a margin of safety arising between the tighter process limit and the limit of the specification. This was in fact at the beginning of the 1980s, a standard parameter in Japanese industry. D shows further progress widening the safety margins, and significantly further reductions occur in E and F. It has been widely suggested that the process capability of 2.0 in diagram E should be identified as a minimum standard in respect of suppliers' quality characteristics and it should be upon this basis that supply evaluation and monitoring might proceed. In the case of F we have a situation

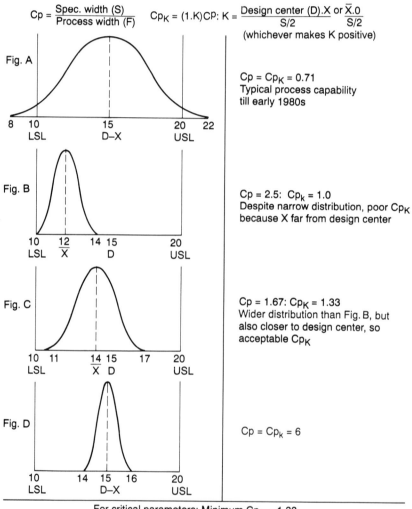

$$Cp = \frac{\text{Spec. width (S)}}{\text{Process width (F)}} \qquad Cp_K = (1.K)CP: K = \frac{\text{Design center (D).X or } \bar{X}.0}{S/2} \quad \frac{}{S/2}$$
$$\text{(whichever makes K positive)}$$

**Fig. A**

8   10        15        20   22
    LSL       D–X       USL

$Cp = Cp_K = 0.71$
Typical process capability
till early 1980s

**Fig. B**

10    12   14 15        20
LSL   X         D        USL

$Cp = 2.5$: $Cp_K = 1.0$
Despite narrow distribution, poor $Cp_K$
because X far from design center

**Fig. C**

10   11    14 15    17    20
LSL        X  D           USL

$Cp = 1.67$: $Cp_K = 1.33$
Wider distribution than Fig. B, but
also closer to design center, so
acceptable $Cp_K$

**Fig. D**

10        14   15   16    20
LSL            D–X         USL

$Cp = Cp_K = 6$

For critical parameters: Minimum $Cp_K = 1.33$
Desirable $Cp_K = 2.00$
Ideal $Cp_K = 25.00$

LSL   Lower specification limit
USL   Upper specification limit

**Figure 4.8**  $Cp_K$ – a measure of process capability

where the process capability figure of 8.0 represents what may be considered to be virtually an ideal situation. The chances of any product arising that fails to meet the product specification is, for practical purposes, zero unless it should happen that the process is itself considerably off centre.

There is, however, a need for a further refinement since non-centring of the process relative to the specification reduces the margin of safety (see **Fig. 4.8**). As can be seen in B, a narrow distribution can still give rise to problems because of the offsetting of the mean value from the design centre. It could indeed be better to have a situation in C where, though the distribution is wider, it becomes more acceptable because it is more proximate to the design centre. In consequence, process capability may be refined to take into account both spread and non-centring. This can be achieved by applying a correction factor giving a formula for the corrected process capability of 1 minus K multiplied by process capability. The correction factor itself is the positive value of design centre minus process average all divided by half the specification width or alternatively process minus design centre all divided by half the process width.

Taguchi's assessment of this problem is that the effects of inadequate process capability are that there is a failure to satisfy the customer, a cost to society and a cost to manufacture. These costs arise either from the purchase of the product or from its rejection. In order to minimise these effects, Taguchi advocates seeking to eliminate noise or error factors from both product and process.

The ideal in a functional quality is for there to be no change in the way in which the product performs in spite of noise. Hence quality can be measured as the degree of variation from the target functional value or from the normal or ideal value as determined in the specification. The approach to this process is similar both for processes and products. Noise can be defined as those factors that cause variability in the functions of product. In the case of a fluorescent light, brightness can vary, and the power supply or voltage can also deteriorate over time. These would be termed as noise.

## Noise

The principal forms that noise can take are termed *external, internal* or *variational*. External noise is caused by a change in the environment or in conditions of use, such as dust or temperature change. The plasticity of many products can vary with ambient temperature. There are, for example, some ten different ingredients in caramel and by varying these, a caramel of greater or less plasticity can be made. Typically customers prefer their confectionery to remain broadly constant whatever the temperature may be and prefer the mix of ingredients that varies the least around some identified target value.

By contrast, internal noise is variation in the internal constants in the product itself. There may, for example, be deterioration with storage or wearing out in use and this can cause the product to fail to perform in the expected way. High stability requires the maintenance of initial performance for an indefinite period and may be seen as of prime importance to purchasers of, say, consumer durables. An example of internal noise lies in the power circuit of a colour television set. This converts input to 115 voltage DC output and over, say, a ten-year period the resistance of the resistor may increase by up to 10%. The manifestation of the phenomenon is likely to reduce consumer satisfaction and be seen as a quality problem.

Variational noise is the difference that can arise between individual units manufactured to the same specifications. In the case of the power circuit, this would lead to different output voltages from the same input voltage and hence to performance changes. This can be a source of major irritation to customers who demand a high degree of uniformity from branded goods. Where those goods are of natural origin, subtle variation gives to the consumer the appearance of uniformity. Blended whiskies, sherries, or tea are all examples of naturally derived products where the reduction of variational noise is essential.

There are a number of ways in which noise can be reduced or even eliminated. The first of these is off line quality control. The objective of off line quality control is to find the cause of variability and to remove it permanently. The types of off line control are systems design or primary control. The purpose of systems design is to produce a process that possesses the functions designated by the planning department. This may be achieved by carrying out a survey of pertinent technology in order to determine, through internal expertise, which is best. This requires wide knowledge both of what is needed and also of market availabilities.

It may also be necessary to carry out studies in order to be able to select optimum levels for system parameters. The objective of parameter design is to evaluate the overall variability due to either internal or external noise for different levels of controllable factors, and then to find designs that are immune to noise as far as possible. The key in the view of Taguchi is to improve process capability by reducing the influence of harmful factors. Through such experimental work it may be possible both to improve quality and to lower cost. It may facilitate the use of inexpensive components and lead to the reduction of the variability of the required characteristic.

Lastly, there is tolerance design or tertiary control. Amongst the various noise factors there will be some that have a disproportionate influence on the pareto basis. It is important that these be identified and it is an objective of tolerance design to ensure that high tolerances are applied to these particular noise factors even though this may mean more expensive components. When combined with the results of system and parameter design, the production department can then be briefed in the form of specifications. It is a means of suppressing variations in quality by directly removing their cause, calculating in the course of this whether additional costs are justified.

# ● On-line quality control

## Product variability

The need for an on-line quality control exercise by the production department arises from the fact that once the production process and operating conditions have been determined, significant sources of product variability will still remain. These arise from the following factors. In the first place, bought in materials and purchased components will themselves be subject to variation. This variation will impact directly but will also have a compounded effect due to interreaction. Secondly, process drift, tool wear and machine failure represent ever present factors. In addition there will be variability in the way that the production process is carried out, as well as human errors.

## How product control is applied

To deal with these contingencies, quality control will be applied in a variety of ways, virtually irrespective of the industry in question. First, the process itself must be maintained through diagnostic checks at regular intervals. This monitoring will be related to preventive maintenance carried out on a systematic basis. It is necessary, when the process appears to be moving out of control, to find the cause and repair it to an acceptable state of balance. In respect of machines, dimensional instability must be reduced and, for example, positioning accuracy improved. Tool stocks need to be rationalised and their quality raised. Speaking of this, D J King of Rolls Royce plc said with regard to aero engine casing manufacture that:

> 'Rationalisation of the cutting tool range within the Automatic Tool Changer capacity was achieved so that tools and tool holders could remain permanently in position thus eliminating another involvement in setting ... Through meticulous attention to detail in developing the method and establishing process capability to give repeatable performance within specification, the product quality has been achieved with minimum operator input.'

Second, the quality characteristics to be controlled must be measured. The resultant values are used to predict the mean characteristic value if production is to continue without adjustment. Should predicted values differ from direct values there must be modification in order to reduce the differences. It may be necessary to augment this action by inspection, since it deals only with the product and not with the process. However, in the sophisticated manufacturing environment of the industrialised nations, it is uncommon to find 100% inspection except where required by government or regulatory bodies. Elsewhere, in developing countries for example, inspection is the norm. Notwithstanding the import of technology in these countries, there is inadequate process capability and consequent poor levels of quality. In order to counterbalance this, inspection therefore becomes a normal feature of the manufacturing scene.

Amongst the many quality prescriptions that are now to be found, Taguchi most explicitly focuses upon variability. This is seen as the prime enemy, defectives are simply a manifestation. Wherever possible Taguchi advocates the use of low cost, off-the-shelf materials, which are generally tailored so that they may work under a wide variety of conditions. One way in which variation can be reduced has been referred to already and this is through experimentation. The objectives of *design of experiments* (DOE) are to identify key variables in the product and in process design, to reduce those variables and to open up tolerances on lesser variables to cut costs. Variation patterns may be positional – for example, operator to operator; cyclical such as batch to batch; or time related. Within the DOE concept, it is intended to seek to test every variable with each level of every other variable in order to determine the main effects or ways in which interaction occurs. Japanese industry has undertaken the significant volumes of work thus entailed as a necessary investment and, partially as a result, has within two decades completely transformed its quality image.

# ● Controlling the process

## Control charts

Within manufacturing industry, control charts are in widespread use. Of themselves, such control charts do not solve problems, they simply confirm their existence. Underlying causes are a matter of process capability and no useful purpose is served by using one if the other does not exist. Control charts represent an advance upon frequency distributions because they add time dimensions. In statistical process control, upper and lower limits of plus or minus 3 sigma indicate a 99.73% chance that values outside these limits are caused by a non-random and assignable cause. Control charts are a means in many organisations of analysing, displaying and providing a background for improvement techniques based on interpersonal reactions. Training in brainstorming techniques or the use of cause and effect diagrams are typical examples of how problem-solving on the shop floor is seen as an important element in controlling processes.

The Ishikawa or fishbone diagram, however, frequently misses interaction effects and even though the use of cards in the so-called *Cedak* approach enhances worker participation, the same judgemental weaknesses remain. All such techniques have a very inherent high degree of hit and miss, and they cannot be considered as substitutes for the fundamental analysis that is contained within DOE. Indeed control charts in the form of pre-control, are advocated by Keki Bhote and others as being a more effective and less costly method of maintaining a process under control, once inherent variation has been reduced through DOE. The rules of pre-control are relatively simple without, it is claimed, impairing either its statistical validity or practical value. Both the risk of over-correcting – stopping a process when it should really continue – and that of under-correcting – continuing to operate a process that should be stopped – are attractively low. Pre-control penalises poor quality by shutting the plant, but only within the limits imposed by absolute necessity.

In his book *World Class Quality*, Bhote alleges that the greatest achievement of Taguchi is to take the design of experiments out of the completely theoretical area and into design laboratories and on to the production floor. It may be the case that the Taguchi method is over-complex and does not build in sufficient randomness within the experiments. In addition, the Taguchi approach may, by comparison with others, fail to identify sufficiently which of the important variables are really essential. A severe structural flaw in Taguchi is the failure

**153**

adequately to consider interaction, but notwithstanding this Taguchi has a high profile not just in Japan but also in the west. Within one Japanese firm alone – Nippon Denso – some 2,500 Taguchi experiments are carried out each year, whilst firms such as Ford and Lucas Automotive have derived considerable benefits from the Taguchi approach to quality. At a minimum, the focus upon variation reduction and the need to use low cost, off-the-shelf components wherever possible, provided they can operate under a wide variety of conditions, represent a significant contribution from Taguchi to the western approach to quality.

## ● The cost of specials

In respect of price there is also the question of the value either of distinctiveness or exclusivity. Taguchi has stressed the need to tighten up vital tolerances whilst relaxing those that are less essential. Standard, off-the-shelf components are significantly cheaper than specials. How

● **Table 4.2**

Costings for a 'special' required by a multinational from one of its suppliers

|  | Original | | Company specific | | Specific |
|---|---|---|---|---|---|
|  | Factor | Cost $ | Factor | Cost $ | + |
| Basic cost |  | 3.25 |  | 3.25 |  |
| Visual inspection |  | 0.25 |  | $1.00^x$ | 0.75 |
|  |  | 3.50 |  | 4.25 |  |
| Yield | 0.9 | 3.89 | $0.5^x$ | 8.50 | 3.86 |
| Assembly |  | 3.00 |  | 10.00 | 7.00 |
|  |  | 6.89 |  | 18.50 |  |
|  | 0.95 | 7.25 | $0.85^x$ | 21.76 | 2.77 |
| Initial test |  | 1.00 |  | 1.00 |  |
|  |  | 8.25 |  | 22.76 |  |
|  | 0.8 | 10.31 | $0.8^x$ | 28.45 | 4.54 |
| Burn in |  |  |  | $2.00^x$ | 2.00 |
| Final test |  |  |  | $1.00^x$ | 1.00 |
|  |  |  |  | 31.45 |  |
|  |  |  | $0.9^x$ | 34.95 | 3.50 |
| Pack |  | 0.25 |  | 0.25 |  |
| Total cost |  | 10.56 |  | 35.20 | 25.36 |
| Gross margin 60% |  |  |  |  |  |
| Price |  | 26.41 |  | 88.00 | 61.59 |
| Direct cost + 25.36 |  |  |  |  |  |
| Contribution + 35.83 |  |  |  |  |  |

much so can be seen from the actual costings for a 'special' required by an oil industry related multinational from one of its American suppliers (see **Table 4.2**). The cost based pricing policy of the supplier ensured that technical enhancements had a dramatically leveraged effect on price. On the assumption that, at the most, the overhead implications of the special were a 10% uplift, the contribution rose from 15.15 to 56.23%, whilst, if one accepts the supplier's own assessment of a 20% margin, 'profits' escalated from 5.28 to 16.2%.

It is precisely to prevent design enthusiasms of this type having a damaging impact, that procurement engineering based upon function-ally integrated terms has become so important. Their impact is not, of course, simply price related.

S.O.S

● Suppliers and quality

**Certification**

It cannot be denied that a supplier should be fully responsible for the quality of his products. Post-BS 5750 and ISO 9000 (see p. 165) this implies that there must not only be an effective system for quality con-trol but that the supplier must maintain and be able to produce on request adequate records both of system use and operational perform-ance. In some fields it has been possible to go further. Either vendor conformance is monitored in a way similar to SPC (**Fig. 4.9**) or, where

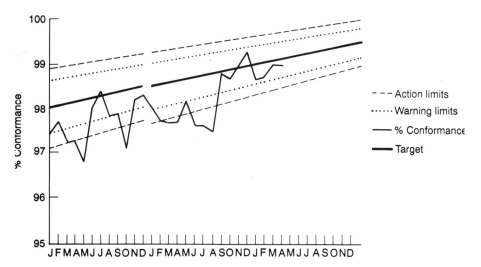

**Figure 4.9** Vendor conformance

suppliers are self-certifying, they have a total responsibility for the control of product and process quality, for the certification of initial sample reports and for the completion of first production shipment checks. In addition, process capability must be maintained. This approach cannot be extended to those areas where government or regulatory bodies, often for reasons of safety, impose requirements regarding product inspection and analysis. There are nevertheless large areas where it becomes possible once suppliers have reached this particular stage of advancement, for items to be delivered direct to the purchaser's manufacturing line. It is in this way that fabrication out of house can be significantly extended as a proportion of total product cost and high rates of inventory turnover rapidly come within reach. The integrity of the supplier is paramount. It cannot be stressed enough that, whatever the process capability may be, it is essential that the supplier be able to assure the purchaser of commitment to the purchaser's cause and that there is a totally transparent approach to all aspects of the purchasing process.

The systematisation of supplier quality systems has been international, national and by corporations. ISO 9000 and BS 5750 both represent attempts to introduce system into the quality process. Based originally upon the requirements of the defence industry, this approach has seen rapid extension throughout the 1980s. In his foreword to BS 5750 – an executive guide for the use of the UK national standard for quality system – the then director general of the British Standards Institute wrote of some 8,000 companies registered to BS 5750 or equivalent defence standards. He claimed that the adoption of quality principles would both safeguard industry and increase the ability to export successfully. 'Fitness for purpose' was seen as a simple summary of the 'totality of features and characteristics of service that bear upon its ability to satisfy a given need'. Understandably stress was placed upon prevention rather than cure, upon getting things right first time and upon the twin pillars of management commitment and workforce responsibility. Both BS 5750 and ISO 9000 aim to make possible the establishment of documentation and maintenance of an effective and economic quality system. This would demonstrate to customers a firm quality commitment.

The operative sections of BS 5750 are three in number. Section 1 is intended for all but the simplest products where the requirements are specified by the customer and subsequently manufactured by the supplier. Its 19 subdivisions cover areas where demonstrable systems are needed, with co-ordination obtained through a single manager with the necessary authority and ability. Where products had already been established in terms of design, either Section 2 or 3 of BS 5750 apply. In

Section 2, some 17 of the 19 parameters were considered to be necessary and in Section 3, that figure was ten.

At first a good deal of scepticism abounded in purchase circles regarding the use of this British Standard, but during the course of the 1980s, particularly with the establishment of many low-cost consultancy advisory services, 5750 came to be very widely developed. Major companies increasingly came to see certification as an essential part of their quality profile. There was criticism, however, and in October 1989, in presentations for the best UK factory award, Sony overtly criticised the British Standard. BS 5750 was described as a total irrelevance. The managing director of Toshiba UK, in agreeing with this statement, said that BS 5750 made little effective difference and that its use was by no means incompatible with the 'them and us' relationship – the adversarial approach that has dominated customer–supplier relationships in the UK. The argument advanced was not that there was something fundamentally wrong with conformance to 5750 but that it was a false benchmark, encouraging complacency, and indeed it is quite true that BS 5750, once established, seems to be regarded as the pinnacle of achievement by many companies. It is therefore not easy to reconcile it with continuous improvement programmes that have as their starting point the allegation that quality achievement is never good enough and that further progress is always possible.

The cost of introducing BS 5750 is rarely used, although in Spain for example, companies in mainland Europe do aver that ISO 9000 has prohibitive set up costs. Registration, in the form of the Department of Trade and Industry Quality Assurance Register is another potential buyer aid. For a modest sum (£125 in 1990) this Register lists companies in the UK and abroad where quality systems have been 'independently assessed and certified by United Kingdom certification bodies'. The publicity for this particular publication claims that the companies listed cover a complete range of manufacturing goods and services. Every one of these has had a quality management system assessed against standard ISO 9000 or its equivalent, and in the words of the promotional material:

'Together they enable buyers to evaluate suppliers before doing business. Whether you are buying toothpicks or torpedoes you can be confident the listed companies are committed to high standards of quality control and thanks to regular rechecking you can be sure that those standards are never allowed to slip.'

The Register is, it is claimed objective, reliable and accessible; a definitive point of reference for anyone committed to quality and serious about doing business. As with certification however, the problem with such an approach is that once in the Register, the dangers of failing to maintain standards are all too readily apparent. In addition, the purchaser may feel less obliged to carry out that close personal examination that, in the case of major suppliers, is necessary.

Certification and registration represent potentially powerful tools. Opinion regarding them has become much more favourable since BS 5750 was introduced in 1978. It is all too easy to point to drawbacks, real or imaginary, but certification does represent a significant advance in the approach to quality and at the end of the day in no way absolves the buyer from responsibility.

## ● The Ford quality system standard

### FMEA

It is common for manufacturing companies to lay down quite detailed procedures in respect of the determination of supplier quality standards. One of the earliest and best known of these is the Ford Q101 system. This model for numerous other organisations has three principal parts and provides a powerful in-house tool. *Feasibility, failure mode* and *effect analysis* (FMEA), and *control* make up the approach, and it will be noted that customer reaction and competitor response do not overly figure.

So far as *feasibility* is concerned, five essential questions are posed: (i) can the part or item in question can be made economically; (ii) in the quantity required; (iii) in the time available; (iv) to the specification required; (v) and with minimum variation? This implies that a team approach to suppliers in this respect is essential since not only must technical dimension be addressed, but commercial and other considerations must also be taken into account. Using a similar framework, Nissan Manufacturing (UK) Ltd approach this stage with quality and the attitude of the supplier as essential threads. At the feasibility stage, many purchase decisions are taken in manufacturing industry. This reflects the nature of the technology and the rate at which changes are occurring. It is essential, where suppliers have been contacted in order to involve their ideas or their concepts within a new design, that the commercial dimension receives appropriate consideration. It is of little value to identify areas where innovatory work has been carried out that can enhance the purchaser's product, if a consequence of that decision is either a restriction on supply or an inability to source economically.

*FMEA (failure mode and effect analysis)* is concerned with the identification of the potential way in which an item or part might fail – the failure mode – with the likely causes of such a situation and its potential effects. Thus it is both diagnostic and predictive. FMEA applies both to design and process, and seeks to identify and address every conceivable potential failure. It is possible to ascribe 1 to 10 weightings to frequency of occurrence, ease of detection and the seriousness of potential consequences. For example, in the case of the latter, values are ascribed on an ascending scale. These range from the situation where faults are so insignificant that the customer may in fact be quite unaware of the defect, to one where serious customer dissatisfaction begins to arise and ultimately to the infringement of safety or other legal requirements. $10 \times 10 \times 10$ weighting gives quantification to the importance of rectification and enables priorities to be established.

The final stage of the Ford approach, the *control plan*, is concerned with all significant features affecting fit, function, durability and experience. Process capability is the measure used and provision is made for parameters that relate the number and size of batches to failure rates and process condition. In this area therefore, Taguchi principles are much in evidence.

The Ford system has been widely publicised and used as a standard not just by Ford with their own suppliers but by many other corporations. Statistical process control features prominently in the approach and, subject only to the reservation that this technique describes a situation rather than prescribes a cure, it represents a highly visible manifestation of the quality culture.

● Customer–supplier relationships in total quality

Total quality transcends statistics. It relies on:

● A focus on customer needs.
● Universal participation.
● Considering everything as a process which contributes to quality.
● A continual process of improvement.

In this context organisations must endeavour to produce products and services that meet customer needs and expectations. In so doing, if they are manufacturers – they must design for maximum manufacturability and reliability with minimum design cycle time. But there is more to it than this. Over and above product and process, human relationships are also an important aspect of the quality dimension. Workers have brains as well as brawn if they are encouraged to use them. Suppliers are not necessarily adversaries but partners. Everyone has both customer and supplier relationships.

## The internal customer

In purchase each group or element must seek to determine the nature of its assignment and its responsibilities. The questions to be answered include: why does the group exist?; what does it produce?; why is it needed?; and what are the goals? Customers must be identified. Exactly whose needs does the group try to satisfy? Who sets the requirement and who is best able to evaluate success? Once requirements have been determined, how should they be met? How can the group ensure that it produces only what the customer wants? Suppliers are also internal as well as external, and purchase groups must determine their requirements with suppliers, performance measures, identify and address problem areas and develop effective feedback methods, and increasingly apply this form of quality approach within the work of purchase.

The concept of total quality relates to the quality of performance in every aspect of the business and not simply in manufacturing. It embraces finance, administration and marketing, as well as purchasing, and seeks to achieve performance against pre-determined standards. Total quality principles are carried through the business to suppliers with objectives such as:

- Riduce supplier bases.
- Establish strong relationships.
- Monitor performance – key measures.
- Set improvement targets.
- Hepl suppliers to apply total quality.
- Targets are ambitious but achievable.
- Changes are visible.
- Agreeing our aims – business/customer and clearly understanding the relations.
- Targets are meaningful and ambitious.
- Targets are moving towards goals.
- Standards are not fixed.

The beauty of the customer–supplier relationship to total quality lies in its adaptability and universality. It can be applied as fruitfully in service industries or in process as in batch manufacture. All purchasing's customers use the functions 'products' and these can, with advantage, be identified and agreed. Latent demand or previously unrecognised need can be activated simply by the circulation of the product menu. For example, where plant maintenance or engineering is concerned, purchase is responsible for generating contracts for front end design and contract services, for providing estimates of cost and lead time and for seeking to identify and display the different commercial implications of various design choices. Enquiries – their preparation and despatch – is a purchasing responsibility. Project teams must be assisted to choose between suppliers and ensure that there is an appropriate balance of technical and commercial factors. Quotations must be refined and compared, and contracts prepared for issue specifying the appropriate terms and conditions. Orders must be progressed and expedited, and where projects are involved, data must be provided for cost monitoring and material management. When new plant has been introduced, purchase should be involved in agreeing essential spare scalings and their source, and the ordering, specification and stock control arrangements. And finally, where such work is to be carried out overseas, packaging, shipping, export documentation all fall within the purchasing brief.

## Management as clients

Purchase's clients are many. To agree formally an internal contract is one step towards ensuring customer satisfaction. Through regular review, it enables the function to remain abreast of changing need and in particular to adapt as corporate strategy evolves. This is of particular importance when a major change of operating mode occurs. For example, in petrochemicals a common response of companies like ICI or Exxon to changing market conditions was to move away from low-cost bulk towards higher value added specialised chemicals. One consequence of this was the development of business units with new style business managers. No longer could purchase be a reactive service department. It needed to show a face much more attuned to market opportunities and to focus upon end market competitive advantage as its goal.

The business manager as an increasingly important customer of the purchasing department sought a different type of relationship with purchase. For its part, the function recognised a need to develop both credibility with this particular sector of the customer base and also clearly to establish new requirements. Business managers looked for a lively professional service providing levels of knowledge and expertise over and above that available in the business groups.

One consequence of the business manager purchase relationship that was less easy to foresee was the clear emergence of another important client group in management at board level. With CEOs and other directors, performance related judgements of purchase are as frequently subjective as objective. Hence it is important that purchase moves rapidly to establish an appropriate form of distinctive identity. This implies a conscious marketing effort, and to this end the purchase department's use both of Crosby-type approaches and of tools such as operational audit, provides a valuable means of establishing a platform from which senior management opinion can be influenced. It is perhaps true that in too many companies senior management is insufficiently purchase-aware and that only by directing a considerable amount of political effort into this domain can the purchase function hope to establish a presence appropriate to its ability to contribute. A good purchase manager is conscious of this need. In the short-term, it is frequently necessary to repair the damage done by a long standing acquiescence in a view of purchase as a subordinate clerical activity divorced from mainstream decision-making.

The customer–supplier approach has obvious relevance externally. It is probably most common amongst organisations whose purchases are not definable in terms of components or sub-assemblies. In areas such as oil, petrochemicals and other process based industries, a Crosby-style approach may be of value in raising the level of interaction between the purchaser and supplier. It will facilitate the reaching of an understanding of motivation and intention, which is of value to the prospective purchaser. This makes possible quality improvements between a purchaser and supplier based upon a common definition of quality. Both parties understand what they mean by it and establish a system that can both measure performance and also be the basis where necessary for positive corrective action. From the point of view of the purchaser, a quality improvement programme (QIP) is the formalisation of this type of relationship. QIPs are only one facet (albeit an important one) in developing suppliers. If it is to be successful, the quality process requires a more interventionist attitude towards suppliers. Cost control and business growth are positive consequences, whilst there is also a diminution of all those problems that give rise both to time wasting and to customer dissatisfaction. Hence there is less firefighting, fewer hassles and less rework. As a result, reputation is enhanced.

In order to make a quality improvement programme work, every individual must be involved and give commitment, and this implies a fully comprehensive programme of training and an explanation as to the reasons why this course of action is being taken. In some companies this is achieved by seminars in which all parts of the company – people drawn from every department and every level – are involved, frequently in mixed groups. Such groups examine the relationships that they perceive themselves having, both with suppliers and customers and the services actually provided as against what *should* be given or what are expected.

Quality relationships are definable in terms of conformance to requirement. The emphasis is on prevention, the only performance standard is error-free work, and the best measurement is the price of non-conformance. Such internally directed efforts are a necessary corollary to better external supplier quality performance. Such performance is enhanced by greater total quality awareness by buyers and by the clear perception that 'everyone is playing'.

## ● Quality functional deployment

Each new application or development in quality thinking represents one more step towards a *receding* goal – perfect quality. The reason for this is that each step has become accepted by the customer as the norm and has awakened new expectations for the future. The ultimate goal of total satisfaction is therefore always receding.

*Quality functional deployment* (QFD) represents, in appropriate circumstances, the state of the art in 1990 being in many ways an amalgam of previously differentiated approaches (**Fig. 4.1**) (see **Table 4.3**). It brings together customer attributes, engineering characteristics and

● **Table 4.3**
Developing quality

| | |
|---|---|
| *The process* | (Design of experiments; variation reduction; statistical process control) |
| + | |
| *Customer perceptions/ expectations* | (Customer–supplier and relationships) |
| + | |
| *Competitor response* | |
| = *Quality Functional Deployment* | |
| *or* *Deming + Taguchi + Crosby = QFD* | |

**163**

perceptions of competitive products. Adapted by Ford in North America, the process has been described by a senior design engineer in the company as totally exhausting. Sometimes called the 'house of quality' from the format of the matrix developed in its use, it embraces the following steps (see **Fig. 4.10**):

- *Step 1*: Identify and group customer attributes, ranking them in order of relative importance in the market-place. For example, the ease with which a car door may be opened and closed is closely linked with the degree of insulation required to prevent leaks, cut out noise and facilitate air conditioning. Each different attribute is then related to the company product and to that of competitors, and ranked by customers in order of preference.
- *Step 2*: Is to identify the different engineering decisions that are

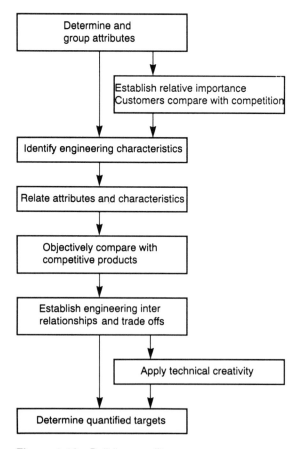

**Figure 4.10** Building quality

involved in bringing about the characteristics identified and that can change the product.

- *Step 3*: Relates those decisions upon the basis of positive or negative correlations to the perceptions of customers.
- *Step 4*: Each of the established relationships can be objectively measured, for example in terms of effort required. This is carried out both for one's own and for competitors' efforts, and provides a technical basis for the views expressed by customers.
- *Step 5*: Relates the different characteristics identified, one to another. This makes explicit the interdependence identified in the first step and establishes a basis for creative trade-offs.
- *Step 6*: Uses the bringing together of all the factors identified in previous stages and the establishment of quantified targets from the improvement or development of one's own product.

It can be seen that these steps call for significant investment in both market research and operational matters. The extent to which QFD is adopted will reflect the relationship between this effort and benefits derived. Its application in the automotive industry is apparent but at the present time the extent to which it will be used elsewhere has yet to be seen. In principle, however, QFD represents a significant advance upon previous approaches to process quality and a bringing together rather than a drawing apart of the disciplines inherent in them.

## ● ISO 9000

### Synopsis

The paper traces the genesis of ISO 9000 and its place in the international scene. It explores the role of ISO 9000 in the market-place from the viewpoint of the supplier and of the purchaser. As such it examines the benefits that both should achieve. The use of third party certification in this trading pattern is discussed with an outline of the additional benefits to be gained and a description and comparison of different types of certification. Finally, the additional factors that arise in trade across frontiers are highlighted, together with an indication of the international activity aimed towards reducing or removing the problems.

### The role of the international quality system standard – ISO 9000 – D. Ware, Managing Director, BSI

#### 1. Introduction

The role of ISO 9000. What is it? Perhaps you will bear with me if I outline the genesis of these standards.

For this, we have to go back to the 1960s. Up until that time many major purchasers exercised controls of one sort or another over their suppliers. Of these, the Ministry of Defence had more activity than any others and their control was exercised through having permanent representatives at their suppliers, responsible for agreeing the release of items. This exercise is believed to have involved somewhere around 12 to 15 thousand staff, clearly an expensive overhead.

The techniques of quality management initiated in the USA were beginning to attract attention and so MoD introduced its Def. Stan 05 series as a means of codifying the required and effective quality management system to determine the capability of their suppliers to produce to specification consistently.

The impact of this approach was to switch the control mechanism to an up-front assessment of quality systems. This reduced the staff levels needed to around four thousand, required particular skills, increased job satisfaction and placed responsibilities where they rightfully belonged – on the supplier.

The success of this approach prompted other major purchasers, particularly in the nationalised industries, to follow suit with the consequential development of slightly different requirements for quality systems.

As a result, work was commenced by BSI Standards to produce a national standard culminating in the publication of BS 5750 in 1978. The standard brought together the requirements of the Def. Stan 05 series for 'quality systems' thus making it possible for its adoption by major purchasers as a common approach. I do not intend to examine it in detail in this presentation but to deal conceptually in the main, to demonstrate the aspects which it covers. BS 5750 became the main plank in the DTI quality campaign, introduced in the White Paper of 1982 entitled 'Standards, Quality and International Competitiveness'.

## 2. International scene

The benefits which can be achieved by the adoption of quality management had been clearly demonstrated by the Japanese trading success. The adoption of BS 5750 in the UK started to demonstrate similar results. ISO, as a result, established a technical committee (TC 176) to produce an international standard. BSI submitted BS 5750 as the first draft and in 1987, the ISO 9000 series were published, substantially the same as BS 5750. BSI immediately adopted the ISO standard and updated BS 5750 to the current 1987 edition. ISO 9000 was also adopted by the European Community and thus we have a standard ISO 9000/EN 29000/BS 5750.

UK industry who already had been working to BS 5750 for many years, were thus placed in a favourable position in the international market-place.

This standard is increasingly being viewed as a major feature in the development of the Single European Market. Worldwide, it is attracting a great deal of interest and being adopted by many countries. At the ISO/CASCO meeting in June this year, a record attendance of some 40 countries and 6 international organisations were represented, all keenly interested in its adoption as a means of improving industrial performance and assisting in world trade.

## 3. Total quality management

We should say something about concepts being described as Total Quality Management (TQM). I find this interesting in that there are two main aspects generally accepted in the definition of TQM. These are the involvement of *all* staff and continuing improvement. There is no doubt in my mind that the concept of applying quality system management to all aspects of a company's activities is the way to progress. I prefer to refer to this as company-wide quality. Equally, I have no doubt that the application of ISO 9000 is only a start towards achieving maximum benefit. Quality improvement has to figure largely in a company's strategy.

However, there is also no doubt in my mind that ISO 9000 is an essential first step – a building block towards achieving TQM, a view shared and supported by many major companies with whom we have dealings with.

## 4. Quality assurance in the market-place

I would like to now spend a little time discussing how quality assurance can be used as a marketing tool.

Let us suppose that a supplier has been convinced that quality assurance is a good concept and that he has established a quality system, which enables him to have a high level of confidence that he has an effective operation producing goods in conformity with specifications. How does he use this to secure a greater penetration into the market-place? For the moment let us disregard the role of third party certification and concentrate solely on the supplier who has established a quality system. In giving this matter consideration we have to think about the supplier himself and how he can utilise quality assurance, but also the customer who we must assume has equally to be persuaded of the advantages of dealing with a quality assured company. We should then look at the role of these two participants in the marketing exercise.

### 4.1. Suppliers

It is useful to start to explore this aspect by looking first of all at the supplier, or, for the purposes of our discussion, a manufacturer. I have used the term 'manufacturer' because in essence he tends to be involved in both the purchase and selling activity. Whilst on the one hand he has the need to safeguard his reputation in terms of the goods that he is selling and hence he has a relationship as the supplier with his customer, he is equally concerned in buying in a number of goods or services in which activity he acts as the customer to his own supplier.

The cost of purchased goods and services often comprises a large proportion of the manufacturer's expenditure and hence his general reputation and manufacturing competence is very much at stake in respect of these purchases and he is likely to want to take prudent steps to ensure that his requirements are met. Interestingly, therefore, whilst he may have one attitude towards the demonstration of conformity of the products which he is selling, he may have a completely different attitude towards the products that he purchases.

He will in consequence consider the merits of carrying out his own checks on bought-in supplies or of relying upon some other agency. The choice may be conditioned, dependent upon whether the purchase is special to him or whether it is purchased by others. He may have to carry out his own checks because he cannot get anyone else to do these for him. Conversely, he may have the work carried out for him because of his own lack of facilities.

We must also not lose sight of the fact that the marketing and servicing functions of the manufacturer form the direct link with his customer and as such provide the main channel for the feed back of market reaction to goods and services supplied. Advantage should be taken of information available from these sources as a means of completing the loop and thus developing the quality programme. Market research should take account of user requirements such as environment, life expectation, wear and tear aspects, etc, together with cost estimates from all major functions to produce, through the quality system, a quality product at economical cost.

Equally important is the control of servicing and in this respect the quality system should ensure that adequate technical documentation and education is provided for the user.

All these aspects form part of the ISO 9000 approach.

### 4.2. Purchasers

Large purchasing organisations, whether in the private or public sectors, conduct their purchasing through their own purchasing department or specialists who are responsible for making the right choice. This purchasing department or specialist is unlikely to have complete knowledge of the choice available to him on the market; nor will he know the reputation of the firms that are offering products for sale. However, his own reputation within his organisation is at stake and decisions have to be made.

Such a large purchasing organisation is more readily able to operate its own inspection of the product or to assess the supplier. This latter activity is frequently known as supplier assessment or vendor assessment.

Thus, over the years the practice by large purchasers of carrying out their own assessment of their suppliers has become well established.

The term 'purchaser' can also include the ordinary domestic or high street shopper, typifying the non-profesional purchaser.

What distinguishes the non-professional from the professional purchaser is the absence of technical knowledge necessary to choose rationally and the impossibility for him to carry out tests.

As such he is, in theory, at a disadvantage. He will tend to make his choice related to personal experience and subjective judgement. His choice is likely to be to the known manufacturer with whom he has had a previous satisfactory experience.

## 4.3. Implications

It will readily be seen that there are disadvantages to the second party activity and subjective judgement. The practice of carrying out their own assessment by major purchasers has a cost implication upon the purchaser and he may therefore be receptive to the suggestion that he could place reliance upon an agency in whom he has confidence, to carry out quality system assessment.

A problem which can arise is that of multiple assessment. This is where a number of professional purchasers are all carrying out their own evaluation of a supplier leading to a multiplicity of assessment visits, which is time consuming and expensive to the supplier and results in wastage of resources.

Similarly, the non-professional purchaser is frequently at the mercy of the salesman.

The benefits of using a third party become attractive and lead to the development of third party systems of acceptable credibility.

## 5. Third party certification

From our consideration of quality as a marketing tool and the cost of supplier assessment we need to look at third party certification as one answer to the problems. This is where a third party certifies that the quality system, the product or the service conforms to laid down requirements in the way of standards or specification. Thus the supplier has a readily recognisable assurance of the quality of his product or service that he can use as a marketing tool; the purchaser for his part knows that the goods he is purchasing come up to a particular level of performance.

## 5.1. Certification

The purpose of certification is to assure a customer that he has received what he specified. A simple concept. Conformity certification in its various forms is a complicated and extensive subject. Certification is a process which may, under certain conditions, take place between two contracting parties as we have already discussed. This takes effect when a supplier 'certifies' to his customer that he has complied with the customer's requirements, possibly through the use of a national standard. Sometimes this two party version of certification is referred to as 'self certification', but more recently has become known as 'manufacturer's declaration'. I favour this latter term as I think it is rather more descriptive of the process which takes place in those conditions.

However, this is not always considered to be sufficient in the market-place, particularly where there is not a two-party relationship. This leads to the role of third party or 'independent certification'. In some instances, a standard may specify the characteristics and related test method without specifying the relevant category or level and without requiring the manufacturer to do more than indicate this on a label giving product information. This allows for variations of categories or grades of the same characteristic within a given standard. In such cases it is possible for independent certification to operate in a way which certifies or confirms the claims made by the manufacturer.

By its very nature, such certification is undertaken by a body independent of all interest, i.e. independent of the manufacturer, user, seller or buyer. Demand for independent certification may be created through a need to extend a supplier's market into areas where his reputation is unknown or needs support; to set the supplier apart from competitors whose claim of conformity with a recognised standard is doubtful or where he wants to provide verification of a claim of superiority; to establish the quality of a new product; or to provide confidence to a purchaser.

The supplier may see advantage in having an independent assessment of his quality system. This may arise for three different reasons:

a) Audit – of an independent nature: here we have an analogy with a financial audit of a company.
b) Liability – it may be a mitigating defence in the case of product liability litigation.
c) Efficiency – independent checks on controls can create greater efficiency of operation.

In addition, stockists, wholesalers and retailers in the marketing chain may also wish to have their reputation enhanced and to have the same measure of protection against liability as that of the manufacturer.

The manufacturer who seeks to have independent certification to assist his own marketing policies, may equally apply pressure to his suppliers of bought in components for independent certification.

Many large purchasing organizations need to assure themselves, for many of the reasons already given, that the products they are purchasing either for use in their own manufacturing processes or for onward sale, are in conformity with appropriate standards.

The consumer often looks for an independent assurance in respect of a manufacturer's claims.

The community at large, either for reasons of consumer protection, safety, legislation, etc, may produce pressure for forms of independent certification.

### 5.2. Certification systems

We have seen that the purpose of a certification system is to provide certain criteria, which would give the purchaser confidence that the product meets his requirements. The oldest form of building this confidence is the salesman's assurance. In this day and age, this is frequently not found acceptable. Even the professional purchaser sometimes feels the need for certification systems, operated by impartial bodies, that are not dominated by the manufacturing influence or the brand image.

Thus a certification system needs to be objective, reliable and acceptable to all parties. It must meet expectations that it will be efficiently and impartially operated.

All certification systems are subject to certain practical limitations. One of the most common limitations is that a total item-by-item check of conformity with the technical requirement is not obtainable. The art of devising a good certification system is to develop procedures which will provide the optimum assurance that goods have been produced under the best practicable conditions of manufacture consistent with the commercial, legal and social situation prevailing at the time, and it thus can minimise the chance or risk of the buyers obtaining sub-standard products.

The eight common third party certification systems identified in the ISO booklet 'Certification Principles and Practice' are:

5.2.1 Type testing.
5.2.2 Type testing followed by subsequent surveillance through audit testing of factory samples purchased on the open market.
5.2.3 Type testing followed by subsequent surveillance through audit testing of factory samples.
5.2.4 Type testing followed by subsequent surveillance through audit testing of samples from both the open market and the factory.
5.2.5 Type testing and assessment of factory quality control and its acceptance followed by surveillance that takes into account the audit of factory quality control and the testing of samples from the factory and the open market.
5.2.6 Factory quality control assessment and its acceptance only.
5.2.7 Batch testing.
5.2.8 100% testing.

Systems 1–5 follow a logical order of progression, each starting with type testing. Systems 6, 7 and 8 on the other hand, have no connection with one another or with systems 1–5, each capable of standing on its own. However, System 6 can, of course, link with any of systems 1–5.

System 6 is in essence a form of certification or evaluation of company performance. The other systems outlined in contrast, are all related to product certification. In this sense, System 6 can be seen to have a rather different purpose and object.

6. Product certification

If we consider System 5 as typical, we see three components:

171

## 6.1. Type testing

When one is concerned with product certification and with particular reference to systems 1–5, type testing forms an inescapable basis for certification.

Any form of product certification must infer that the product in question will be tested. It may be tested for conformity to a specification or tested in respect of previously stated requirements contained in the document by a specified test method. The disadvantage is that it does not in itself provide any information about the subsequent production of other articles made to the same specification.

Although it could be assumed that the conformity evidenced by the result of type test leads to the probability of conformity of subsequent items, experience indicates that this assumption may be unjustified or that there are factors other than the test itself that can influence this assumption.

I would argue that a type test achieves one purpose and one purpose only; namely that an article has been produced, which is in conformity with the specification and that such a conclusion can only be drawn in respect of the actual article which has been tested.

## 6.2. Assessment

For any certification system which involves making statements about subsequent production, i.e. systems 2, 3, 4 and 5, and for System 6, assessment is again an inescapable feature of the procedures. The word is used in the context of an evaluation of the factory quality management arrangements concerned with the products to be certified. The assessment is concerned with whether the system of quality management is such that the manufacturer has adequate control over his production facility, purchase of material and checking procedures, that the products should consistently be in conformity with the specification.

In a third party product certification system, its main purpose is to give the certification body the confidence that the manufacturer seeking to use the mark of the certification body has such control over his activities that he is able to clearly identify non-conforming products, which can then be isolated from conforming products and remedied, before the mark is applied. In other words, it is the certification body's assurance that it can exercise its responsibility for its mark in a competent and credible fashion.

## 6.3. Surveillance

We have highlighted the importance of ensuring that the manufacturer has the management system to ensure continued conformity with the specification. Although a certification body has carried out an evaluation of the manufacturer's quality system and has satisfied itself that the manufacturer has the system in operation, it is borne out by experience that even in the best organised operations, things can go wrong. It is frequently the case, therefore, that the certification body would exercise some follow-up evaluation on the manufacturer's performance. There are, in general, two ways in which such surveillance may take place. One is by re-evaluation of the manufacturer's quality system to check that the system is still being applied correctly. The other, by independent testing of samples of his production, often referred to as audit testing.

There is much debate on the relative merits of each method and in general, a combination of the two as defined in System 5, is used.

The proponents of surveillance by means of independent testing would argue that a test is the only precise method of judging conformity. Certainly, the use of this method enables the identification of non-conformity. It suffers from the disadvantage that such identification is likely to take place subsequent to the shipment of non-conforming items with the problems then of recalling, if necessary, defective items. Surveillance through third party inspection of the manufacturer's quality control system should indicate whether or not the manufacturer is continuing to exercise adequate control and has merit, but suffers from the disadvantage that in itself it does not necessarily provide the precise identification of non-conforming items as is the case in audit testing.

Hence, the advantage would seem firmly on the use of both systems, each of which will back up the other, and the use of the first tends, with the build up of confidence, to reduce the necessity for extensive audit testing.

## 7. Quality system assessment

As we have seen the basis of quality assurance is the development in a company of quality management procedures. System 6 gives the two essential components of a third party system; namely; assessment and subsequent surveillance.

The basis for this assessment and surveillance is exactly the same as I have just described for product certification. We have outlined the benefit to the company of (a) putting in a quality management system and (b) utilising third party assessment.

The basic advantages inherent in such a system is that it can be applied to any company and is not dependent upon there being a national standard or other generally accepted specification which would enable product certification to be applied. It can therefore give confidence to a purchaser as to this supplier's competence.

Increasingly, we are seeing that these techniques can be applied to all forms of supplier. Amongst the 9,000 or so registrations current by BSI QA, an increasing proportion is in service industries such as transport and distribution; professional services; banking; hotels; education and training; to name but a few.

It is this technique which has attracted so much interest world-wide, following from the adoption of the ISO 9000 series, and I believe that there will be an ever increasing demand for this form of third party certification.

## 8. International competitiveness

We have talked about the need for purchasers to satisfy themselves that their supplier is competent and able to supply goods or services to meet their requirements. We have seen that by the introduction of effective and credible third party assessment and certification schemes, purchasers can develop sufficient confidence substantially to reduce the level of their own assessment, with benefit to all. What, however, happens when the customer/supplier link crosses national frontiers?

The essential confidence of the purchasers in the third party may be missing. There is likely to be a return to the previous situation of carrying out assessment by the purchaser. Alternatively, if the supplier has the certification of an acceptable certification body in the purchaser's own country, this may be acceptable.

Thus we see the potential classic development of barriers to trade which have been and in many cases, still are, prevalent. For many years a manufacturer in Europe, particularly of products where safety is a consideration, has had to have his products certified by the appropriate certification body in each country. Whilst in some areas, notably that of electrical appliances, measures have been taken to reduce this problem, it is probably the concept of the Single European Market which has done most to focus attention on the need to resolve this problem.

It is not easy and depends on the development of mutual trust and confidence. ISO/CASCO had foreseen the need for common criteria as a means towards this goal by providing guides on the structure and operation of testing and certification bodies. Clearly, if two bodies wishing to enter into a mutual recognition agreement are both structured and operate in the same way, there is common ground for the development of operation co-operation and eventual mutual recognition. These guides have been adopted in the EN 45000 series standards for use within the EC.

The industrialised nations are grappling with these problems and making steady progress. The developing countries need to follow these developments in preparation for eventual discussion on mutual recognition. At the recent ISO/CASCO meeting and the CASCO/DEVCO Workshop that preceded it, the problems of recognition of the competence of Certification Bodies in developing countries was a major item for discussion. Further work will be done during the forthcoming year to assess the problems and make recommendations to ISO if it is felt that steps should be taken in one direction or another. Clearly, as world trade develops and as developing countries become more competitive, the need for resolution will become more pressing.

In the meantime, the approach must surely be twofold.

First – to encourage and support industry in adopting ISO 9000 as the basis for sound management of quality.

Second – establish effective and credible third party assessment procedures through bodies which can demonstrate compliance with appropriate ISO/IEC guides.

Trading patterns will inevitably determine the need for mutual recognition. Preparation through the two actions I have mentioned above will have created the common ground from which progress can be made.

## Glossary of terms

1. BS 5750 1987 Quality Systems
   - Part 0 – Principal concepts and applications
     Section 0.1 Guide to selection and use
     (identical to ISO 9000, EN 29000)
     Section 0.2 Guide to quality management and quality system elements
     (identical to ISO 9004, EN 29004)
   - Part 1 – Specification for design/development, production, installation and servicing
     (identical to ISO 9001, EN 29001)
   - Part 2 – Specification for production and installation
     (identical to ISO 9002, EN 29002)
   - Part 3 – Specification for final inspection and test
     (identical to ISO 9003, EN 29003)
2. ISO International Standards Organisation
3. IEC International Electrotechnical Commission
4. ISO/CASCO ISO Council Committee on Conformity Assessment
5. ISO/DEVCO ISO Council Committee for Developing Countries

# 5

---

# Electronic data interchange and the supply chain

*David Jackson*
*Digital Equipment Company*

David Jackson is a management consultant with Digital, where he deals with the business implications of information technology.

The views in this chapter are those of the author and not of Digital Equipment Company.

## ● Introduction

Supply chain operations involve vast quantities of information. Physical movements are accompanied by movements of information. In fact, the number of information movements outweigh the number of physical movements by a large margin. Efficient supply chains demand efficient means of moving information. It is logical, therefore, that companies should seek to use information technology (IT); indeed IT has been, and is, used extensively in certain sectors of supply chain activities. Inventory control, manufacturing planning, distribution, purchasing and sales order processing systems are commonplace. In some organisations, these functionally-based systems have been integrated more accurately to reflect internal supply chain operations. With *electronic data interchange* (EDI) we see this integration expanding across organisations. This continues the trend (see **Fig. 5.1**) of directing IT investments to facilitate greater degrees of integration.

Electronic data interchange will significantly improve the efficiency of information across the supply chain, bringing great benefits to supply chain operations. By creating a link between business processes in different companies (or disparate parts of the same company), EDI will result in significant changes. Not since the discovery of just-in-time has

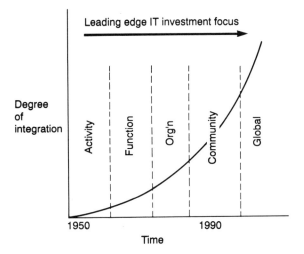

**Figure 5.1** Electronic data interchange

a concept been devised that will have such far reaching implications – and for once, the west leads Japan.

Interest in EDI has grown as a result of its ability to help organisations respond to the competitive pressures facing them. EDI can help shorten product development life cycles by facilitating the rapid exchange of information. Customer satisfaction can be improved by reducing delivery times and making it easier for customers to do business with their suppliers. And of course EDI contributes to the constant drive to reduce costs. EDI's greatest value, however, is its ability to help organisations focus on the value adding activities within the supply chain. Breaking the shackles many organisations face from outdated business processes, cumbersome computer systems and masses of red tape is where EDI really scores in the value stakes. These benefits, however, are only available to those who are determined to obliterate before automating.

● What is EDI?

Fully to appreciate EDI, it is helpful to understand the way in which information is currently managed in the supply chain.

Any supply chain is a series of closely related activities. A purchase order on a supplier triggers actions to supply the required product or service. This in turn triggers a need for transport, with the associated

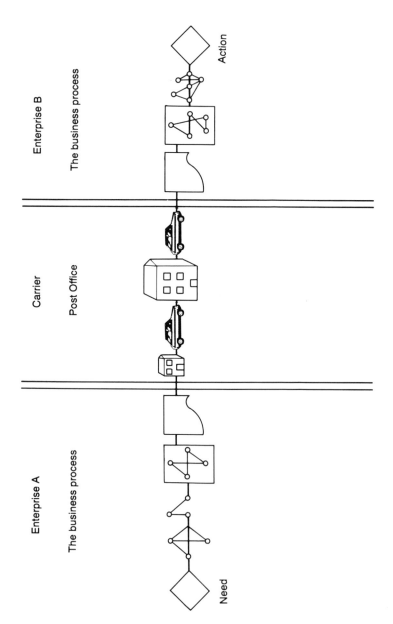

**Figure 5.2** Pre-EDI

delivery and advice notes. Invoices are submitted, which require payment; the list goes on.

In a macro view (see **Fig 5.2**), each link starts with the recognition of a need.

This need is subject to businesses processes – analysis, decisions, approvals – which are often an interaction between manual and computerised processes. The end result is an instruction, increasingly computer generated. These instructions (purchase orders, invoices, customs declarations, etc) are passed to a carrier, the Post Office, which delivers the document to the recipient. Research shows that approximately 70% of all computer output is re-input to another computer system. The recipient therefore takes the document and passes it through their manual and computer processes. The required action is eventually effected, and the cycle passes to the next link.

There are inherent weaknesses in this approach. Time, an increasingly critical and scarce commodity, is wasted in communicating the need to the organisation taking the action. Errors occur in the entry of the data into the receiving system. Different formats for dates, units of measure and part numbers provide many opportunities for transposition and interpretation errors. Statistics from European customs authorities suggest that over 50% of all documents they receive are inaccurate or incomplete. Direct costs include stationery, postage, mail handling and data entry and correction. Inventory holdings (related to delivery times), the costs to the business of undetected errors (wrong parts or quantities delivered) and the inability to provide accurate information also have their costs. They may be intangible but more significant in their impact on the ability to capture and keep customers.

Viewed in a simple way, EDI (see **Fig. 5.3**) replaces the postal system with a telecommunications system between applications.

Automating the postal system involves setting up a link between the two organisations. This may be a direct (leased telecommunications line) link between the two organisations, or, more typically, through a *value added network* (VAN). In an EDI context, VANs act as a telephone exchange, allowing an organisation to create one physical link and through the 'exchange' communicate with any number of trading partners. The only constraint is that the trading partner must be connected to the same VAN.

A widely accepted definition of EDI states:

'EDI is the application to application exchange of business and technical data using recognised standards to define the structure of the information.'

There are three important elements of this definition.

**179**

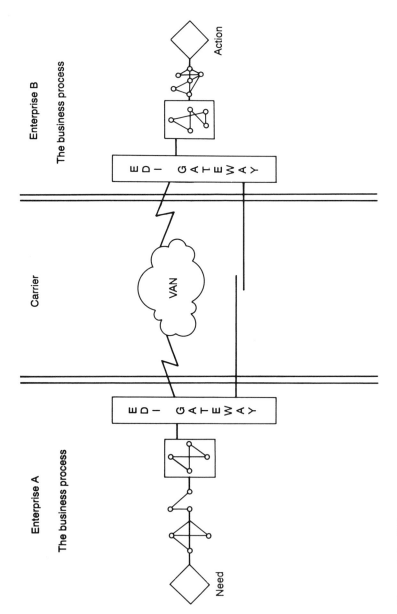

**Figure 5.3** EDI

## 1. Application to application

EDI is application to application exchange of data, not to be confused with electronic mail, which uses computers to facilitate communications between people, or videotext (Minitel or Prestel), which is application to person. The connecting applications without manual intervention is a central objective of EDI and essential for obtaining the maximum benefits. The manual interfaces of the current paper-based systems account for a significant element of the costs associated with it. Mail handling, data preparation and entry and data correction all add time and cost, and create opportunities for error to occur.

Linking the applications not only removes costs; it enables business to transact at short cycle times 24 hours per day, 365 days per year. Time zones become unimportant; computers do not need to sleep. Consider the impact on supply chains if all transactions could be effected within two hours of their origination. Processing of transactions overnight would be a significant improvement for most businesses. Without a change of the length of the working day, the time available to work the real issues increases. Orders are available 'in the system' at the start of the working day, rather than midday, as is so often the case.

The concept of application to application processing can apply to applications within an organisation as well as across organisations. Many organisations have developed their supply chain management and other systems around business unit and/or functional boundaries. They are looking for EDI to integrate their disparate systems. This brings significant benefits from the closer linking of elements of their internal supply and information chains. For example, large organisations often buy and sell from/to themselves. The information flow behind these transactions is often very similar if the trading partner was an external company. EDI provides a mechanism that can service both internal and external exchanges with a common interface. This makes system development and change easier and cheaper.

## 2. Business and technical data

Business documents – purchase orders, invoices, price lists, delivery notes – are the type of data most people associate with EDI. Indeed the documentation around the order–delivery cycle comprises most of today's activity. It is estimated that in the UK, purchase orders and invoices account for over 95% of all EDI transactions. An increasing number of documents can now be transmitted via EDI.

Banks are established users of EDI. Organisations like the Society for

Worldwide Interbank Funds Transfer (SWIFT) and the Bankers Automated Clearing System (BACS) have been exchanging structured data electronically for some years. They have not, however, been effectively integrated into the business cycle. Pressure from customers has pushed banks into closing the order cycle through EDI-based payment services. This pressure has also led to a significant change in the responsibilities banks are taking. Previously they only concerned themselves with effecting payment. The new electronic market-place is forcing them to transmit the associated remittance information. In this way, payment and transaction data coincide throughout the payment cycle.

Technical data, CAD information, engineering specifications, recipes, advertising graphics, etc, often reside on computer systems and have to be transmitted to other organisations. Whilst EDI applied to this type of information is in its infancy, it has massive potential to deliver real benefits. Automotive and aerospace industries with co-makership, consortium development and shorter product life-cycles demand a quick, accurate and effective means of exchanging data. The EDI systems they employ are currently independent of other forms of data exchange and are proprietary (1–1) systems rather than open, many–many systems typified by EDI. The availability of standards and increasingly sophisticated and cheaper telecommunications networks will contribute to a growth in this area. Sending the purchase order with a drawing attached, both electronically, will become commonplace.

## 3. Standards

Standards are the last of the three elements of the definition needing explanation. They provide the common language – a form of application Esperanto. EDI standards define the content of the message being passed between trading partners. Unfortunately in EDI, Esperanto comes in several varieties. Industry groups, the driving force behind developments, reflect their own industry. Whilst many, but not all, are using the same basic rules (the EDIFACT syntax), their implementations differ. Coupled with messages developed by geography, we have a confusing, complex collection of messages. **Table 5.1** lists the major message sets in use.

The issues of choice of standards and their implementation will be discussed later.

## ● Why use EDI?

Most companies get involved in EDI because of pressure from cus-

- **Table 5.1**

EDI messages

| Standard | Geography | Industry | Comments |
|----------|-----------|----------|----------|
| EDIFACT | Global | All | Recognised around the world as the standard of the future. Highest use in Western Europe. Most messages still under development. Numerous industry-based implementations in use. |
| ANSI X12 | Essentially USA | All | The leading US standard currently with more users than any other standard. Developers have committed to move to EDIFACT in an unspecified time. |
| Tradacoms | UK | Retail | Leading UK-based standard. Is used outside the retail industry. Currently being amalgamated with EDIFACT. |
| Odette | European | Automotive | Available in two forms – one EDIFACT-based. Used extensively outside auto industry. |

- **Table 5.2**

Reasons for involvement in EDI

| | Small/medium | Large |
|---|---|---|
| Customer pressure | 75% | 30% |
| Operational benefits | 20% | 50% |
| Proactive marketing | 5% | 15% |
| Strategic | 0% | 5% |

tomers. Research by Price Waterhouse (see **Table 5.2**) suggests that few companies are proactive in their use of EDI.

Customer pressure usually emanates from companies operating at the end of a supply chain. The leading protagonists are the major retail chain operators and the automobile manufacturers. Both operate close to the ultimate consumer and have significant purchasing leverage. The success of their EDI programmes is dependent on their ability to move from pilot to high volumes. Only then can they scale down their manual operations. Once they have been 'persuaded' to introduce EDI, the poacher turned gamekeeper syndrome comes into play. To leverage the benefits of their investment, these companies apply pressure on their suppliers, and so on – like ripples on water.

Operational benefits are the reason most large companies quote for getting involved in EDI, although the author suspects many of these companies have already heard the 'suggestion' of their major customers. The reductions in operating cycles, savings in paper (yes, EDI is a green technology) and improvements in data accuracy are what most commentators focus on, but are only the beginning. People who see EDI as a means of replacing the Post Office and the data entry clerks are missing the most important point. EDI is like an iceberg; cut off the top and the iceberg refloats. After implementing EDI, new problems come to the surface, and those usually relate to the effectiveness of the business processes surrounding EDI and the relationships with trading partners. These processes and relationships were often designed for a completely different, usually outdated business environment. The improvements made in the 'post office' function will probably pale into insignificance compared to the benefits available from changes here. EDI does not create these problems; it does, however, bring them to the fore. As such it is a major catalyst for change – an opportunity not to be missed.

Marketing proactiveness and strategic use of EDI are terms that are regularly used, often by people who have no understanding of them. Be very clear – EDI is not a strategy; it is just one of the many tools used to craft strategies, offering the best service through excellent logistics, just-in-time, quality, lowest cost producer. These are strategies; and EDI can help them all. Whilst it is not a strategy in itself (nor ever should be), EDI is of strategic importance. Although it cannot deliver long-term competitive advantage, failure to use it can deliver lasting competitive disadvantage. As companies seek to shrink their supply base to a more manageable size, only those companies who can offer the best products and services at the lowest cost will survive. Coupled with an environment where long-term relationships are being sought, it will be difficult, if not impossible to win a second chance.

'EDI helps you lock in your customers and suppliers.' This is another popular myth. EDI systems and networks today are built around openness and accessibility – the exact opposite of systems designed to lock in partners. Why is this so? Rather than create one-to-many relationships essential in systems that seek to lock in partners to the hub company, EDI creates many-to-many relationships, facilitating the building of communities. Hubs do exist. They are the large companies, often at or close to the end of a supply chain possessing substantial leverage. Their actions to roll out their own EDI projects create communities. Whilst the communities may seem to be proprietary in the early days, they evolve over time as shown in the following sequence of diagrams (see **Fig. 5.4**).

In stage 1 (**Fig. 5.4(a)**), connections tend to be simple; a series of one-to-many connections with hub companies driving the process. These hub companies often share a common supply base. For example, most retail chains buy from Heinz, Elida Gibbs, Procter & Gamble; most automotive companies buy from Bosch, Champion and Chloride. In the second stage (**Fig. 5.4(b)**), these common suppliers create links with their other customers. In stage 3 (**Fig. 5.4(c)**), hub companies begin to create links with other hub companies. Automotive companies buy

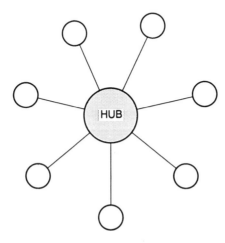

**Figure 5.4(a)**  Primary communities

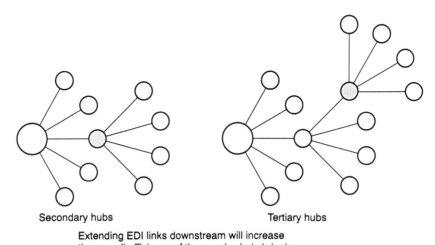

Secondary hubs                                    Tertiary hubs

Extending EDI links downstream will increase
the overall efficiency of the supply chain bringing
even more benefits to the primary hubs

**Figure 5.4(b)**  Increased penetration

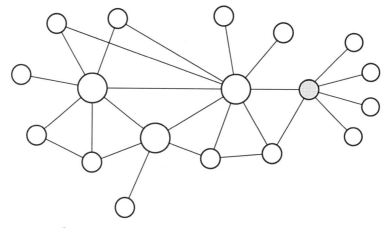

Standards issues become more critical

**Figure 5.4(c)** Community interconnection grows

chemicals, chemical companies buy construction services, construction companies buy vehicles, and so on. Eventually, different industries will be connected together in a web of EDI links. Many companies will be a *prime* player in one community and a *secondary* player in others. Monitoring the activities of the leading players in your respective supply chains can provide early indications of developments that can have substantial impacts on those involved with that chain.

One word of caution. Some major companies used to calling the shots impose proprietary approaches on their suppliers. A common supply base can find itself supporting complex EDI links, squeezed between the big players (see **Fig. 5.5**)

Modern software packages can manage the technical aspects of this

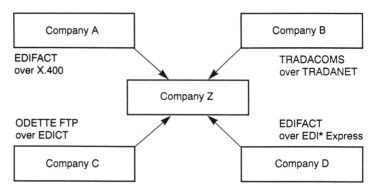

**Figure 5.5** The squeezed supplier

connection but the cost – particularly in management time – is either squeezed out of already thin margins or passed on to the customer. Lobbying aside, there is little the suppliers can do when faced with this situation other than comply.

## ● Putting EDI to work

EDI is a business tool. The skilled manager knows how to use the tool. He also knows that other tools are needed to do the job and when to use each tool. The first, and by far the most important step in introducing EDI, is to establish the business case; to ask if this is the right tool for the organisation. Most failures of EDI (in common with other IT projects) result from the lack of a business case and a business manager as the sponsor.

The keys to success with EDI is to establish a sound case, taking a long-term view and develop and implement an aggressive plan to roll out EDI to trading partners.

EDI is a very flexible tool. It can be used in a variety of areas of the supply chain. Identifying the possible applications and the contribution they can make is an important step. This can be done at the corporate, business unit or functional level. A simple matrix (**Fig. 5.6**) helps assess the relative value of each potential application.

The vertical axis lists the possible linkages to suppliers, customers, other divisions, banks, carriers, etc. The horizontal axis lists the business objectives. Each link can then be examined to identify what contribution it makes to the objectives. This exercise will give a list of priorities for EDI – priorities based not on expediency but on contribution to the business. The process focuses on information flows and an essential prerequisite is critically to examine the value of those flows, constantly asking 'is this information flow necessary' and 'what does it achieve' 'what is the effect of removing it'? This follows my two fundamental laws of computing – 'Do not automate the existing process' and 'Don't automate – obliterate'.

It is through this fundamental review process that EDI becomes a driver of signficant change. EDI of itself does not force change. It does, however, make the need and the opportunity for change much more visible. Digital Equipment Corporation use EDI to pass demand information from their manufacturing plant in Galway to suppliers around Europe. The initial implementation of EDI required the automation of a purchase order approval policy. As experience and confidence in EDI grew, Digital questioned the premise of the purchase role. When

**Business objectives**

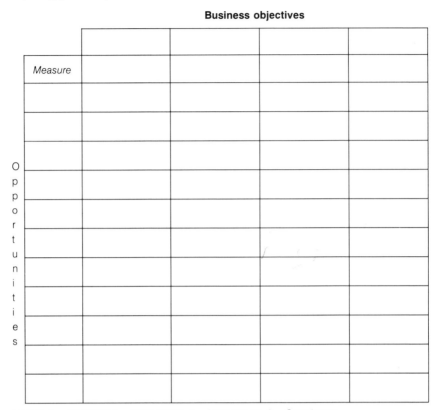

Legend: 0 – No impact, 1 – Small impact, 2 – Large impact, 3 – Great impact

**Figure 5.6** Matrix to assess relative values of applications

analysed, the demand trigger for new supplies was identified not as the buyer, but as the manufacturing plan. Moves are now planned to move the demand trigger (using EDI to link processes) from purchasing on to the shop-floor. This will remove at least one task from the cycle.

The scale of change presented by the EDI opportunity can be significant. The three-transaction order cycle is now being discussed. A demand signal or purchase order is issued by the buyer. The supplier issues a despatch advice to notify delivery and a bar-coded delivery note to accompany the goods. This delivery, when verified, is used to issue payment. Acknowledgements and invoices have no place in this cycle because they serve no purpose.

Such fundamental changes in business practices are only possible when three conditions are fulfilled. First, the relationship between the parties must be stable. Redefining basic processes is difficult, if not impossible, when significant problems such as quality performance cloud the relationship. Second, the opportunity for change must exist.

The availability of EDI coupled with severe competitive pressures provide not just the opportunity but also the driving force. Finally, the creativity of business managers has to be harnessed to the power of communications and computing technologies. EDI has facilitated this by providing a concept and technology that is easy to relate to business need.

The end result of this process of analysis of information flows is a list of opportunities for applying EDI, each of which can be subject to further investment appraisal. **Table 5.3** lists the costs and benefits that should be considered.

Organisations have claimed a wide range of financial benefits from EDI. British Coal estimate a saving of £11,000 per 50,000 invoices processed and a substantial inventory reduction. Philips Components' well-documented savings are shown in **Fig. 5.7**. This particular case is interesting because it displays benefits for both sides.

Digital Equipment Corporation in Augusta, USA, where inventory is measured by individual buyer have seen reductions from $880,000 to $43,000. More significantly, the time spent on purchase administration fell from an average of seven and a half hours a week to 30 minutes per week. The greatest benefit for Digital was probably the reduction of purchase cycle time. The time between placing an order and receiving confirmation of supply from the supplier was slashed from five weeks to three days. This has contributed to a 30% reduction in manufacturing lead time. Tallent Engineering, a small manufacturing company based

● **Table 5.3**

Costs and benefits

---

*Costs − Initial*
EDI system design
Consultancy, including training
Hardware
Software − EDI gateway
                 Application system changes
Telecoms equipment
EDI service charges
Management time

---

*Costs − Ongoing*
EDI service fees
Telecoms charges
Hardware rental/depreciation
System management and support
Development

---

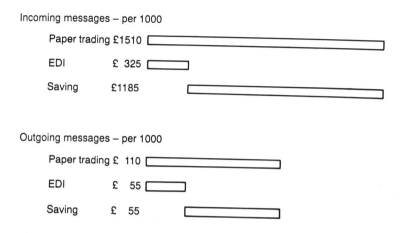

Incoming messages – per 1000

Paper trading £1510

EDI          £ 325

Saving       £1185

Outgoing messages – per 1000

Paper trading £ 110

EDI          £ 55

Saving       £ 55

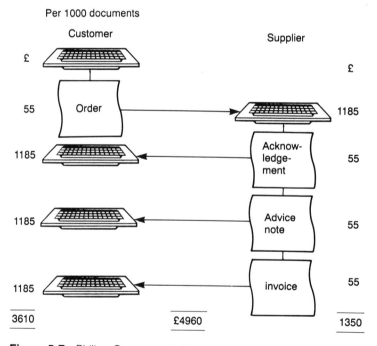

Per 1000 documents

**Figure 5.7** Philips Components Ltd – savings

in the North East of England estimate savings of £150 per month. Vestric, a pharmaceutical wholesaler, suggest postal savings of £160/day from a multi-warehouse, multi-supplier operation.

● Trading partners

Having identified the what and the why, the next question is with whom. EDI is a partnership activity. Selecting the trading partners – particularly the initial EDI partners – is important. New investments always attract attention. Early wins help to ensure the longer-term success of the programme. Experience has shown that the best partner for a trial or pilot is one who can make a significant contribution to the chosen business goal, has some experience of EDI and a stable trading and commercial relationship.

A simple way of identifying the right partners (suppliers, customers, distributors, etc) is to assess their contribution to the business and their readiness and willingness to establish EDI links. The contribution must be assessed against the appropriate measure: inventory reduction; administrative cost reductions; delivery time reductions; customer service improvements, are just some examples. In some cases a composite measure may be needed. Detailed statistics are not necessary. An approximate figure, which enables realistic rankings, is all that is needed. EDI readiness is usually assessed by collecting data from trading partners. Questionnaires are a favoured and effective way of collecting the data about current and planned EDI activities, standards and VANs to be used. This information can be converted into a rank by allocating values to the different parameters. These values are then mapped on to the matrix shown in (**Fig. 5.8**).

The key trading partners are those that fall into the upper half of the matrix. They are the first candidates for EDI. They are ready now and can provide the results needed to ensure continued development of EDI. They are the companies to *embrace*. High readiness, low impact partners (*fallback*) could provide a pilot project where no *embrace* partner exists. The *ignore* quadrant are unimportant. They are not in a position to introduce EDI and any link would have little impact on the business.

The top left hand quadrant – high impact, low readiness – are critical to the long-term success of any EDI programme. They have to be *educated* about the benefits of EDI. Bringing these companies into the EDI fold is critical for achieving the full benefits of EDI. Only when the necessary critical mass is achieved will climbing the benefits curve (see **Fig. 5.9**) be possible. The shape of the curve demands a long-term

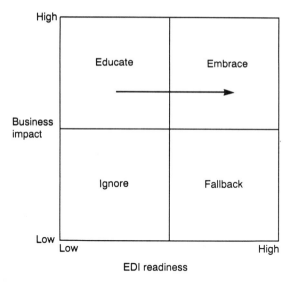

**Figure 5.8** EDI Readiness Matrix

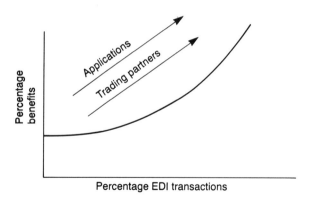

**Figure 5.9** Benefits time-lag

approach to be taken. The first EDI link is an important milestone, but only the first step.

Approaches to convincing trading partners in the *educate* sector to join the EDI programme will differ according to the type of relationship. EDI conferences overflow with companies who have been pushed into EDI through the power of what is politely called purchasing leverage.

Force is not an approach that can easily be used with customers and is not always the right approach to suppliers. Creativity must replace coercion. Some customers will be quick to identify the benefits from EDI. For those who don't fall into this easy to convince category, effort has to be invested. The key questions are what are my customer needs and problems, and how can EDI help them? The most successful approach is to bundle EDI as part of an improvement in service – making you easier to do business with, providing additional information or services, reducing customers' costs. These are benefits customers can relate to and will invest in.

In an effort to maximise the take up of EDI, some organisations have helped their trading partners introduce EDI. The most popular scheme is to hold seminars introducing EDI and the role it plays in the trading relationship. Others have given financial and technical support or equipment. British Coal embarked on an aggressive EDI campaign with its suppliers. Their three-pronged approach linked education with low-cost EDI software and reduced EDI VAN service charges. The software package, Supplyline, provides a PC-based data entry and printing facility along with communication to British Coal's chosen VAN. BC also negotiated a substantial reduction in VAN charges for trading partners linking only to BC. They were able to do this because of their position as a hub company. VAN operators define a hub as a large organisation who are at the centre of a large trading community. BC have approximately 12,000 suppliers, 4,500 of whom are potential EDI partners. VAN operators signing one hub on to their network can watch that company market their EDI service. It is perhaps surprising that network operators also call these hub companies 'honey pots'.

### ● Legal considerations

The information being exchanged in the EDI chain is, in some instances, part of a legal process. Purchase orders and invoices and some freight documents have legal as well as business purposes. If nothing else, EDI eliminates the battle of the forms. Documents with terms and conditions referenced now disappear. The legal structure and rules, however, are built to serve a paper-based trade system. It has not caught up with the technology.

In the UK there are no restrictions on the use of EDI in the legal code, save for the requirement that land and bond purchasing be effected under seal. No one has yet found a way of applying a seal to an EDI message. The Finance Act 1981 was changed at the request of the EDI lobby to amend sections that would have outlawed EDI-based invoices. Whilst there are no significant restrictions on EDI, it must be pointed out that, to date, EDI has not been tested in the courts. The validity of EDI log files as valid documentary evidence is therefore questionable.

To help remove the uncertainty created by this lack of legal precedence, the UK-based EDI Association has produced a model interchange agreement. The agreement is designed to supplement existing terms and conditions of contract when EDI is used. It includes clauses covering security and integrity of data, use of intermediaries (EDI service providers) and disputes. Copies can be obtained from the EDI Association, Almack House, 26 King Street, London SW1Y 6QW.

Whether the EDIA or another interchange agreement is used, it is important to review existing terms and conditions of trade. Many include references to paper and postal systems, which will have to be removed.

Organisations seeking to use EDI in an international arena will need to be particularly careful. The legal status of EDI differs, even within the European Community. The United Nations has produced guidelines (the UNCID rules) to help draft interchange agreements. The Commission of the European Community is currently trying to harmonise the Community's legal position on EDI but that work is not yet complete. For further advice, contact the International Chamber of Commerce or the Trade Electronic Data Interchange Systems group of the Commission of the European Community (Directorate-General XIII)

## ● Implementing EDI

Having identified the what, why and who, only the how remains.

Implementing EDI is little different from implementing any other IT project. The only significant difference is that it often involves co-ordination with other organisations – the trading partners and the EDI service providers. Sound project management is essential.

The key decisions are what form of 'EDI gateway' is needed, what EDI standards should be supported and what form of communications should be used.

### Gateway

EDI is a mechanism for exchanging data beween applications. Most organisations have multiple applications – inventory management, purchasing, accounts, transport, sales order processing – all of which could take advantage of EDI. The planning process defined earlier will have identified the key links. In many cases this is not one, but several possible options. This could be true for several parts of the organisation; division, business unit, function, geography or corporate-wide. It is important to understand this scale. Obviously the greater the scale, the greater the complexity and the initial cost. This decision is a trade-off but must also reflect the trading environment.

## Standards

EDI message standards define the structure of the content. They are the common language that enables one application to understand the information passed to it from another application. Unfortunately, there is no single EDI standard. Different countries and industries have defined their own. This proliferation is likely to exist for at least five years, and more realistically for up to ten years.

It is often said that choice of standards is a crucial decision. On the contrary, choice is the questionable privilege of the few. Most organisations find that their choice of standard is dictated by the trading partners and the communities they operate in. For companies operating across industry and continental boundaries, coping with multiple standards is inevitable. This is true at both ends of an organisation's supply chain. As indicated in **Table 5.1**, EDIFACT is emerging as the most popular base for standards in Europe, indeed around the world. This is a complexity caused by multiple standards that can be managed by many modern EDI software packages.

In this volatile standards environment, it is important to ensure that core applications are not affected by changes in standards. The user should be totally unconcerned about which standards are being used.

When determining the precise implementation of a standard with a trading partner, a 'hierarchy' of agreements is needed. At the top level – the business level – it is important to determine what information is needed by the two parties to support the transaction. It is best to pare this to the minimum, avoiding the desire to include something for the unlikely event, which rarely, if ever, happens. Free text is taboo. If true application – application EDI – is to be implemented, free text is impossible. Codes should be used to handle alternatives if they are essential.

The next level of agreement is the standard of which syntax and message is to be used. The final level is the detailed message design. These stages demand detailed knowledge of the appropriate EDI standard.

## Choosing software

It is not the intention to describe in detail the functionality of EDI software.

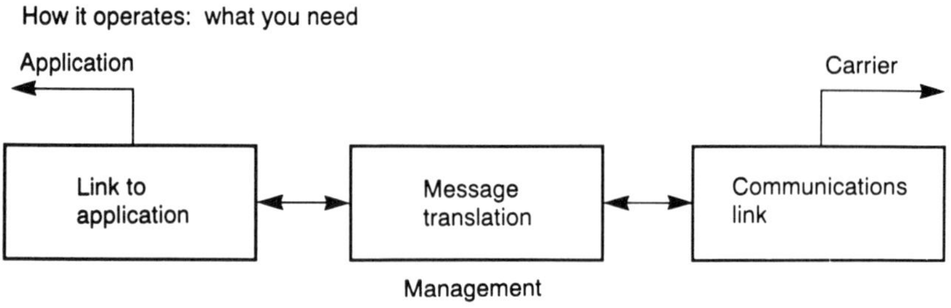

How it operates: what you need

**Figure 5.10** EDI gateway

All EDI gateways (see **Fig. 5.10**) perform four activities – a link to the application; translation between the data formats used internally and the EDI standard; transferring the message over the chosen network; and managing and tracking the whole activity.

When selecting software it is important to ensure that it meets current and future needs. **Table 5.4** provides a checklist of factors that could be used to compare available packages.

When selecting a VAN, three elements should be considered. Most important is the available community – the VAN operators' existing subscriber base. Several trading partners may already be using an EDI service; it would therefore help take up of the project if this service was used. As important as the number of trading partners using a service, is the profile of the subscribers. An existing base within an industry sector will attract other subscribers, increasing the number of users available. In an EDI context, like attracts like. The facilities offered by the VAN operator is the second selection criteria. This includes factors like message standards and communication protocols supported, policy of service development, support offered, geographic coverage and other

- **Table 5.4**

  Selecting software and services

  When selecting EDI software and services it is essential that a complete evaluation is performed taking into account both current and future requirements. The following is offered as the basis for you to develop your own checklist:

  *What's on offer?*

  Does the package support all the functions needed to operate a robust EDI system in one, integrated package, i.e. applications link, translation, communication and management? If not, what work is required to build a complete system? Does the package link to other messaging products?

  *Audit facilities*

  What audit facilities are included in the package? Can you check the status of documents sent, received and in process? If yes, how? e.g. can document contents be examined?

- **Table 5.4**

*(Continued)*

---

*Validation of data*

How does the package validate the data processed? How will you manage the control of documents to/from trading partners?

---

*New partners*

How are new trading partners added to the system? How do you change the agreements with existing partners, e.g. add new documents?

---

*Testing*

Will the package automatically check for the correct operation of all functions? Is there a comprehensive error logging and exception reporting system?

---

*Security*

How does the package control access? Can different types of users be created with differing levels of control?

---

*Access*

How do you access the package? Are commands consistent across the package?

---

*Recovery procedures*

If the system fails, what is the recovery procedure? How much work will be necessary to recover failed or lost documents?

---

*Standards management*

What standards does the package support? How are standards updated? What tools are available to help define the standards implemented with different trading partners?

---

*Communications options*

What communications options does the product support? Can you use different communications options with different trading partners? What happens if the communication link fails during transmission of data?

---

*Growth*

How can the capacity of the EDI system be increased with this approach? What happens if you change or upgrade the host machine?

---

*Future developments*

What are your company's plans for developing your EDI systems?
What are the software supplier's plans and long-term commitments for developing their EDI systems?

---

*Support and service*

What training is available for the package?
What documentation is supplied with the package?
What help is available for planning, designing and implementing the EDI package?

---

*Coverage*

Is the product supported in all the countries where your company operates?
Can you manage and support multinational projects?

---

messaging services available (e.g. EDI). The third criteria is cost. This can be difficult to assess because different companies have differing approaches to calculating costs. It is important to look at all the costs involved for both current and planned volumes of data.

## ● Impact of EDI

One of the most frequent questions asked is 'How will EDI affect my organisation?'.

At a simple level, EDI will quickly highlight inadequacies of the existing application systems. Many information exchanges prove to be a combination of the formal, often form-based, information and informal information and processes. Sales order process clerks interpret purchase orders, knowing that when customer A orders product Y, he really wants Z. Part numbers, units of measure, date of delivery, are often changed before they are input into the receiving system. Information not sent is added. This intelligence is lost, and, if essential, has to be added to the formal information flow.

Many are concerned that introducing EDI will remove a point of contact with a customer, thereby reducing the opportunity to sell. It is true that EDI removes the need to collect the order. It does not mean, however, that the contact has to be stopped. Instead of collecting orders, sales personnel can spend the time understanding the customers' needs, problems and plans. The same is true of links with suppliers. Buyers are able to use the time previously spent chasing paperwork, on cost reduction, sourcing quality improvement and product development. If used correctly, EDI actually brings organisations together. This has implications for the number of people employed and the quality of those people. Removing the administrative element of tasks will reduce the workforce. The invoice clerk is about to become an endangered species. Those that remain will focus on the value added content of jobs, requiring a higher degree of professional and interpersonal skill. Those who have climbed up the organisation based on their ability to manage the paperwork feel rightly threatened by EDI.

## ● Summary

EDI has been described as the data equivalent of the telephone. It will become as commonplace – a competitive necessity.

EDI can help many organisations, probably most of them involved in the movement of goods through supply chains. That is not to say all such organisations should rush off and implement it. EDI is one tool in the business manager's toolkit. Skilful managers know how to use it. They also know that different jobs need different tools. Investing in EDI has to be assessed against other investments and needs.

Those who gain most from EDI will use the technology creatively to find new ways of doing business. It is this combination that provides comprehensive advantage. The supply chain provides many opportunities for those with vision.

# 6

## Supplier relationships

● Purchase portfolio

The trend in the 1980s towards a progressive reduction in the size of the vendor base has made it imperative to analyse carefully the constituents of the supply portfolio in order to ensure not only that the most appropriate suppliers are chosen but that leverage is maximised wherever possible. The most commonly used analytical tool in purchase is still the pareto curve.

A typical example is shown in **Fig. 6.1**, relating invoices by quality and value. With a total spread of approximately £450 million a distribution that is more skewed than would normally be the case can be seen; 31% of all invoices carrying a face value of over £1,000 account for slightly over 95% of the values involved. The prime uses of this tool are to ensure that it is possible to identify those suppliers where the volume of business may give leverage to the purchaser, and also the ability to identify the vast quantity of small orders that must, through a process of rationalisation, consolidation and systematisation, be reduced from being a major impediment to the working of the purchase department to one that is controlled carefully by means of well-validated procedures.

Pareto analysis is, however, static in the sense that it is a snapshot taken at a point in time and does not readily lend itself to restructuring the purchase portfolio in order to gain commercial advantage. It was therefore an important landmark when, at the Copenhagen Purchasing Conference in 1983, Peter Kraljic explained the development of a matrix form of portfolio analysis. Kraljic pointed out that a company's need for a purchase strategy depended upon the importance of purchasing in terms of value added and percentage of costs by product and upon complexity, current state, and rate of change of the supply market. It is not simply a powerful tool for analysis. It is an important aid in the determination both of short-term strategies and also in arriving at a policy for the more fundamental restructuring of the portfolio as a

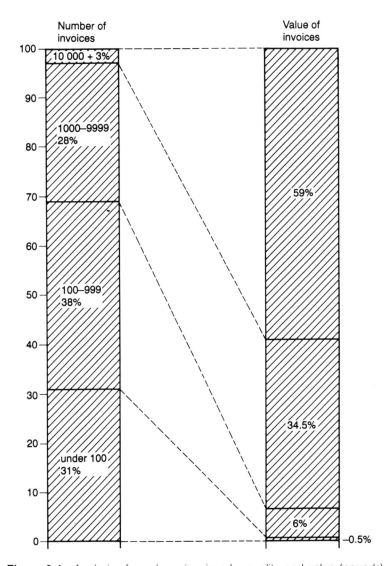

**Figure 6.1** Analysis of purchase invoices by quality and value (pounds)

whole. Both applications add to the purchase director's armoury but it is probably the latter that is of the greatest innovative value in the development of a proactive approach to purchase.

## The purchase matrix

The purchase matrix analyses the supply base according to supplier risk factors and the impact upon profit of the purchasing organisation. The

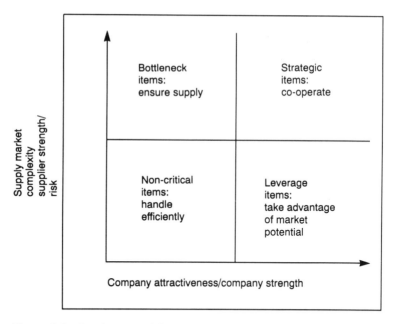

**Figure 6.2** Purchase portfolio

aim is to group suppliers within the four areas of the matrix (see **Fig. 6.2**). In the quadrant that is labelled non-critical products, will normally be found general stores and other items, which have a low face value but which are a dominant activity by virtue of the high volumes that are involved. There is normally a wide choice of suppliers, and the principal challenge in this area is how to develop systems that will ensure that the many transactions do not overwhelm the purchase department. If they should so do – and regrettably this is frequently the case – then individual buyers can find themselves so inundated with paperwork and with follow-up action that, inevitably, they are not able to stand back and systematically analyse the processes that bring this state of affairs about. Non-critical products are always going to be a major problem, although as systems, particularly EDI, develop, they may well in the future be dealt with on a computer-to-computer basis. This type of item, whether held in stock or called off, lends itself to forecasts upon the basis of past consumption using one of the varieties of exponential smoothing techniques available, and then, on an EOQ basis, for the purchasing computer to scan the supply market and choose from the list of offers that become available. EOQ orders or call-offs can then be made to suppliers selected by competitive tender.

With very similar characteristics, in so far as the purchaser's demand is concerned, are bottleneck items. These can be important, however, where they represent essential items since, inherent to this area, is shortage of supply and high risk of non-availability. From time to time, many items (steel products were for many years a prime example) enter the bottleneck category. Political factors impinge heavily since, patented items apart, supply will normally expand to meet demand. Both here and with non-critical products, the leverage available to the purchaser is limited and inventory levels can rise either as a consequence of minimum order quantities or as a strategic insurance.

As spend increases, the buyer–seller relationship naturally changes. Leverage products are those where significant buying power is exercised in favourable market conditions. The purchasing organisation has a choice of ways in which they may exploit this position, bearing in mind the need to be aware that the matrix has a dynamic characteristic and with changes in the supply market or in the purchaser's pattern, the leverage product of today could become either the non-critical or the bottleneck product of tomorrow. Power carefully used is the key. (See **Table 6.1.**)

Strategic products are those where, at a high value level, a broad balance exists between the power of the buyer and the power of the seller. Indeed both parties may be crucially dependent upon each other. The strategic area calls for high level negotiations. Where purchase has fallen behind corporate need in terms of this development, senior line management may reserve this area to themselves and it may in any event be necessary for purchase to operate within umbrella arrangements set up at CEO level.

## Constructing the matrix

In developing the matrix there are problems regarding the ways in which different factors will be used and the weighting that should be given to them. To refer first to the supplier axis, this axis – this evaluation of the supply market – is intended to give a view of the capacities involved, of utilisations, of competitive structure and of financial factors. It is also concerned with the uniqueness of the product and the degree of technological stability inherent within the area. Entry barriers in the form of capital or know-how and logistic stability are also important. Some of these data are published whilst other information can be internally generated by buyers. However, significant difficulties in terms of the availability of information can arise and indeed when data are available then there are problems of weighting in order to form a view as to an appropriate positioning. **Table 6.2** illustrates the different factors to be considered. A 'do-it-yourself' version, developed by the author, has

- **Table 6.1**

Classifying purchasing materials requirements

| Procurement focus | Main tasks | Required information | Decision level |
|---|---|---|---|
| Strategic items | Accurate demand forecasting. Detailed market research. Development of long-term supply relationships. Make or buy decisions. Contract staggering. Risk analysis. Contingency planning. Logistics, inventory, and vendor control. | Highly detailed market data. Long-term supply and demand trend information. Good competitive intelligence. Industry cost curves. | Top level (e.g. vice-president, purchasing) |
| Bottleneck items | Volume insurance (at cost premium if necessary). Control of vendors. Security of inventories. Back-up plans. | Medium-term supply/demand forecasts. Very good market data. Inventory costs. Maintenance plans. | Higher level (e.g. department heads) |
| Leverage items | Exploitation of full purchasing power. Vendor selection. Product substitution. Targeted pricing strategies/ negotiations. Contract/spot purchasing mix. Order volume optimisation. | Good market data. Short- to medium-term demand planning. Accurate vendor data. Price/transport rate forecasts. | Medium level (e.g. chief buyer) |
| Non-critical items | Product standardisation. Order volume monitoring/ optimisation. Efficient processing. Inventory optimisation. | Good market overview. Short-term demand forecast. Economic order quantity inventory levels. | Lower level (e.g. buyers) |

- **Table 6.2**

Purchasing portfolio evaluation criteria

| | Supplier strength | Company strength |
|---|---|---|
| 1. | Market size versus supplier capacity | Purchasing volume versus capacity of main units |
| 2. | Market growth versus capacity growth | Demand growth versus capacity growth |
| 3. | Capacity utilisation or bottleneck risk | Capacity utilisation of main units |
| 4. | Competitive structure | Market share with regard to main competition |
| 5. | ROI and/or ROC | Profitability of main end products |
| 6. | Cost and price structure | Cost and price structure |
| 7. | Breakeven stablility | Cost of nondelivery |
| 8. | Uniqueness of product and technological stability | Own production capability or integration depth |
| 9. | Entry barrier (capital and know-how requirements) | Entry cost for new sources versus cost for own production |
| 10. | Logistics situation | Logistic |

been to identify that the key element on this axis is the number of suppliers who are able and willing to supply *now*. This much simpler approach is based upon information that is readily available. It takes into account the number of suppliers in the field and their capacity utilisation. The impact of the purchaser's business in terms of financial return will also find reflection in the willingness of suppliers at a point in time to be in the market-place. Competitive demand is similarly catered for. Accordingly, in the second illustration of the purchase portfolio (see **Fig. 6.3**), the market index reflecting supplier risk and the strength of suppliers identifies a maximum of 12 companies as representing for all practical purposes as wide a degree of commercial freedom as any buyer would normally desire. The middle point of the axis has been arbitrarily fixed at six, which in most cases would represent the approximate point of transition from a supply market in which appropriate choice was available to the purchaser to one in which the risks caused by shortage of supply became more pronounced. The axis therefore covers the spectrum ranging from highly competitive conditions to monopoly.

In terms of the evaluation of the buyer's position, a range of factors must be considered, and once again questions arise as to the availability

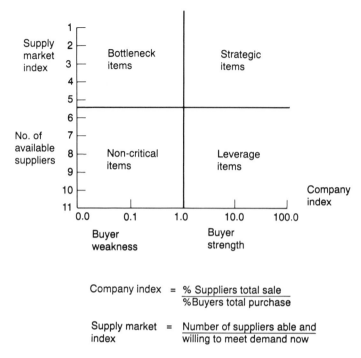

**Figure 6.3**  Purchase portfolio

of information and to the way in which the different factors should be weighted. The most important factor to be taken into account is the current level of purchases and the forecast for the future. It is a sad reflection that there are too many organisations where the only accurate way to get data upon the value of purchases is to ask the supplier how much has been spent. Needless to say this can neither be defended as professional nor admired as a prelude to commercial negotiation. Amongst the elements that should be taken into account, therefore, are the current purchase volume and the future forecast.

In addition, however, factors such as value added and the contribution to competitiveness in the end market expressed in terms of market share, will affect the purchase position.

The value of the purchase spend has a relative significance. It is relative both in terms of the total value of purchases and also in the sense of the degree of importance attached to any particular sum by the seller.

In an attempt to place spend into perspective a modified matrix uses an index ranging from 0.1 through to 100. This index relates the spend on any particular item or commodity to the buyer's total spend and the same amount to the supplier's total sale of the commodity in question. The availability of data of this type varies from organisation to organisa-

206

tion and is a pointer towards the need for a database of information gleaned through interviews and visits to suppliers. Similarly, the buyer's total purchase must also be related to the overall spend of the company or the business unit, which, whilst more readily available, can still present problems of allocation. Given these details, the buyer's index may therefore be expressed as the percentage of the supplier's total sale divided by the percentage of the buyer's total purchase. As is so often the case with such a measure, the extreme values can be unreliable and should be excluded from consideration. That caveat apart, the index is a relatively straightforward means of reducing a complex operation to terms that can be handled by the less sophisticated organisation.

When **Fig. 6.4** is superimposed upon the matrix, three principal options emerge. These are exploit, balance and diversify. They guide the treatment of each of the quadrants which have been defined and are indicative of the strategies to be followed and of their implications for both staff and systems.

### Definition of risk position and strategic thrust

In the weakest of all situations from a buying point of view – where bottleneck items are concerned – shortages can arise either through deficiencies on the supply side or through excessively buoyant demand. Items within this category may represent a small proportion of total

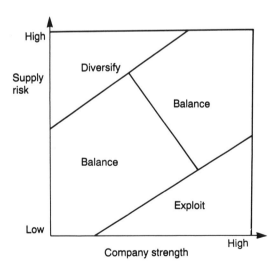

**Figure 6.4** Position in purchasing portfolio matrix defines risk position and strategic thrust

spend but they can be fundamental to the manufacture of a product or running of an organisation. Prudence dictates the maintenance of a strategic inventory. There is also a need to support this inventory if possible by a reasonably close relationship with the supplier and to have contingency plans in the event of non-availability. In the longer term, the purchaser should aim to reduce the dependence of his organisation upon suppliers in this quadrant by minimising the number of bottleneck elements in new products. It is important, through close liaison with or involvement in the design team, to ensure that as far as possible, bought in items are purchase friendly.

Particularly where innovation is seen as a major aspect of competition, differentiation must not lead the design teams into adopting company specials when standard components would suffice. Taguchi has drawn attention to the implications of injudicious specification, not least it its escalatory impact upon price. **Table 4.2** (p. 154), typical of high technology engineering, shows not only the dramatic price increases that result from company specific items, but also the vigilance that purchase must display when dealing with products that are apparently related by formula to the cost base. A clear balance between the market appeal of innovatory design and sourcing needs must be struck, and this can only be achieved by the close working together of the functions concerned.

Turning to those items that are labelled non-critical, here the essential problem is one of transactions volume. With a good choice of suppliers and with the probability that the products are standardised, the purchaser will aim to optimise the inventory situation and to reduce the capital employed. Routine purchase, using economic order quantity approaches, is valid with costs passed to the supplier as far as possible. Above all other areas, this is the one in which the traditional buying mechanism using competitive tenders is most valid. The workload

● **Table 6.3**

Purchase strategy

| Situation | Focus | Elements of strategy |
|-----------|-------|----------------------|
| Non-critical | Balance | Optimise inventory: routine purchase |
| Bottleneck | Diversify | Insurance: close relationships fall-back plan |
| Strategic | Balance | Strategic inventory: long-term relationship |
| Leverage | Exploit | Competition: spot and long-term deal |

involved makes system investment essential, together with the letting of frame contracts against which call-offs can be made directly by users. Most major organisations adopt this course of action, and in some – ICI and SADAF, for example – the number of frame contracts let and the take up against them is an important performance indicator.

Elsewhere within the matrix, a higher spend normally increases purchase power. This is greatest where leverage items are concerned. Here there is a high profit impact and low supply risk. There is a good choice of supplier, there are material substitutes and the high purchase volumes are attractive. Power lies with the buyer. How can this best be used? Traditionally, competition will be used to the maximum effect. This may mean contracts based on spot pricing or a succession of transactions, which by their nature are of a one-off type. Dangers of antagonising suppliers by over-ruthless use of the power that is currently possessed need to be recognised, since this could produce hostilities that, under changed circumstances, might prove damaging. Consequently the buyer should use the power of the present in order to purchase protection for the future. It is perhaps a truism that at this point the attractiveness of the purchaser makes suppliers who look beyond the immediate, anxious to enter into long-term agreements that can be mutually beneficial, and this should be regarded as an important option for this area of the matrix. Provided that the other requirements are in place, leverage products are fertile ground for just-in-time contracts.

Finally, strategic items. Balance is again the key characteristic. Notwithstanding the volume of business available, buyers do not have things all their own way. Goods may be scarce; there can be an absence of substitutes; or few suppliers and significant entry barriers may exist. The purchaser needs accurate forecasting and it is almost certain that a strategic inventory will prove an appropriate investment. Whilst alternatives both of product and supplier may be sought, the overall strategy that is most likely to be attractive to the purchaser is to seek long-term relationships based upon top level negotiations. In the case of the British Telecom portfolio, which is illustrated over three decades (see **Fig. 6.5(a)** to **6.5(c)**), the current strategic approach envisages the building of long-term alliances with key suppliers. This corporate goal has involved the search for a meeting of minds at CEO level providing a basis for understanding within which purchase will operate.

### Building a portfolio

The purchase portfolio matrix is prescriptive of action with regard to individual suppliers. It is also, however, a powerful tool for restructuring

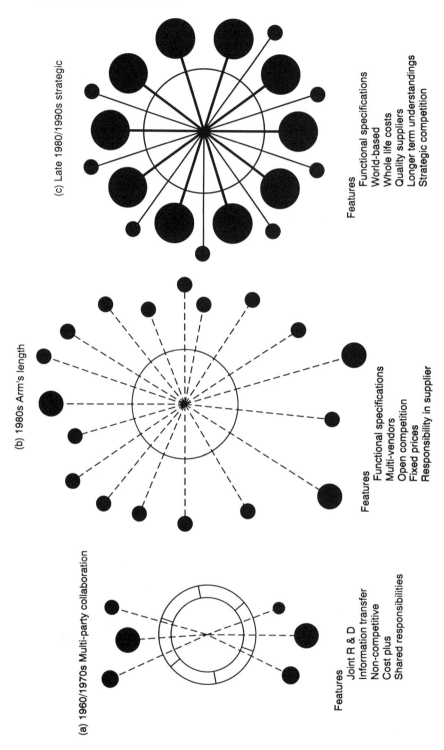

(a) 1960/1970s Multi-party collaboration

Features
Joint R & D
Information transfer
Non-competitive
Cost plus
Shared responsibilities

(b) 1980s Arm's length

Features
Functional specifications
Multi-vendors
Open competition
Fixed prices
Responsibility in supplier

(c) Late 1980/1990s strategic

Features
Functional specifications
World-based
Whole life costs
Quality suppliers
Longer term understandings
Strategic competition

**Figure 6.5(a), (b), (c)** Changing supplier patterns at British Telecom

the portfolio as a whole, or in the case of greenfield activity, designing from scratch. The *'volume analysis'* sheet is one of the German activities of a multinational company in the electrical/electronics field (see **Fig. 6.6**). It portrays a well-ordered portfolio of a progressive purchase department playing an important strategic role within the organisation.

Non-critical products are 15,000 in number. This would appear to indicate that substantial rationalisation has occurred, a fact borne out by the surprisingly small number of vendors employed. An overall spend of DM 2,000 million amongst 600 suppliers is the total position, with only 350 being responsible for the 15,000 non-critical items. In purchase, one of the main generators of cost is the number of suppliers used, this being one of the factors behind rationalisation of the supplier base. EDI becomes much more viable as the number of suppliers reduces and it may be concluded that in this case the non-critical sector has been effectively systematised.

The bottleneck quadrant reflects a value/volume profile similar to the

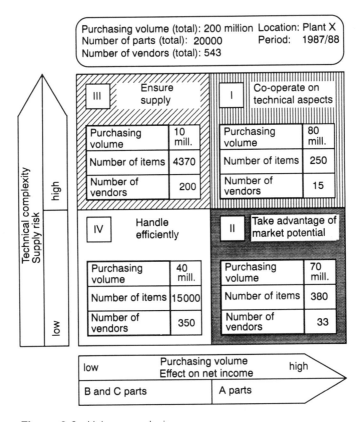

**Figure 6.6** Volume analysis

non-critical area. The distribution per vendor, however, is significantly lower, demonstrating the existence of supply difficulties and market complexity. The marriage of low volume to high supply risk is one that, of necessity, absorbs purchase effort to a degree that makes the desirability of escape from this area virtually self-evident.

As we now move into the two right hand quadrants of the matrix, referred to as 'A parts', strategic importance and purchase clout grow. In an ideal portfolio or one consciously restructured, purchase will be substantially freed of routine procurement to concentrate on these areas. The processes of procurement engineering or more prosaically of standardisation and rationalisation are intended to move the portfolio towards these areas. The outstanding characteristics of the leverage and strategic quadrants are high spend and a low number of suppliers. Purchase's main thrust varies from taking advantage of market potential to supplier co-operation. The win/win approach to negotiations ultimately rests upon the perception by both buyer and seller of mutual benefit through co-operation. These are the quadrants of just-in-time and supply chain integration. The spread of these approaches must therefore be parallel in portfolio terms by a freedom to develop in these sectors of the portfolio. This freedom will result from commercial restructuring possibly allied to the distinction (as in Siemens or Procter & Gamble) between commercial aspects of buying or purchase marketing, and procurement or purchase logistics.

From a greenfield point of view it is technically possible to design a purchase portfolio virtually from scratch. Whilst it is true that there will be always the problem of low value items, this can be minimised not just through systems but through the use of umbrella or focused suppliers. It would appear that part of the Nissan Manufacturing (UK) strategy has been to optimise leverage by using suppliers to develop and be the sole source for, for example, whole systems rather than for individual components within the car. It would, on this basis, be quite possible to envisage having a very limited number of key suppliers some of whom would in effect be both manufacturers and super stockists handling multi-item ranges. Each of the focus suppliers might be regarded as the umbrella for a supply base, which although not directly dealing with the purchase organisation was also wedded to its end market success. In other words the purchase portfolio is a means of strategically designing or redesigning the shape of the vendor base. Properly used it does not reflect simply what is but it acts as a blueprint for what might be.

Although proactivity is a much over-used term, it can be applied with merit to the idea of addressing the supply market in a positive and direct way. The term favoured by McKinsey, of 'reverse marketing', may perhaps be a little ambiguous but nevertheless it does convey to a degree the notion that the purchaser must go forth into the supply market and positively manage it. The purchase portfolio does in fact provide the basis for both a supplier development programme and also for a supplier enhancement programme. These are both ways of developing supplier capability, not least to meet the higher quality and performance standards now demanded.

The matrix approach should be used as a positive tool and provides a means of moving purchasing from a relatively passive and reactive state into one where it is capable of sharing the supply market better to meet its needs. That there are dangers cannot be gainsaid and it is quite possible for dominant buyers to fuse their leverage to their own detriment. A rationalised vendor base may be reduced to a point that tilts market structure against the purchaser. Some years ago in the British coal industry, the rationalisation by the purchaser of aspects of the cable market produced a situation where leverage that had favoured the purchaser, changed in such a way that the supply market became dominated by few major suppliers to the buyer's detriment.

In summary therefore, purchase portfolio analysis is a powerful tool, which has many uses in a proactive sense. It is not simply diagnostic but also has important prognostic powers. Within limits it can be used by all purchase departments. Clearly the use will vary in terms of sophistication and in terms of effort, but even on the very simplest level it is an important means of progressing beyond the pareto curve. It can be said that this represents perhaps the most important single diagnostic and prescriptive tool available to purchasing. If we are indeed to heed the maxim of the Harbour Committee – 'get closer to fewer' (bearing in mind that they must be better) – then there is perhaps no more appropriate place to begin than by analysing the purchase portfolio upon these lines. It is a powerful, even a formidable tool, whose value has long been recognised by marketing and whose adoption by purchase goes some way to redress the analytical balance.

Portfolio analysis reflects the business situation. It has nothing to say about the factors that bring about that situation, into those aspects of quality, delivery or price, which determine how business is placed. For purposes of negotiation, other underlying characteristics and the potential for improvement need to be examined. Confidence in suppliers is the product of many factors and as it grows, the portfolio will change to reflect it. Continual monitoring is therefore necessary. The matrix reflects the position at the end of a period of time. It must be continually updated if it is to retain its usefulness and relevance. The pay-off for this investment in analysing the supply portfolio and for restructuring it, lies in the form of lower costs and better supplier service. It is, in fact, the essential prelude to any form of co-makership, sole sourcing, long-term agreement or just-in-time. It is an *essential* prelude, and without this, to embark on any of these programmes, is in fact to be aiming in the dark without really identifying the nature, form or intent of the target.

● Developing suppliers

Rationalising the supply base has been a front rank issue for purchase since early assessments of Japanes practice highlighted significant differences in approach to this question. However, implicit in the move is the question of quality and of supplier performance. Confidence in suppliers reflects both purchase need and industry type. **Fig. 6.7** is representative of high technology engineering. Many major buying organisations rightly perceive the scarcity of really good suppliers as a major limiting factor and as a consequence develop strategies designed to improve the position. This is a tendency that must inevitably be re-inforced as competition intensifies. Indeed one of the most striking features of many purchase portfolios is the relatively low number of suppliers who are consistently excellent.

Supplier selection *ab initio* has been characterised in the European off-shoots of Japanese firms by a willingness to invest time and effort in getting it right first time. Nissan Manufacturing (UK) Ltd has a programme of supplier selection, which aims to harmonise what could so easily be conflicting aims. On the one hand there is a clear imperative to achieve specified levels of UK and European content. On the other hand, the quality dimension stands predominant. Nissan regard supplier selection as the buyer's most important task. It is, however, also a multi-functional team effort, with quality and real commitment the ultimate benchmarks.

Building a portfolio from scratch is in many ways analogous to a greenfield factory site. For many companies, however, the question of 'where are we going?' needs to be ranged against the mirror image of 'where are we coming from?'. Digital Equipment Corporation is one of those who recognise that supplier development must be comprehensive, systematic and continuous. Their key supplier quality development programme, **Fig. 6.8**, represents the corner-stone of a five-year rolling approach. Suppliers move from basic approval, which features inspection-based quality control and full piece part qualification, to ship to stock status. Emphasis here is on control of the product and a full assessment of quality systems. Weekly deliveries are programmed

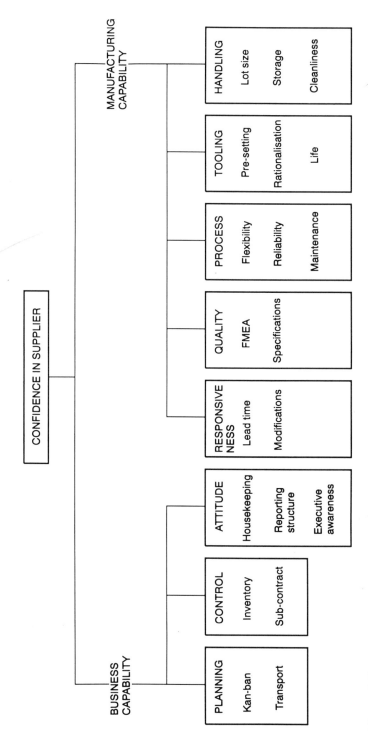

**Figure 6.7**

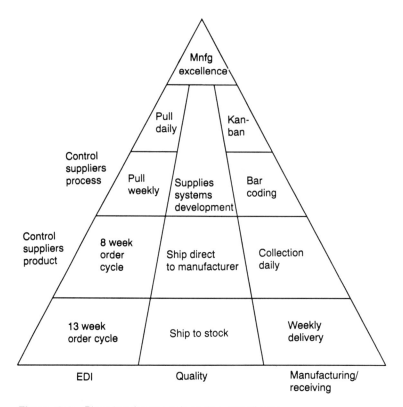

**Figure 6.8** Planning for manufacturing excellence

within a 13 week replenishment cycle. With only modest improvement it is possible to move to a position where shipment is direct to line, with a daily sweep truck regime installed.

In the third stage, a supplier systems management programme (SPC) is fully operational. Quality agreements are signed with an emphasis now upon process rather than product. SPC is installed as a control mechanism and supplies are pulled, Kanban-fashion, daily or weekly. Finally, with full certification, total quality based upon small group activity and continuous improvement is achieved.

This systematised approach represents not just a well thought out and directed methodology, but a realistic assessment of the current position. With over 80 key suppliers, DEC in Europe expect elimination of the basic approval category by 1994. Certification of perhaps 50 suppliers is the highest hoped for target, but the reality was when development began, no single supplier had achieved that status.

It must follow from investment of this kind, that a continuous relationship based upon careful selection is anticipated. In the process, negotiation plays a key part as indeed it will do for all organisations who seek explicitly to restructure their portfolio.

## ● Negotiation

### The need to negotiate

Changes in the role and scope of the purchase function have manifested themselves in many ways. One of the most apparent is that in the purchasing climate today a great deal of emphasis is placed on the role of the purchaser as a negotiator. Part of the reason for this is the movement towards rationalisation of portfolios, the selection of single suppliers and the attempt to obtain long-term working relationships. Of necessity this implies that the purchase negotiator concentrates his attention on those areas of the purchase portfolio where the simple use of competition will not bring about the desired result. Depending upon whether items are defined as *bottleneck, leverage* or *strategic,* a rationale for negotiating will vary.

In the *bottleneck* area, the principal problems are those caused by shortage of supply either due to overall shortage or due to competition in the supply market. The negotiator's objective here is primarily to ensure supply and to reduce the risk to the organisation of non-availability. Notwithstanding the fact that quantities involved may be small, there can be a case here for high level negotiation as a result of the criticality of the items concerned. Normally, however, the negotiation process is best carried on at a lower level. In respect of the areas where there is a *leverage* advantage, negotiation will take place where it has been concluded that this advantage is best exploited by the negotiation of a longer-term arrangement. This is the alternative to spot purchase, where immediate advantage is obtained from the disproportionate balance of power and where this situation is expected to continue. Spot buying calls for a trader approach with price, rather than quality or availability, being the key. Only where the longer view is being taken are more sophisticated methods needed.

Finally, where *strategic purchases* or *strategic alliances* are needed, and where horizons may extend to ten years or more, the need for win/win calls for substantial experience. Almost by definition, such activity implies substantial research activity and development costs. Mutual end market advantage in the face of strong competition is frequently the stimulus. With vertical integration, apart from a few significant exceptions now generally out of favour, the construction of supply chain

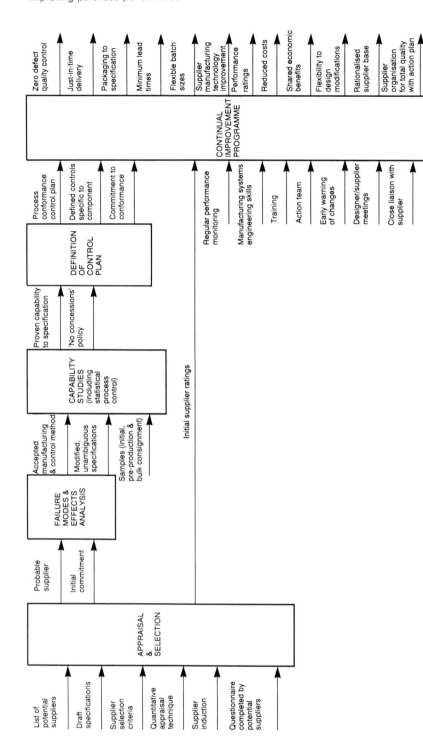

**Figure 6.9** Systems approach to supplier development input–output analysis

relationships is a major challenge to the buyer. Space and time to negotiate is generated by disaggregating from the purchase portfolio matters that are either repetitions or concerned with day-to-day logistics.

## The types of negotiation

Negotiation is an interactive, competitive decision-making process in which it is necessary to try and achieve a balance between scientific integrity and political reality. As a science, negotiation lends itself to systematic analysis. As an art, it calls for powers of judgement, a sense of timing and an array of interpersonal skills.

Negotiation may take the form of distributive bargaining with, in the purest form, two parties debating one single issue. Their objective is to reach an agreement that will be implemented rather than aborted or avoided. The characteristics of form of negotiation include a high degree of probity and an absence of favours to be called in. There is no linkage with other negotiations and ratification is not necessary. Although both parties are opposed to each other, threats will not form part of the process. There are no time constraints, and the outcome will normally be legally binding. This is the commonest negotiation form, between non-antagonistic adversaries.

Much more complex is integrative bargaining. Here, whilst there can be two parties, negotiation will be more sophisticated, frequently involving aspects of coalition analysis. The process is multi-issue and the parties need not be true competitors. It is not the case that if one gains the others must necessarily lose, and hence it is possible, through co-operation, for all the parties to obtain more. This is the form of negotiation that leads to win/win, and whilst this may be the only way in which certain issues can be resolved, it is difficult for buyers reared in the adversarial tradition to adapt easily to its requirements. The attitude change required represents a major challenge to the trainer and in many organisations obeisance is not widely reflected in practical application.

## Organising a negotiation: structural considerations

The frameworks for commercial negotiations reflect both general economic considerations and the dispositions of both purchase and market portfolios. Different interests may exist as much within negotiating teams as between them. Coalitions rather than monolithic bodies are virtually the norm and it is not uncommon for the different members of negotiating teams to have widely differing objectives and values. These

internal differences can be exploited by the other parties to the negotiation and indeed frequently the internal negotiations in the group may
present more problems than those that are carried on externally.

Negotiations that are repetitive introduce elements akin to those
linked to other issues. Where negotiation is repetitive, atmosphere and
reputation become much more important, and materially affect both
apparent strengths and weaknesses. Issues themselves may interact and
through this interplay produce linkage. Value trade-offs therefore arise
adding a new and much more complex dimension. In discussions, multi-
issues will be perceived by different parties in different ways. Not everything will seem equally important and even relatively minor concessions
may appear to have much more significance in the eyes of the other
parties and may therefore affect outcomes in a disproportionate way.

A failure to agree has different implications for the parties and the consequences will influence the stances and reservation positions taken up.
The acronym BATNA – *best alternative to no agreement* – reflects the perceived downside of no agreement and it is an ultimate arbiter. Absent
arbiters or ratifiers may be a source of strength to negotiators bringing
into play the need for further concession finally to seal an agreement, or
providing space to effect a tactical withdrawal. Time may be used in a
similar way or as a forcing mechanism.

A party that negotiates in haste is often disadvantaged, not least when
haste is self-induced through the creation of artificial deadlines. Delay
penalties can be quite different for the parties to the negotiation.

Underlying all forms of negotiation is perceived power. A characteristic of western negotiators is the reluctance to share information, which
may apparently affect the relative power positions of parties. It is the
case that certain negotiations are only a search for a mutually necessary
basis for collaboration, and that a willingness to go more than half way
is an essential condition for success.

## Structuring negotiations – preparation for negotiation

In any given situation, there are a set of possible outcomes. Each participant has their own subjective view of the situation, which is derived
from the interpretation of information available to them, and their view
of the preferences of others. At the start of the negotiation, each participant will estimate potential gains and disadvantages, and the benefits or
costs involved. From these factors will flow a series of benchmarks or
levels. Although, with experience, many buyers neglect this aspect of
negotiation, they are in truth fundamental to the negotiation process
(see **Fig. 6.10**).

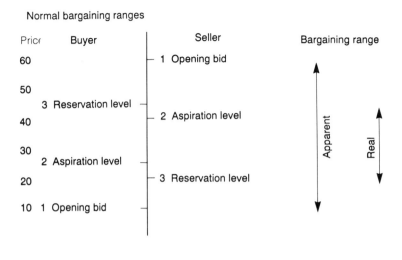

Normal bargaining ranges

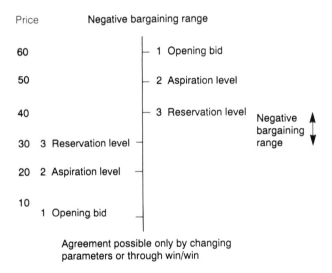

Negative bargaining range

Agreement possible only by changing
parameters or through win/win

**Figure 6.10** Normal bargaining ranges

Reservation levels are the ultimate bottom line. For the buyer, in price terms, it is that at which the cost of purchase exceeds perceived value. For the seller, it is that level at which a sale ceases to be attractive. The best alternative to no agreement dominates the thinking of both parties. The ability skilfully to perceive an opponent's assessment can materially affect negotiation outcomes. Aspiration levels represent what we would normally hope to achieve, and research has suggested that high attainers have high aspiration levels. Unlike the reservation levels, aspiration levels can be revised and readjusted, based upon views of the behaviour of the other parties. They are much more fluid and much more flexible than other aspects of the negotiation process. They may appear to be the major influence in deciding opening bid levels. This is a crucial step because, well done, it will provide a focus leading to our aspiration level. Badly done, it will draw us towards the reservation level. Well timed, it will focus negotiations in an advantageous way. Badly timed, it can represent a major and possibly unreciprocated concession. Negotiations take place within a bargaining range.

The apparent bargaining range lies between our opening bid position and that of our opponents. However, that it is this gap that must be bridged is an illusion. The real area of difference lies between our respective reservation positions or bottom lines, and part of the early exchange when negotiation begins is designed to identify this *true* range as opposed to the *apparent* position. Normally agreement is possible because an actual area does exist, which will meet the views of both parties. If, however, the reservation levels are mutually exclusive, then a negative bargaining range will exist and agreement will be impossible without altering one or other of the principal parameters. Only through a win/win approach will this be possible and an early appreciation of this fact is therefore essential.

## The negotiation process

Howard Raiffa used the term 'negotiation dance' to depict the varying stages by which the opponents move from their initial stated positions to a zone of agreement and the end game. The process by which this is conducted is through communication that may be tacit and indirect or explicit and direct. The objective of communication is to influence the other participant, and the degree to which success will be achieved will depend not just upon the nature of the message but also upon the manner in which it is delivered and the perception of the recipients.

The moves that can be made are a combination of verbal or written modes, structural changes, and a conscious impetus towards coercion or accommodation.

Skill in negotiation makes it possible to alter perceptions and preferences. This implies passing information, making promises or issuing threats. A threat is intended to coerce by indicating how non-compliance will be punished, and has an advantage in that it need not necessarily be carried out. Accommodation, on the other hand, which takes the form of promises, implies reward, and here a key difference is that it must in fact be implemented or carried out.

In contrast to pure communication, structural changes alter the framework by introducing concessions for which reciprocation is sought. It is skill in using concessions that justifies the description of negotiation as an art as well as a science. Good powers of judgement are needed to determine the size and the timing of concessions, whilst an understanding of psychology may assist in eliciting hoped for responses.

## Coercion and accommodation

Frequently, negotiations begin by using coercive tactics. This is an attempt to modify perceptions of one's own commitment to the position and perhaps to alter the appearance of the different risks if settlement is not reached. One method of using coercive tactics is to increase the apparent valuation of the stakes. Perhaps this may be done by coupling the issue with something that is more important through, for example, emphasising the degree to which one's own prestige and reputation is at stake or even the extent to which one occupies the moral ground of the debate.

Another method is to assert one's determination to stand firm. This may be by making some irreversible commitment, which eliminates any possibility of retreat – the classic 'burning of bridges' case. Alternatively, it may be possible to alter the opponent's estimate of the cost of failure or indeed to reduce the opponent's value of winning. Saving face can be achieved by this form of downgrading and there could be nothing further from the truth that this is a concern exclusively of those from the east. The drawbacks of coercive tactics are not simply that they may have been anticipated and discounted. It is that the advantages offered are more apparent than the costs involved. If coercive tactics fail, then the postponed bills may be much larger than those that might have had to have been paid if this approach had not been followed. The degree to which coercion is used reflects therefore not simply the power or perceived power of the players, but also the temperament of individuals and their view of the significance of different outcomes. Threats may bolster the ego of the utterer but in fact they are 'the last resort of the bankrupt negotiator'. Too many negotiators habitually adopt this approach, leading to an escalation of issues and to the elimination of win/win as an available option. Hence they should be carefully balanced with alternative approaches. Above all, threats must not be allowed to become an organisational norm.

Accommodation tactics are designed to heighten the awareness of common interests. Usually they involve concession and a search for reciprocation. When making concessions, it is necessary to balance the chances that the opponent will accept, with the costs of acceptance and with the costs of non-acceptance. If concessions evoke no response, can the situation be retrieved? Will they simply be interpreted as weakness and, above all, when a concession is made, can the other party be convinced that one will stand firm in the new position?

Any form of escalation carries with it increased risk. If raising the stakes should become self-fuelling, negotiations are getting out of hand. It is therefore part of the negotiator's task to determine the likely location of such thresholds. This will depend to a large extent upon personal relationships and upon the skills with which subjective judgements are made. The blending of hot and cold, the minatory and the conciliatory,

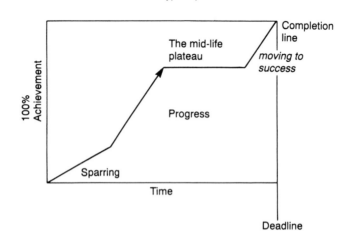

Situation 1 : consistent progress

Situation 2 : a typical pattern

**Figure 6.11**  Time maps

is a common ploy in negotiation acquiring, where different players are involved – the 'good guy/bad guy' designation. Such personal skills involving speed of response to changing situations are the product of experience and training, and are one reason why no area generates quicker or more attractive returns to training investment than this one. In part, this is because timing is of the essence, never more so than when the pattern of structural change or concession is planned.

## Time maps

*Time maps* effectively chart the progress of negotiations, demonstrating with almost monotonous regularity the ad hoc approach that in practice

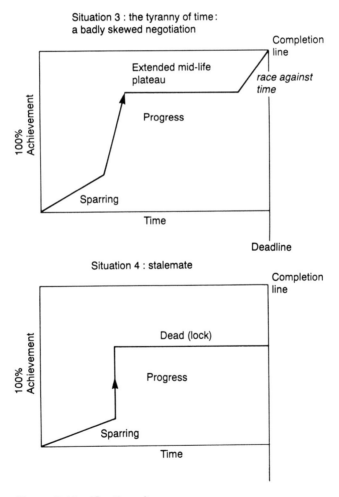

**Figure 6.11** *(Continued)*

is favoured by so many. An insight into this kind of analysis is valuable in pacing the intervals between concessions and also in judging the points at which pressure may be applied (see **Fig. 6.11**).

Time maps raise fundamental questions regarding the flexibility or otherwise of the frame proposed and of the validity of the resulting deadlines. Many unsatisfactory outcomes are the product of badly skewed discussion patterns, which replace structured and systematic negotiation by bazaar-style haggling. Clearly the consistent progress depicted in Situation 1 of **Fig. 6.11** is a thoroughly unlikely scenario – unlikely ever to be found in practice. Much more realistic is a pattern that follows preliminary exchanges by solid progress, interrupted only for a relatively brief period by what may be termed the mid-life plateau. At this stage, the useful exchange of information, the assessment of participant priorities and substantive progress come to a temporary halt. During the mid-life plateau, tangible progress is made and frequently negotiation becomes becalmed on matters of detail. Where deadlines exist and are so recognised, the importance of curtailing the mid-life plateau is apparent and with a re-focusing upon the realities of the issues involved.

A very real danger does exist, however, when, as in Situation 3, an extension of the plateau leads inevitably to an undisciplined scramble for agreement. Two scenarios frequently appear. On the one hand, a race against time begins and more concessions are made at the end of the negotiation pro rata to time, than at any other period. This is usually a recipe for, at worst, disaster or, at best, a suboptimal agreement. Alternatively, it is possible that the negotiation becomes locked into deadlock. Neither of these two situations is desirable. Plateauing should therefore be controlled and negotiators need to consider the incidence of concession as something that can be planned to a degree in advance. Time must be a servant of the negotiator rather than a master, and Situation 4 ought in consequence to be an exception. Changing the composition of negotiation teams can help to avoid some of the more obvious time pitfalls, but equally the newcomer can easily return matters to square one. It is all too easy for matters, which have apparently been settled, to be placed once again in the melting pot.

The need for expertise in negotiation rapidly increases with changing purchase focus. Much of the current vogue for training in this area stems from this fact and has given rise to a proliferation of programmes. There is a need to understand structure and the fundamentals that underline a successful outcome. It is perhaps unfortunate, therefore, that a great deal of training concentrates almost exclusively upon the use of tactics. In his book *Give and Take*, Chester Karras, one of the most successful of trainers, lists over 200 different types of tactic. He terms this an 'arsenal of ideas'. Their names are as exotic as the list is long: 'big pot tactics'; 'bogey tactics'; 'low ball'; 'tangling with an elephant'; and many more. No one should assume that an armoury of such tactics is all the skill the negotiator needs. Useful, and at times amusing, they may be, but by themselves they are only a gloss, which can distract attention from underlying reality.

## Negotiation – cultural elements

As supply markets become wider and more global in their scope, differences arising from culture ot national background grow. This is reflected in the underlying disposition towards, for example, adversarial or co-operative approaches, in matters of ethics, or in manifestations of temperance. Similarly, different cultures have different criteria for the selection of their negotiators. It may be company competence or substantive knowledge, it may be personal skills or qualities such as loyalty or trustworthiness. It can be status, seniority, or other types of group tie. The nature of an issue will have a varying significance. In some countries, substantive issues are regarded as more important than those that are relationship-based. Elsewhere procedures may dominate, or personal factors, or a concern with protocol. The employment of non-verbal signals and even different concepts of the nature of argument complicate matters. The French fascination with Cartesian reasoning and Russian concerns with ideology are well known.

Views of risk also vary considerably, frequently seen in the willingness to divulge critical information where the counterpart's trustworthiness is questionable. It also manifests in a willingness to adopt novel approaches or creative solutions, in a preparedness to go beyond a superior's directive or authorisation, and in responses to proposals involving unknown or unforeseen contingencies. It will affect the desired form of the final agreement. In some cases the agreement must be explicit, legal, detailed, written, and covering most contingencies. In others, it is implicit, verbal, broad, covering general principles. Views of the sanctity of a contract are also important. In the Pacific Rim, a contract may be valid only whilst the conditions that prevailed when the contract was negotiated are maintained. Should there be a fundamental shift, then re-negotiation may be perceived as a precondition of continued implementation.

It is all too easy in international negotiation to fail to understand another person's viewpoint simply as a result of the different thought processes that prevail in different parts of the world. Insufficient

**227**

knowledge of the host country, of the different ways of reaching decisions and of the layering of decision makers is common. Whilst generalisations are a frequent cause of misunderstanding, some key differences between national characteristics can be readily discerned. Frequently the essential preoccupation of the British negotiator is with achievement of a task, rather than with building up relationships. Hence a relationship is just one factor in the development of a contract. It is a way of achieving results rather than evidence of a real interest in a person. Many non-Britons see the British negotiator as being very tenacious, displaying cleverness, pragmatism and fighting spirit. British negotiators on the whole tend to be very self-controlled and polite. As a pragmatist, the British negotiator is apt to take a view of 'let's try it and see' but this very flexibility can be seen as continually confusing issues and of weaving a subtle fabric through sly and devious manoeuvres. The British sense of humour, used at the right time to ease a difficult situation, can quite rapidly shift the tone of negotiation and indicates that the British negotiator on the whole is less tense and more casual than many others. The British negotiator sometimes gives an impression of superiority, which is reinforced by long standing views of language unequalled even by the French. The British like to give the appearance of being less gifted in languages than others, and even if they speak a foreign language they are frequently seen as not making much effort to do so. To a desire to negotiate in English is added no concession to accent and willingness to foreswear idiomatic expression. Equity, as an element in the English legal system, is in many ways an embodiment of pragmatism and as a result there is a tendency for British negotiators to be frequently interested in the spirit of the agreement rather than in its letter. It seems to foreigners that British negotiators often consider that changes in a contract are justified if circumstances change. Even quite minor alterations appear to open the floodgates to faxes and telexes seeking amendments.

In sharp contrast is pride in race or homeland. The French like to feel that they are meeting people who are sympathetic to their own country. It is essential to conduct at least the first few minutes of a discussion in French, showing insights into the French way of life. There is a great sense of pride in French art, food and wine and accomplishments. The French value their Cartesian background – a product of the French education system and a reflection of the codified law that prevails in France. The French therefore appreciate logical, well-structured, well-organised discussion; a formal approach. Conflict and debate come naturally to the French – in a way they are part of the game – and it is quite common for the French to contradict or to negate a proposal with more vehemence than might be necessary. Interruption or vehement bargaining are favoured, and time is seen as necessarily flexible. Negotiation should not be rushed. Since sound decisions are frequently based on past experience, logically they depend on complete information and since this takes time, French negotiators resist any attempts at time pressure. However, once a decision is taken, it will be implemented and schedules and deadlines will be met, a reflection of a self-perceived view of national efficiency.

It is sometimes said that Mediterranean related nationalities have temperaments distinguished as much by emotion as volatility. Relationships have an intrinsic value and should not be used lightly. The French do not have the same view of fair play as the British and Americans, and frequently work to tight briefs with relatively little freedom of action. They tend to act on strict orders and are carefully mandated. This tight link with a higher decision-making body can be a drawback. Since it affords little room for manoeuvre and makes compromise more difficult, few enjoy the feeling of losing. Many who do see this as the result of duplicity or perfidy.

American negotiators are highly tolerant of ambiguity. There is no incompatibility in their eyes between hostile confrontation and a care for other people's needs. Goal orientation and achievement are frequently more important than how things are done. The 'what if' approach shows a pragmatism that is also reflected in a disregard for precedent or history. Only when agreement is reached does a legalistic attitude rise to the surface. Agreement in principle does not generally satisfy an American. Details must be spelt out, for Americans have confidence in their legal system, and respect contracts. Once the contract is signed, they are not open to renegotiating parts of it because the situation has changed. A contract is seen as a lasting item. With the Americans, where there is a will there is a way. The baseball cry of 'let's get going' typifies their underlying attitude.

In the course of negotiations it is usually found that Americans are very concession conscious. They may make early concessions but always expect concessions in return. Negotiation is seen as a process of exchange through trade-offs, with an initial concession a means of contributing both to the climate of trust and also to a successful result. The Americans may express this as saying 'it was my turn to play and I did, now it's your turn'. There is a strong view in the value of proceeding step by step: one concession will lead to another but a refusal to make concessions will also lead to a refusal to make concessions. An impatience with those who seem unable to think in these terms quickly manifests itself, for time is all important. The adage that 'time is money' is firmly believed and this is one factor that leads to the attempt to progress matters by putting people at ease through informality. It is a way of escaping from procedural traps and in no way detracts from an awareness of power, an awareness easily interpreted as arrogance. Americans affect a strong belief in competition and in the virtues of success. They expect to win in negotiation whilst at the same time feeling that neither side should completely lose. The desire to win outweighs any wish that the other party should lose.

The opening up of greater trade links with what was formerly the Eastern Bloc has focused attention in particular upon export possibilities. Purchasing from this area immediately raises questions of quality and delivery reliability, which in turn defines potential areas of development. The stereotype negotiator from the old communist domains is formal and unsmiling, conscious of status and rigid in approach. A stylised seating arrangement is the norm, with the two parties facing each other symbolising the forms of exchange. There is little room for expediency and improvisation, and very little flexibility in matters for example such as specification. Facts are at a premium with detailed documentation in both languages. Terms and conditions can be major points of discussion. To the extent that decisions on the whole are reached by consensus, detailed work is seen as important in reducing risk. Continually to amend positions or documents is an acceptable practice and even 'final' versions can be changed if conditions arise that were not foreseen at the time of discussion.

Perhaps, however, it is with the Japanese that cultural gaps combine with weight of contact to produce the biggest problems for western negotiators. It is here that mistrust can be at its most potent. Westerners are seen as people who easily make demands and criticise but do not understand other people's needs.

To the Japanese, negotiation is a process both of reaching an agreement and of building up personal relationships. The two cannot be separated and throughout all discussions, courtesy is of fundamental concern. Respect and face saving are also important and any failure of a western negotiator to respect these values is an afront to basic norms of civilised behaviour. The Japanese place very great store in status and hierarchy and, in consequence, feel that negotiation must take place at the appropriate level with a clear role differentiation. The preoccupation with saving face and respecting status means that it is difficult to say no in so many words. The natural unit of organisation to the Japanese is the group, which matters more than the individual. Should a conflict of interest situation arise the group will be given priority. The implication of this is that prior to any negotiation the group will carefully consider its position at all levels. Preliminary talks to reach consensus will be held and this principle will also pertain throughout the negotiations proper. These are a ritual, social event. Situations are seen, however, in terms of yes or no, rather than with the ambiguity of the either/or approach. The long term dominates rather than the immediate. Approaches are meticulous in their attention to detail, every aspect being probed. In particular, this includes information. The Japanese are aware that westerners are frequently reticent or unwilling to disclose information. In consequence, they frequently send different teams at different times to check and recheck, to gain information.

The Japanese on the whole do not like or expect to bargain. Face can so easily be lost. The price they indicate, for example, is the one they wish to settle at and they would see differences of more than 10% as difficult to agree to. Negotiations are not time constrained and form is important. With due formality, a Japanese team will advise the other side that agreement has been reached by repeating the other side's offer several times. Once the agreement is signed they feel bound by it but again, as with other cultures, it is the norm that if circumstances change, for the agreement or part of it to be renegotiated.

There can be little doubt that changes in purchase, in particular the long term, single source movement, will produce an ongoing need for greater skills in the area of negotiation. Insights into structure are essential and it is in this area that the greatest value of simulation and training lies. The Harvard negotiation project has focused attention in the issues involved and provides valuable experience in the types of case example to be used. Far more than more superficial exposure to behavioural traits or to tactics exotic in name but lacking in rigour, structural experience is an essential element in the professional purchaser's negotiating armoury. The meeting of cultures is now an everyday experience and exposure to television and other visual media reduces the element of shock at the time of first encounters. It reduces but it does not eliminate, and it is certain that formal provision for bridging this type of gap will remain necessary not just for the immediate future but for the longer term.

# 7

---

# Measuring purchasing effectiveness

● Introduction

There can be few questions that have, in recent years, been of greater concern to purchasing professionals than measurement and account-ability. In part this stems from a realisation that in many organisations the scope and role of the function do not adequately reflect its potential contribution to the bottom line. The transition from a reactive service department to one that is at the centre of strategic decisions is a slow and in many cases a painful one. The process can be aided, however, by a conscious effort to market the function, but this presupposes the exis-tence of benchmarks against which changes may be measured and the formalisation of a systematic continuous improvement programme. Such a programme must reflect the principal areas of purchase contribu-tion. Purchasing has, for example, a very significant impact on costs both in the form of direct inputs to the manufacturing process and also by virtue of the way in which its actions can affect the level of capital employed. But it is not just simply a question of financial implications. There are also factors such as risk reduction, flexibility, and, today, the all important quality dimension. In all these the expectation of corporate management can be identified under a number of quite specific head-ings, which should find reflection in purchase performance.

On the whole there is less systematic measurement performance than might be expected within purchasing. There are clearly major problems where large volumes of transactions are involved unless appropriate management information systems are in place and it is probably under-standable that management by exception in the form of shortage report or in the form of quality reportage is the general position. This can make it difficult to produce any overall and meaningful indices, which register the changes in the level of purchase attainment. It is therefore a matter of observation that fully developed and effective systems of performance measurement are to be found only in more advanced organisations. Few can point to a well thought out, systematically used array of performance measures. Those who can – Dow Corning, for example – find in them an important contribution to professional performance which more than justifies the costs involved.

The arguments for measuring performance are easily marshalled. Performance measures should lead to better decision-making. Of that there can be little doubt. They should lead to better communication and to the extent that things are made more visible there should be a contribution both to improved motivation and also to influencing top management. The marketing of the function, particularly to the latter, is now assuming greater importance and on balance there seems little doubt that systematic performance measures play an important role in this.

Indeed without them it is impossible to aspire to excellence if this is defined as fully satisfying both the end user and the immediate internal customer. Excellence demands benchmarks and the careful monitoring of progress towards their achievement.

## ● What should be measured?

One of the problems that arises in respect of the purchase function is that there is no common opinion about what should be measured. There is no single index of performance and no universal way of evaluating that can be seen to have a general justification. Attempts so to do invariably produce complex indices, flawed by problems of calculation and weighting. The extent to which the purchase function's actions cannot be seen in isolation is a further complication. For example, are improvements in levels of price paid necessarily the result of purchase action? They may easily reflect rationalisation programmes, in which design or maintenance or production also play a major part. Is it appropriate simply to co-relate changes of the performance levels in purchase interfacing elements to the function itself? There is also a temptation to lean towards particular measurement factors on the grounds of ease of compilation. Neither this nor accuracy of measurement is of itself a major consideration. Usefulness is more important than either. In addition, time horizons taken into account for the contribution to long-term profit growth may be more significant than contribution to short-term advantage.

The enormous range of approaches to the measurement question is a further complication. There are organisations that simply count and monitor the number of transactions. Others, by sophisticated means, seek to identify and illuminate exceptional performance. The statistician, Wouter Faes, produced one such example for Janssen Pharmaceutica NV, part of Johnson and Johnson. The Belgian operation introduced 'spectra mapping' – a form of multi-ratio measurement – in an attempt to identify the relationship between purchase parameters, and to sift out elements that were the result of action by other departments. By this means it was alleged that it was possible to identify the gains from negotiation in terms of individual contributions. Spectacular to look at, difficult to comprehend; spectra mapping appears to have more in the way of presentation to commend it than in the way of actual impact upon events.

## Transactional focus

As an underlying principle, what is appropriate to measure rests to a very large degree upon the focus of purchasing (see **Fig. 7.1**). Focus is a matter of perception, not simply of those engaged in the function but also of its customers and in particular of senior management. Changes in focus can come about without the active intervention of management and simply as a result of the changing nature of the organisation and of movements in the economic and commercial environment. As has been

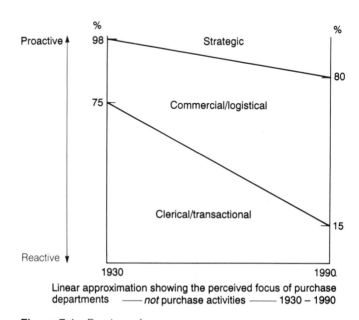

Linear approximation showing the perceived focus of purchase departments ——— *not* purchase activities ——— 1930 – 1990

**Figure 7.1** Purchase focus

indicated earlier, some years ago the predominant purchase mode was clerical rather than commercial or strategic, with possibly 75% of all purchase departments falling into this category. Today the position has changed. The transactional mode, and updated clerical focus, can be seen to apply to probably no more than 10 to 15% of all organisations.

Some of these are, for example, in the public sector and reflect the bureaucratic tradition. Others are major manufacturing or extractive firms of high repute and great size. The emphasis is upon systems, upon the number of transactions and the speed with which they are carried out. Such emphasis may be wholly appropriate given the nature of the operation and the purchase function comes to be dominated by this element. British Coal, ICI Chemicals and Polymers and the major oil companies, all come into this category.

## Commercial focus

Perhaps some 70% or even more of remaining purchase departments have a commercial focus with an emphasis upon price, quality and delivery as the main parameters. In this area are to be found those departments that have a highly aggressive image, which rejoice in the combatorial nature of supply relationships, and which demonstrate their power in the supply market. A highly successful entrepreneurial company like J C Bamford (Excavators) Ltd would fall into this category. There, the purchasing department demonstrates those characteristics that were perhaps characteristic of the founder, with a strong emphasis upon the ability to get results through the use of competition. Finally there are organisations – perhaps 10% of the total – where the purchase activity is central to the organisation's competitive position. It is not only central but it is perceived as being proactive in nature. Purchase activity is not of course the same thing as the purchasing function. For example, where bulk purchases of commodities or fuel are fundamental to an organisation's purpose, as in the electricity generation industry whose major expenditure is on fuel, whole areas of buying may be carried out by other than specialist purchasing.

This poses the question of the range of purchase activities and the basis of authority. There is a significant variation of practice. In some organisations the mandatory use of purchase effectively means that the overwhelming proportion of requirements for all goods and services pass through the hands of the specialist function. British Coal in its previous form as the National Coal Board through the purchasing and stores directive mandated that all goods and services should be obtained and all commitments to expenditure made through the purchasing and stores department. There were exceptions – for example, insurance services – but for the most part the National Coal Board presented a clear procurement focus to the outside world. Elsewhere, in ICI Chemicals and Polymers Ltd for example, no such mandatory statement exists and the use of the purchase department depends upon its ability to project and market its services. Such an approach is as brave as it is uncommon, particularly given the problems of any purchase department seeking an identity in a marketing driven company.

Perhaps the principal determinant of the purchase status is the degree to which top management sees the range of goods and services bought as being wider rather than narrower and its need to use fully the distinctive competence of the purchase department. This competence may be perceived as lying primarily in the area of supply market knowledge and in the area of personal skills, such as the ability through negotiation to perform better than others within the organisation. These factors form the essence of the purchase process. Where materials or logistics are also within the function, however, it is clear that a high degree of systems competence is also a necessary feature of purchase's specialist appeal. In sum therefore, how purchasing is seen is a reflection of the scale, the magnitude and the critical importance in the final product of bought in items. It is a reflection of trends in the make-up of products between in-house fabrication and bought in components, of the surrounding commercial and environmental position, of top management's view and, it must be said, of the quality, the determination and the orientation of purchase management itself. When J W Robb, in his then capacity as purchasing director of Rolls Royce spoke to the International Purchasing Conference in Brussels in 1987, he delivered a blueprint of his vision for the development of the purchasing function within his company. This clearly showed that when management addressed this issue in a positive and proactive role, purchase could quite rapidly be brought to a level at which it could be seen to be a leading edge among the competitors in the particular field.

● Efficiency and effectiveness

As organisations change their purchase focus, so this is reflected not simply in terms of the strategies and the policies that are pursued, but also in terms of measures of performance. When setting out to evaluate purchase performance, clearly it is necessary to distinguish between those activities that relate to the efficiency of an operation and those that relate to its effectiveness. Derived from engineering, efficiency is a relationship between the efforts of achievement and the results obtained therefrom. It is an operating ratio. Effectiveness, on the other hand, is concerned with whether or not the course of action adopted is or is not appropriate for the end in view. The two concepts are not mutually exclusive and many activities reflect a compound of them. Changes in their relationship do occur, however, and in broad terms, as purchasing departments evolve so the emphasis gradually moves from those performance areas that are primarily efficiency oriented towards those that are essentially concerned with effectiveness. This corresponds to a degree to a transition from that which can be easily quantified to elements that are either much more difficult to measure or are essentially qualitative.

## ● Implications of clerical or transactional focus

The first stage of purchase development is where the purchasing function is primarily concerned with obtaining what is asked for in the most cost-effective way. If we term this a clerical function the very expression may be seen as derogatory since, as a clerical function, it will be seen as being low in the organisation and will have a reportage level that reflects that. Performance measures such as the number of orders placed, any backlog that develops and the purchase lead time, are all subject to quantification and are all clearly efficiency oriented. A pre-eminent concern with authorisation procedures is clearly indicative of a function limited both in scope and in ambition.

At one time a significant number of buying departments fell within this broad category, but the number has in fact decreased, and whereas at one stage it might have been said without exaggeration that most public sector departments could be regarded in this light, today, particularly with privatisation and with the introduction of the commercial ethic, this statement would no longer hold good. Factors such as the introduction of professional purchasing through Diktat, such as the Fleck Report, or through transition to the private sector (e.g. British Telecom), provide powerful and major stimuli to change. The movement of any organisation into a situation where its overall performance can be related to its profitability makes it necessary that the purchase function also adopt a similar orientation. No longer is it sufficient simply to execute the intentions of others, it becomes necessary to make commercial judgements, particularly upon such factors as price, delivery and quality. Overall efficiency, as judged by the performance related to budgets, will always be a continuing process and as part of assessment it is also necessary to measure the volumes of work passing through a department. Of course questions do arise as to the purposes for which control information is being collected, the benchmarks that may be set and the types of remedial outcome that can be expected should there be significant variations. There can be little doubt that in many organisations, particularly those with transatlantic connections, head count remains a popular measure with the performance of the department assessed largely against this. It is of interest to note, for example, that in Procter & Gamble over a ten-year period, the size of the purchase department has fallen in Europe to roughly one sixth of what it was before, in spite of increase in the overall parameters governing the company.

As a general proposition, head counts have fallen and volumes of business risen across the entire scene. It might therefore be thought that if an organisation focuses upon these measures, it is by that fact establishing itself as being an organisation that perceives purchase in a particular and fairly low level light. This is not necessarily the case and there are situations where it is not in fact so. One of these is where the purchase department has long ago moved its focus elsewhere to the commercial or strategic mode but nevertheless remains committed to an ongoing evaluation of the volume of work undertaken, in view of the important part played by transactions in its day-to-day activities. For example, in the petrochemical industry it is recognised that the sheer volume of transaction is an important and difficult aspect of the purchase area. More than in many other fields, a key and overriding problem is how to handle massive transactions without on the one hand impairing operational efficiency through delay or failure to supply whilst, on the other, without submerging the whole department in the task of endeavouring to maintain a constant flow of materials to users.

Virtually all purchase departments face a call-off or small order problem. The ratio between the number of orders placed with a face value of £100 or less and those of over £10,000 can easily exceed 20:1. Each order placed represents an addition to cost just as a broad vendor base imposes similar strains. A failure or an inability to reduce these numbers can lead to the view that the strength, appeal and distinctive competence of the department is focused upon transactions. To avoid this, reorganisation may lead to a division of the purchase department essentially into a purchase marketing or purchase commercial activity and into a purchase logistics activity. In London in 1991 T Kowalski outlined the approach in the Siemens organisation towards this particular problem. The position in three German plants revealed the following results on time divisions, as shown in **Table 7.1**.

- **Table 7.1**
  Time divisions

|  | Purchase logistics | Purchase marketing |
|---|---|---|
| Plant 1 | 58% | 42% |
| 2 | 73% | 27% |
| 3 | 65% | 35% |

Kowalski identified the logistics function as embracing database management, materials management, order processing and such special tasks as the sales of an active inventory and logistical connection to suppliers. Purchase marketing, he considered, was concerned with research including the selection of new suppliers, with material cost reduction in the widest sense and with the purchasing interface with accounting manufacturing Quality Assurance and R&D. Performance measures reflect this organisational division and to the relatively straightforward quantification measures already referred to, may be added those steps that reduce the logistics impact. The provision of rationalising mechanisms is important in this context. Principal amongst these are term or frame contracts, which imply getting out in effect of the process of order placing and of expediting and of allowing users to call-off against departmentally negotiated contracts. This is a model that finds favour in organisations across the whole purchase spectrum.

For example, in Sadaf, in Saudia Arabia, the number of frame contracts placed each year is regarded as an important benchmark to be co-related to changes in volumes with regard to ordinary, day-to-day commercial transaction. Procter & Gamble have sought successfully to concentrate the essential purchase function on a restricted number of high level decisions and to systematise and remove from the portfolio the many day-to-day elements that call for intense involvement in detail and frequent contacts with, for example, users and/or suppliers.

## ● Emphasis upon 'commercial' aspects

As organisations change so the focus of purchase activity also changes and the second principal grouping in terms of evolution is where purchasing is seen as virtually a stand alone and essentially commercial activity. Generally speaking the management reportage level will be higher than in departments primarily concerned with the clerical aspect, although not necessarily higher than those where transactions are deemed to be a more appropriate term to describe focus. The purchase manager, in a commercially oriented activity, will generally report either at operational director level or on some occasions to the finance director.

In essence the three key areas that are targeted in order to consider performance, are price, quality and delivery. In broad terms there can be little doubt that purchase people are happier with the concept of price and with attempting to measure it than with the other two, although in recent years the quality initiatives that have become a commonplace in Western European industry have made it necessary for purchase departments to look increasingly towards this area. It is very difficult to obtain accurate information regarding the number of companies who measure these different parameters, or indeed how they address the problem. As with so many things, what is claimed is not always the reality and organisations who profess to have well-established and purposeful systems in place, on examination can sometimes be seen to have less than what they claim. Across major Western European organisations, some 50% of all companies use price measures of some sort. Another 30% systematically assess supplier quality performance, and 25% regularly monitor deliveries. These monitors relate to the purchases handled by the purchase function itself and are, in consequence, much lower if all purchase activities are taken into account.

## Savings

'Savings' are naturally a major preoccupation with those employed in purchasing. Cost savings are attractive to many buyers. This is in part because it is, in their view, the first and foremost element of their activity. Buyers enjoy discussing and agreeing price. Many see it as the specialism in which they can excel. In practice, however, there are a good many problems. In the first place, and perhaps the most intractable, is the question of how a cost saving should be defined. Among sellers it is accepted that buyers need to justify their existence as a specialist function. To the extent that many companies, perhaps most companies, have a price preoccupation, to give a buyer an opportunity to claim price successes is a way of ensuring future business.

Of course this is not simply altruism, and sellers trade on the fact that prices, far from being easy to assess, are in fact opaque. Quantity related discounts, payment terms, credits and subsidies, and currency fluctuations no less than changes to specification have the effect of blurring price. This renders price comparisons and measures of performance much more difficult in practice than might be imagined. An examination of companies in Holland revealed that the most common price benchmark was of price paid this time against price paid last time. Whether this, as a measure, has any great merit depends of course upon the relative success that had been obtained on the previous occasions. For example, an organisation at a time of relatively easy conditions in its own end market, may afford little priority to keen purchase prices, preferring to concentrate upon innovative design, quality or delivery. To benchmark upon such prices, revising by a coefficient of inflation, becomes quite inappropriate as surrounding competitive conditions change. Roller-coaster oil prices from the mid-1980s forced companies providing services to oil, such as Schlumberger EPS, to revise their approach, recognising that what was paid last time was no real guide to performance.

Over a number of years preoccupations with inflation have meant that many companies have seen the upward drift of prices as being virtually an inevitable fact of life. Simply to relate the rate of price increase to generic or global indices such as the wholesale or retail price indices, may be totally inappropriate for their own course of action except in cases of, say, traded commodities. Simply to be better than an index is no guarantee of profitability. This approach may be likened to taking a snapshot but in fact this is the mechanism employed every time competitive tenders are used. A competitive tender, provided the specification ensures that like is being measured against like, is no more than a means of evaluating a price against a benchmark valid only at a particular point in time. It is comfortable to buyers because it has an objectivity about it, which ensures that the buyer cannot readily be held responsible if, at the end of the day, the price paid means that the company's own product becomes uncompetitive. It was the best that could be obtained at the time. The emphasis upon tenders, often supplemented today by post-tender negotiation, encourages buyers to see price in terms of competitiveness and encourages them to view the process of obtaining prices from suppliers as a form of gladiatorial combat.

A third method of assessment is to determine the price paid in relationship to that which is budgeted. If one is pricing backwards from the market-place, from what the market will stand, then upon any given set of assumptions it is possible to determine the precise value of purchase inputs that can be allowed for any given commodity. The buyer can set as a budget a specific target that must be achieved. The value of this approach is that it clearly relates purchase prices to the needs of the end market and ultimately this is a true relationship, and one that should be the subject of the prime focus. It does require that assumptions be made regarding availability and conditions in the supply market which, if not valid, necessitate budget revision or repricing the end product. It also means that buyers are encouraged to move away from the view that *only* by competition can the best deal be obtained and the best price obtained.

Although this approach is not appropriate in all areas, nevertheless where it is applied, striking gains can be made. The approach concerned is the co-operative or win/win approach with suppliers. It must be stated clearly from the first instance that the structure of the purchase portfolio will determine the potential for success. Both parties' actions reflect fundamental need. It is clearly not a strategy, therefore, to be applied willy-nilly, but where suppliers can be seen to have a vested interest in ensuring that their purchase's product is highly price competitive and the two view this as a joint problem, then there is merit in the approach.

In many fields of consumer electronics the real price of the product in the end market – for example, a television set – has fallen substantially in recent years. Where have these real price reductions come from? They can in part be attributable to greater manufacturing efficiency and to the application of the learning curve, but they are also due to the fact that the input from suppliers is being driven down in price terms and driven down in many cases by the collaborative effort of purchaser and supplier. Moving to the field of automobiles, Nissan Manufacturing UK, with the advantages of sustained volume purchase, systematically seek to drive down purchase costs through negative pricing. Through the process of long-term relationships, Nissan endeavour to establish a means whereby both buyer and seller work jointly upon a pricing problem and aim in so doing to make sufficient impact upon cost that over time real prices can be reduced, without necessarily damaging profit margins.

Even if it were possible to gain agreement upon how prices were defined, it is still necessary to ask whether the price is in fact one that will hold firm in the longer term. It is a fairly common practice among selling organisations to seek to enter a market at a low price, confident that it will be possible to enhance margins at a later date. From the purchase point of view, it is necessary to be able either to hold prices firm or to forecast the rate of price change over a whole of life cycle. Price stability is much prized and is one factor promoting both whole of life costing and life of product pricing.

## Who originates 'savings'?

Even given adequate definition of what appears to be an ongoing price saving, the question will still arise as to whether or not this was due to unusual action initiated by purchase, and how accurately it can be verified. If the purchase function embraces the issue of competitive tender, for example, then to claim credit for price falls, which are in fact a reflection not of purchase expertise so much as change in the supply market, is to claim credit for things that would in any event have been achievable even if no specialist purchase function existed. Similarly, price savings may result from actions in no way stemming from purchase. For example, it is possible design or operations may change specifications.

If these result in a lower price, who should be able to claim the credit from them? As purchase works more and more closely with these other functions and as purchase forms part of the procurement and engineering teams, it becomes increasingly likely that it is by joint action that savings are generated. Integration of effort renders functional claims virtually obsolete and calls into question their underlying justification. There is, additionally, a question of what risks may attend undue emphasis upon targeting price as a major determinant of purchase success. Price hunting, just as much as dubious measurement procedures, can distract from the fundamental purpose of quality, fitness for purpose and value for money. Price hunting is indeed a dangerous occupation. It can so easily give rise to the need to threaten, that competition involving a change of supplier will inevitably be the result of a failure to meet targets. This can endanger long-term relationships and make more difficult any move away from adversarial relationships.

In broad terms then, the purchase price area is not the simple and easy to handle area that it might at first sight seem. The tension that exists between parameters determined by the end market and complexity on the supply side underlies the pricing area. Conventional purchase approaches should not be ignored. Standardisation, rationalisation and co-ordination of company requirements are important. In particular, design pressures for company specified items must be weighed against the advantages advocated by Taguchi of adopting standard commercial specifications. Above all, however, there is a need to reject the notion that inflation necessarily means ongoing price increases. It is no longer feasible to think in terms of simply passing such changes on to the customer. The *Financial Times*, for example, alleged in September 1990, as the spot price for Brent Crude reached $34 per barrel, that beyond that price ICI would be forced to absorb 70c out of every additional dollar increase. This, it was estimated, would cut company profits at the rate of £10 million per additional dollar.

When just-in-time became a more common approach in Western Europe, it was believed that this would imply that additional price increases would be necessary in order to sustain the higher levels of quality and delivery called for by this approach. Today that is certainly not the case. Particularly where price competition in the end market is very significant, such as in many areas of electronic consumer durables, real price reductions have become an essential factor.

Consequently for companies like Toshiba, real prices have fallen in the end market and this has meant that not only has manufacturing efficiency needed to be raised, but that other parts of the supply chain have had to play their part in the process of price reduction. Where the supply chain is a coherency, the purchaser needs to work together with suppliers in this process. Such a course of action implies a longer- rather than a shorter-term relationship. No purchaser is going to invest time and effort in seeking to reduce the cost base of his supplier, if that reduction is then going to be used for the benefit of his competitors. Joint price reduction campaigns are clearly a team activity calling upon the resources not just of purchase but of design and manufacturing. Clearly the determinants of action are competitive pressures and industry practice. Price is today coming to the forefront once more, as a key issue no longer subordinate to quality considerations. The debate between those who argue that it is necessary to have a choice of vendor and carry out regular assessments of the market through competitive action, and those who see the joint approach to the question through integration of the supply chain, has been fully and clearly joined. For long relatively quiescent, the advocates of aggressive adversarial approaches to supply issues have regained their voices and 'beating suppliers' is once more respectable.

### Delivery

The second major area of measurement, which is of great importance in a commercially oriented purchase organisation, is delivery performance. This is particularly true as organisations move into small batch manufacturing and possibly adopt just-in-time. In all those approaches that seek to minimise the amount of inventory required and the amount of work in progress required, to sustain any given manufacturing operation, there will be a need to pay close attention to the time related performance of suppliers. A key strategy at the heart of modern purchasing is the reduction of manufacturing lead time. This implies that all those components of the supply chain that feed the manufacturing process must similarly be subject to close and careful scrutiny. In terms of supplier lead time, clearly the factors that are involved concern the transition of information, the availability of product and its physical shipment. Each of these can be subject to significant variation, but if one assumes that electronic data information interchange will soon become the norm, then there should be less room for fluctuation in that element.

The adoption of flexible manufacturing, identifying the batch of one as its key factor would also, subject to schedule stability, lead to significant lead time improvements. The congestion of the 1990s will always pose a significant problem in terms of physical transportation, but even well in advance of the Single European Market there have been rapid improvements in the rate to which goods may flow across national frontiers within the Community. An organisation such as Cerestar, which has invested heavily in the improvement of logistics, would not expect excess delay due, for example, to frontier bureaucracy. A delay of more than two hours would be regarded as totally unacceptable.

### ● Time related performance

The outward looking nature of purchase reflects the interdependence of buyer and supplier. From the point of view of users or of stores, delivery reliability is one of the most obvious parameters of success. The principal variables that must be taken into account when seeking to assess the delivery performance of a supplier relate first to the date requested by the purchaser and the degree of stability inherent in the schedule. But the ability to meet any given requirement is not just a question of shipment date – it is also one of logistics; for example shipment and transit time. It is, however, the first factor that explains why many buyers are reluctant to examine over rigorously the delivery performance of vendors. Many organisations suffer from extreme instability of required by date. If that requirement is subject to very significant variation, it would clearly be difficult to hold the supplier to account if the result poses problems for the buyer. It is the case that many attempts to integrate the supply chain may founder on this particular rock.

Many major purchasers are psychologically averse to sharing in an open manner much of their own production scheduling material or information regarding sales with suppliers. In the case of manufacturers one reason for this is the fear that schedule instability or false information can lead to a major loss of credibility with suppliers and as a consequence it would be more difficult in the future to hold suppliers to account for a failure to meet any given delivery promise. It was recently asserted that the Philips organisation, one of the major pioneers of co-makership, had found that their own inability to guarantee this type of information, when allied to the difficulties of selecting suitable suppliers, had led to the failure of this approach. Many instances therefore of apparent supplier unreliability can be traced to the purchaser's own inability to give reliable requirement dates. As a consequence, suppliers can claim that the goalposts have moved.

Schedule stability also impacts upon this supplier since it affects the ability to give sound delivery information to their customers. Few suppliers in the world of manufacture are dedicated. The greater the degree of competition for that supplier's product and the greater the degree of variation in the schedule supplied to the supplier, the more potentially unpredictable the deliveries will be. With small batch manufacture and with lower inventories, this can become a major problem. This is just one of the reasons why just-in-time includes tight logistics amongst its preconditions.

## Customer service

In any event there is, in addition, a major measurement problem for the purchasing organisation. Focusing upon total customer service is a relatively new development. Its assessment involves such factors as the completeness of orders, the length of the delivery cycle, the reliability of delivery patterns and system interfaces. Rowntree of York, now part of Nestlé, define a series of quantifiable service objectives against which performance is measured. These afford an insight into not just the main parameters but also the importance accorded to them. First and foremost is the proportion of deliveries that were not received as ordered. This is in the long run a major factor in deciding how much business should be placed with any particular supplier.

A second area of concern is the proportion of orders that are incomplete. Incomplete deliveries are a major cause of dissatisfaction and depending upon the nature of the purchasing industry, the whole production process can be dislocated by a number of incomplete orders. In the context of major cost generating activities part deliveries or quantities that vary from those specified by the order figure prominently. So serious can the problem be that in some companies – Toshiba Audio Visual in the UK, for example – a major purchase requirement is precise adherence to the amount requested.

Another prime consideration is the length of time taken to deliver an order once it has left the supplier's works. The responsibility of the supplier to guarantee speedy and safe transit is of course crucial, and significantly this aspect of logistics has seen fundamental changes in the last decade. Own transport milk runs are a feature of companies like DEC in Scotland, moving towards just-in-time. DHL claim more scheduled flights per night than any airline in Europe, whilst to a firm like

Cerestar shipment is the life blood of the business and must be treated accordingly. Skills in routeing and scheduling characterise leaders in the field, together with the setting up of dedicated facilities. Transhield, a subsidiary of British Oxygen, handle chilled goods on an exclusive basis for Marks and Spencer. This helps to achieve that element of reliability of timing that is essential in matching the shelf life of perishable goods to peak daily demand periods.

Finally, normally at a level of irritation rather than fundamental dissatisfaction, is the number and value of invoice adjustments. Rarely would this lead of itself to a change of supplier but it is a significant element in damaging the climate of a relationship.

## Quality measures

Within all these areas it is possible to construct a series of service objectives and measure performance. This facilitates the detailed analysis of particular patterns as a framework for discussion with the organisations concerned. The sheer volume of transactions, however, in many cases presents the greatest problem to purchase organisations and the costs of quantification discourage some companies. But total quality is not achieved by leaving things to chance. A reliable picture of the performance of suppliers is essential, and management by exception, based as it must be upon damage limitation in times of crisis, is no form of substitute.

Of course, quality has been the major area of development in Western Europe in the 1980s and there can be very few companies that do not have or purport to have quality programmes in place. Whole of life costs and the passing of warranties to suppliers are increasingly common, whilst through the use of measures like BS 5750 and ISO 9000, many companies have established procedures that extend the frontiers of certification. Historically the number of purchase departments that maintained accurate quality measures in place has been surprisingly small. However, with the move away from inspection and delivery straight to line, it clearly becomes much more important to ensure that the quality dimension is properly addressed. The argument in favour of purchasing maintaining an assessment in this area is not simply that the final product is enhanced but also that production or manufacturing are reassured and suppliers are kept up to scratch. Continuous improvement and the elimination of unsatisfactory suppliers is the purchase aim. This can be largely achieved by adopting the classical approach to quality. This is to set the standard, determine the measurement method

**247**

and the aspects to be measured, carry out the process and then implement such remedial measures as might appear necessary.

In the past the reasons why quality measure have been more limited in use than might have been expected may be summarised as follows. Buyers might argue that, where there are relatively few suppliers, they are known on a personal basis and no need to quantify exists. Similarly, if the product range is relatively narrow, then any product with a quality problem would automatically be known to buyers. Quality standards, particularly where company specifications required enhancing the commercial norm, might be suspect, and in any event, simply measuring something does not of itself identify problems. The example of the weight watcher, who each day regularly carries out a measurement exercise but without then seeking to implement any remedial measures, is well known. In the last analysis many purchase departments will also claim that head count pressure means that some things, and in particular measurement, enjoy less than the highest priority.

The search for a total index of purchase performance continues to haunt purchase managers notwithstanding the almost universally held view that overall performance ratings cannot be a reliable guide to departmental performance. Nevertheless there are attempts from time to time to produce indices that address content and weighting problems. Price, quality and delivery reliability represent the simplest combination. From British Aerospace comes the following example (see **Table 7.2**).

Any such performance indicator raises as many issues as it solves; over a period of time trends do appear however, and, provided appropriate discounting is made of temporary causative factors, herein may lie its value.

A not dissimilar approach can be seen in Japan as part of a programme designed to ensure constant commitment to efficiency.

Professor Daniel Jones of Cardiff Business School has outlined a grading system by which suppliers are rated by the number of defective parts delivered to the assembly line, by the percentage of on time

● **Table 7.2**

Total index

| Factor | Calculation method | Weightings |
|--------|--------------------|------------|
| Price | Lowest quote/price paid | 50 |
| Quality | Rejects as a percentage of total delivery (Items or transactions) | 25 |
| Delivery | 100 − 7 points for each failure | 25 |

deliveries of the quantity required and by performance in reducing costs. With multiple sourcing the general basis of supply, the scores of suppliers can be evaluated. Although intended to highlight performance, this comparative approach is also a measure of the success of purchase in supplier selection and management.

## ● Operational audit

The strategically oriented department has, by definition, passed through the stages of bringing systems up to an appropriate level and of achieving those commercial objectives that seem to be most suited to the end market in which the company operates. Many of the policies and strategies – for example on *make* or *buy* or *functional* integration – have significant qualitative dimensions. Simple qualification may indicate little, for the true assessment of the success of such elements lies in the contribution to end market competitive advantage or in non-commercial environments, to value for money.

An evaluation against global objectives calls for a wide-ranging, systematised approach and may best be made by an independent operational audit. In the absence of such an approach the danger exists that subjective views, based upon personal perceptions that may not be well informed, may prevail.

Subjective departmental evaluation is almost invariably a process that leads to a focus upon complaint and difficulty. Senior management may be unduly swayed by the number of problems that purchasing clearly has with other departments, particularly problems that cannot be resolved at local level. In manufacturing, changes in schedules due to purchase action and more important, actual interruptions to production, have an impact which may be out of all proportion to their real significance.

Operational audit can address those issues that cannot easily be reduced to routine measurement. Its application is now much more frequent than a few years ago. In purchase terms a combination of reluctant management, budgetary factors and lack of awareness inhibit its use. The characteristics of a purchase audit are that it is essentially broad in focus, seeking to evaluate all aspects of the purchase function. It needs to be impartial and systematic, and to have real effect ought to be repeated out on a regular basis. A good audit is both diagnostic and prescriptive, and lays a foundation for activities to improve performance towards benchmarks set in relation to good practice elsewhere. It should not therefore be seen as a threat by purchase management but as a positive way to better aligning the function with organisational need. It is also a basis by which a marketing plan can be developed and formulated with a view to influencing decision makers in the organisation and to creating a more purchase friendly environment.

## Elements of purchase audit

The basic forms of purchase audit embrace at least five major components. Underlying all of them is a need for awareness and for the collection and use of both hard and soft information. Economic trends, technical innovation and financial turbulence are all factors that call for anticipation and not simply reaction.

Strategy is the starting point for the audit. The trap of seeing purchase as an ongoing activity, unchanging with corporate development must be avoided. Purchasing departments can very easily find themselves broadly out of line when there are significant changes in corporate policy. Purchasing may be seen over much as a process, and a process that does not of itself need to be modified as objectives change. Purchase explicitly needs a clear alignment with corporate thrust. Its overall mission statement and the degree of corporate sanction that it enjoys should reflect the organisational ethic. Purchase should be the authority for expenditure upon goods and services. Exclusions are frequent and services, such as pension or insurance matters or property purchases, come easily to mind; but many professionals look to a clear mandate in all other regards. But purchase can be placed in a situation where it must 'sell' its services upon the basis of quality to its customers. Supply market knowledge, expertise in negotiation and high grade systems may provide an effective base.

The next aspect of audit is organisation. Organisation must follow strategy formulation although often this is not the case in practice. All too frequently, structures are devised *before* the formulation of strategies. In purchase terms, a number of organisational issues arise. These centre around the need to achieve both focus and leverage without sacrificing leverage – a problem frequently acute following a merger or an acquisition. Such developments do not simply pose questions of inventories, of coding or of policies. They also bring into focus the need to bring about a fusion of supply bases. It is easy to see in companies like Rolls Royce for example, that for long periods of time this simply has not happened. It is quite possible therefore for a situation to arise in which different parts of the same company compete with each other in the supply market for the same type of product. Investigations in the engineering industry where companies have expanded, and not integrated their purchase department, have shown that the price differ-ence between the best and worst cases in any one company purchasing identical items from the same supplier, can be as much as 30%.

A further complication, which renders more difficult the task of audit, arises as the impact of shortening product life cycles becomes more and more apparent. A higher degree of functional integration is then likely to take place since purchase decisions will increasingly be taken at a much earlier stage of the planning process. Team decisions are more difficult to evaluate, as is the contribution made to them by the purchase element.

Perhaps more difficult are the systems used by purchase in cases such as vendor evaluation, or assessment, or the determination of 'shield cost'. The implications of change may not necessarily be great. The growing use of electronic systems for transactions, or inventory man-agement is a different question. The disruption effect of change comple-ments the financial factor to make anything but modification or enhancement impractical. In very large organisations the term 'systems dominance' has acquired a new meaning. In ICI for example, a reduc-tion in the material control systems in use to two systems – NEWPS and PISCES – reflecting historical origins as much as anything else, still left unsolved questions of, for example, focus with regard to suppliers. Not-withstanding purchase's needs, however, it was perceived as simply impossible on the twin grounds of effort and expense to contemplate further harmonisation for a term of years. Audit can therefore be increasingly constrained both by complexity and by the need for consideration of its implications.

The Crosby approach that all relationships have a customer/supplier element is clearly compatible with and complementary to the oper-ational audit. The purchase department should, as an ongoing exercise, develop a 'product list' and seek to identify the ways in which their customers use that particular range of services. Many companies feel comfortable with this approach perhaps because of the high accept-ability of behavioural-based techniques. Oil companies – Shell, for example – Rolls Royce plc, and very many much smaller organisations find in this an appropriate way to proceed.

In terms of performance achievements, good audit permits bench-marking based upon experience across a variety of organisations. The merits of different kinds of comparison, against indices, sister com-panies or against competitors may depend upon circumstances and availability of information. In general terms, however, 'best of breed' is the goal and 'best of breed' should be the target indicator. Not for nothing has this method become associated with IBM, but it does require insights that small organisations may not have. This is thus another reason for the use of the informed outside specialist.

Customer responses are a good indicator of the impact that purchase makes upon its internal customer. An audit interview with major internal clients is designed to establish how those clients really feel about the service provided. A frequent reaction is that a given service – suppliers' safety data, for example – is valuable but has never been offered before by purchase. Managers are of course naturally apt to focus upon those things that appear to have gone wrong; to focus upon those things that give irritation; and in the first stage of the interview it is quite easy to form an impression that the purchase department is singularly failing in its activities. Positive virtues tend to emerge later and it should be borne in mind that the user manager often perceives any fault in a product or delay is due to the last element in the supply chain. To the extent that this is the stores or the purchase department, it therefore follows that many of the problems that cause irritation on the shop floor are attributed to purchasing failure. This provides one reason why the issue of materials by stores could be seen to be an important purchase function. It is common for physical storage to be the responsibility of departments other than purchase and it is not necessarily the case that failures attributed to purchase by internal customers should be attributed to the function. Customer/supplier analysis nevertheless gives operational audit a dimension not to be gained solely by looking within the department.

# 8

# Positioning the purchase department

## ● Introduction

As a prelude to a programme of continuous improvement based upon audit or ongoing measurement, it is first necessary to assess the current position of the department. Purchasing positioning can be illustrated by relating purchase focus to the extent to which the primary tasks of the function are discharged (see **Figs. 8.1** and **8.2**). Each of the foci – transactional, commercial and strategic – is appropriate to sustaining commercial advantage for different types of enterprise. In terms of effectiveness, the key question is whether the correct focus exists. In terms of efficiency, how well are key tasks discharged? It is therefore necessary to relate the purchase strategies, current or planned, to the requirements of each type of focus. Initially in the transactions focus, key tasks are to develop the systems and the underpinning of coding that is the essential prelude not simply to running the purchase operation, but also to ongoing rationalisation programmes. Efficiency, the relationship of output to effort, underlies such strategies. As organisational needs change and purchase acquires a commercial focus, such factors as the use of capital employed, cost savings and quality initiatives become important.

One of the dangers faced by functions within this area is that as its role changes, time horizons need to move in harmony. Cost savings, for example, are initially perceived simplistically as being related to invoiced price and it is only with greater maturity that whole of life costs are seen as more appropriate. The commercially oriented department needs to develop longer time horizons and in this context company-wide vehicles such as *total quality management* can be helpful, even as purchase develops a more strategic orientation.

The heartland factors of price, delivery and quality will continue to be seen as areas where improvements will continue to be made. They are

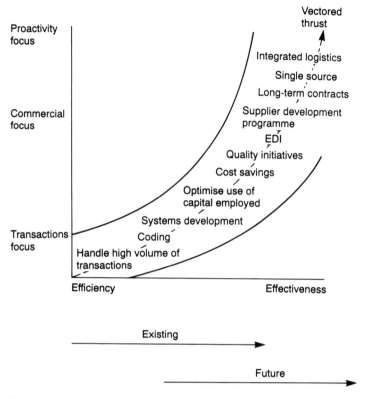

**Figure 8.1** Positioning graph: strategies/policies

very much the upfront aspects of purchase. It is not in every company that purchase will aspire to a strategic role. Only where purchase activities can be clearly related to end market advantage or where commitments to suppliers have an extended or indefinite time horizon can this apply. Single sourcing and make or buy decisions can clearly be evaluated on a short-term basis but integrated logistics or just-in-time need to be assessed in terms of their impact upon the competitive position of the organisation. It is therefore possible to establish the position of any department, first by examining the crude measures of performance in use, second by establishing which policies are current or projected, and finally by the use of the operational audit. The latter will clearly show how purchasing's customers perceive its focus and, more important, how they think purchase sees itself. Purchase often lags (at least to an extent) behind what an organisation needs, and it is the awareness of the need to change that must be demonstrated. Without such an awareness it is more difficult to create the kind of climate necessary to underpin a programme of continuous improvement. The

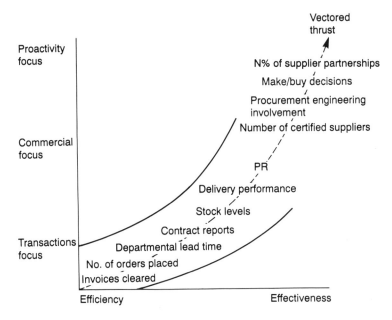

Vectored
thrust

Proactivity
focus

N% of supplier partnerships

Make/buy decisions

Procurement engineering
involvement

Number of certified suppliers

Commercial
focus

PR

Delivery performance

Stock levels

Contract reports

Transactions
focus

Departmental lead time

No. of orders placed

Invoices cleared

Efficiency

Effectiveness

**Figure 8.2**  Positioning graph: measures of performance

ultimate goal of continuous improvement is *excellence* as defined by contribution to competitive competencies. As such, purchase has an aim
derived from the widely publicised Peters' theme of excellence.

In the market-place, real achievement requires both commitment and
understanding. There must be a commitment to building a powerful
competence in the company and an understanding of how that may be
used to gain a distinctive edge. There must also be an understanding
both of the part to be played by top management and of the way in
which total customer satisfaction can be achieved through superiority of
product, of service, through value for money and through the development of an enterprise culture. In terms of purchasing, excellence does
pose a variety of problems. The first is that, as has been shown, in many
companies there is insufficient alignment between corporate and purchase strategies. Effectiveness is often subordinate to efficiency since the
latter has historically been purchase's main preoccupation.

In the second place, for the purchasing function, the historical orientation has naturally been upstream towards the supplier. Too many
purchasing people have an inadequate knowledge of the end user
market and are unable to relate supply characteristics to the distinctive
competence claimed for or required by the product. Too few know
enough about the competitors' products and of the ways in which these
competitors add value. The process of comparison is essential to the

**255**

systematic planning of change and it is from best practice that benchmarks should be derived.

'Best of breed' is a standard towards which progress can be measured. The target will be a moving one but for the purposes of positioning it represents the best that is available. The task is how to move from what is now to what should be. Focus can be vectored against the relative levels of efficiency and effectiveness, and a programme tailored to bring about the desired changes. Where proactivity and strategic buying is the norm, more complexity is necessary than in simpler purchase modes.

● Purchasing contribution

The overall objective is to maximise the contribution of purchase to company competitiveness or, in the public or government domain, to achieving value for money. This can be done by identifying and placing in priority order the key contributory factors (see **Fig. 8.3**). Normally these are likely to be:

- Cost reduction.
- The optimisation of working capital.
- Improving customer satisfaction.
- Developing and maintaining capabilities.

When systematised, in the course of annual review, each of these elements is exploded into its constituents considered by the management of purchase (see **Fig. 8.4**). Priorities and weightings ascribed to each of the separate subjects together comprise each of the four areas. Management determine what goals must be achieved within each. Each is allocated a manager who is charged with meeting, within an agreed budget, the objectives specified. In some companies – Rolls Royce, for

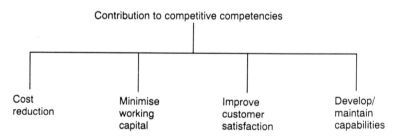

**Figure 8.3**  Overview chart

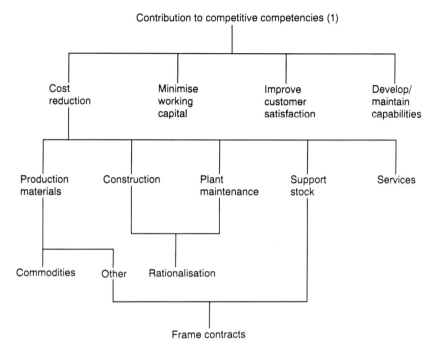

**Figure 8.4** Contribution to competitive competencies (1)

example – all programmes must be capable of quantification in order that measurement be carried out on a regular and systematic basis.

## Cost reduction

In respect of costs, purchases can be considered under the five principal types of item found in manufacturing:

1. Production materials.
2. Project materials.
3. Maintenance items.
4. Support stocks.
5. Contracts for services.

In distribution, resale items may be added. Among the mechanisms that might be targeted are the generation of frame contracts on a fixed or regulated price basis. This is probably one of the oldest but also one of the most successful means of impacting, not just on price but also upon workloads, which helps purchase to concentrate on dealing with commercial or strategic factors. Over a period of ten years, Procter & Gamble in Europe have reduced head count in purchase by approximately 80% through the divorce of commercial and logistic elements of purchase, which enable greater concentration on much more fundamental aspects. Frame contracts in mandatory or optional form were largely pioneered over 30 years ago by British Coal.

Today they constitute an essential part of the strategic portfolio of any major industrial organisation. To a company like ICI Chemicals and Polymers Ltd, the number, success and pace of generation of this type of contract can be an important barometer of commercial success. The complexity of such exercises usually increases as industries become more mature and particularly when they diversify or expand. Behind every frame contract lies a rationalisation of items bought, based upon agreed specifications that, from the point of view of price competitiveness, should usually be as close as possible to industry standards or 'off the shelf' – the Taguchi prescription in fact.

### Working capital (Fig. 8.5)

In respect of working capital, the key business objective of optimising the amount that is tied up in operations, will always remain. Internally

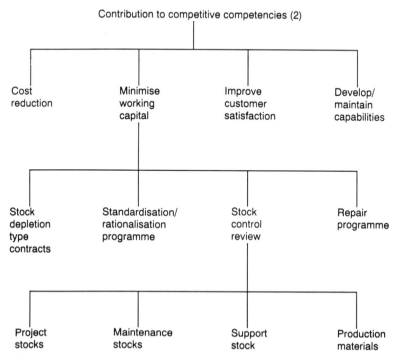

**Figure 8.5**   Contribution to competitive competencies (2)

stocks may be analysed as normal usage, safety stocks and buffer stocks. Firms that drive down the just-in-time road, or seek to adapt its principles to their own operation, aim to impact simultaneously upon all three areas. So far as internal demand is concerned, 'pull' type production and small batches invariably reduce average working stock whilst the rationalisation of manufacturing processes has a similar effect on buffers. Purchasing, however, can make its contribution through the use of devices such as stock depletion contracts whereby suppliers take inventory off the user's balance sheet by retaining financial responsibility until issue.

An even more significant impact, however, can be devised from the selection of better suppliers. Safety stocks reflect the interaction of the factors shown in **Table 8.1**.

The historic approach may be compared to risk analysis and insurance, with stock levels generally based upon a worst case analysis particularly in process industries or where manufacturing management is very strong.

By contrast today, the Japanese example and the impact of total quality management have ensured a focus upon causative factors. If user demand can move nearer to high street or end consumer requirements, or where 'pull' manufacture becomes a reality, one of the two factors can become less turbulent. But perhaps more important from the buying point of view, better suppliers have, by definition, improved quality and delivery reliability profiles. The element of safety stock that therefore pertains to these factors can be substantially reduced. Working stock is also dramatically cut as batch of one capability is approached, but without any overall deterioration in the risk profile since even with a significant cut in safety stock greater supplier reliability provides appropriate protection. Although the model portrayed is simplified for purposes of illustration, this is the principle that relates a reduction in

- **Table 8.1**
  Safety stocks

| | | |
|---|---|---|
| *User driven* | : | Service level as measured by percentage of demand met |
| | | Accuracy of forecast as measured by standard deviation of forecast error |
| *Supplier driven* | : | Quality level |
| | | Lead time reliability |
| *Finance driven* | : | Inventory holding cost |
| | | Run out cost |

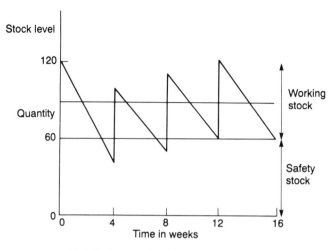

Historical approach with:
　　Fixed order quality of 60 units
　　Fixed delivery period of 4 weeks
　　Safety stock of 60 units
　　Average working stock of 27 units
　　Average total stock of 87 units
　　4 deliveries in total period
　　Variable average consumption rate

**Figure 8.6** Addressing the symptoms

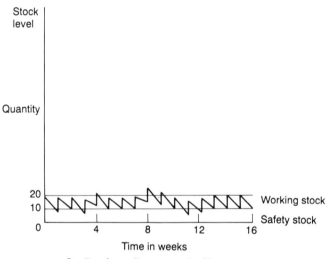

Quality of supplier approach with:
　　Fixed order quantity of 10 units
　　Fixed delivery period of 1 week
　　Safety stock of 10 units
　　Average working stock of 11 units
　　Average total stock of 21 units
　　12 deliveries in total period
　　Variable average consumption rate

**Figure 8.7** Addressing the cause

working capital to direct purchase led action and is one example of continuous improvement in this field.

## Customer satisfaction

Consumer satisfaction is the third major factor. Although many elements combine to create or destroy user confidence, the principal components are delivery reliability, consistency of delivered produce and total quality of service. The first two of these are hallmarks of purchase no less than they are of industry in general. It is the third, however, which transforms tangible delivery and quality gains into a wider purchase responsive environment. For too long purchase has seen its in-house customers as, at best, difficult and prone to fault finding. A customer focus programme, by aligning purchase with the total quality movement, capitalises upon the strong current that is now

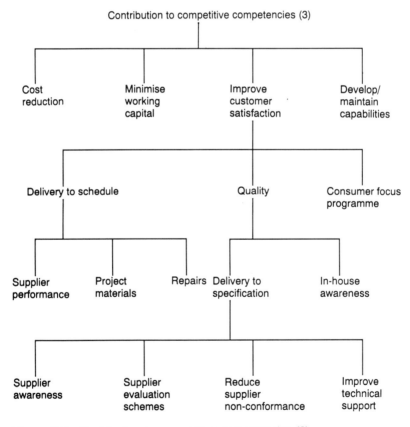

**Figure 8.8** Contribution to competitive competencies (3)

flowing and makes for even better service through the very act of giving better service.

## Developing and maintaining capabilities

In the generalised model proposed, a fourth and last strand of competitive competence concerns the development and maintenance of essential capabilities. In most organisations the development of an effective supplier base, staff recruitment and training and the creation and maintenance of appropriate systems represent the priorities. Certainly for much of the last decade many organisations have pursued strategies

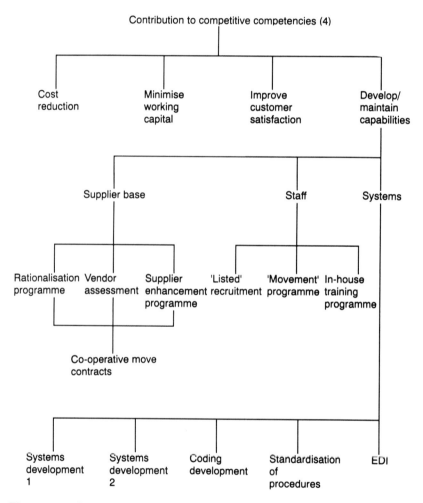

**Figure 8.9**   Contribution to competitive competencies (4)

aimed at reducing the number of suppliers. To a degree this is a natural result of quality initiatives and of the development of closer relationships with suppliers in the interests of product development. It is also, however, a major cost driver and therefore an attractive means of improving purchasing efficiency. Opportunity plays a major part in such rationalisation programmes but they should always be viewed within the context of purchase portfolio analysis. Restructuring the shape of the supplier base by the use of these tools provides the essential structural framework for the exercise.

## ● Development programmes

It is not, however, simply a case of reducing the size of the portfolio but also of enhancing it. Excellent suppliers are in short supply and many organisations therefore invest in development programmes. This naturally implies that both parties perceive continuation of their relationship as a matter for the longer term, and this investment in equipment, training and systems is more likely to be found in industrial sectors where the concept of supply chain management based upon commonly agreed interests in the end market is found. These will include electronics, aerospace and the automotive industry.

### Equipment

In the case of equipment the process will move through successive stages beginning with basic approval on the basis of inspection-based quality control and piece part qualification. Ship to stock will follow as soon as quality systems have been developed sufficiently to give acceptable product quality control. As emphasis moves from product to process, with statistical process control complementing process capability, the supplier has reached a position where all the management systems in place may be assessed. This is the prelude to full bilateral certification recognising total quality based upon excellence in manufacture and continuous improvement. Real impact upon the supply base may require upwards of five years' investment and, as sights are raised, the process may be seen as without finite time limits.

### Training

The cliché that 'people are the business' in one way represents the essential purchasing dilemma. For a long time the perception of purchase as a reactive, service driven function lacking glamour and removed from the essential decision-making process, has acted to dissuade able young people from joining the profession. Hence at a time when purchase is increasingly being called upon to play a more proactive role, efforts must be made to enlist a higher calibre of staff. At a senior level, marketing is an obvious recruitment ground but there is also a pressing need for more graduates and professionally qualified new entrants. Increasingly there will be transfers on secondment between functions whilst for those who are potential high fliers, or 'listed' personnel, purchase experience of three or four years will increasingly be an essential experience. Such people will be, as a result, 'purchase aware' and this will lead to the development of cultures better able to understand and use purchase expertise. Nor is this a one way development process. Notwithstanding older views of the time needed to gain an insight into markets, current experience suggests that well-qualified entrants quickly begin to make returns on investment, gaining high levels of proficiency and skill in less than one year.

Training, of course, is an essential feature of any improvement programme. It is commonplace to say that investment in this area varies very significantly from country to country, and it is noteworthy that in the Siemens organisation in Germany the normal target per year for continuous education of staff is an average of 5% of the 1,620 hours per annum actually worked; i.e. two weeks per year. In the case of Siemens, for the 750 negotiating purchasing officers in Germany, this gives a target figure of 50,000 hours per annum of management development. Few other countries can match this type of achievement and it is an open question as to how far governments need to cajole through tax incentives, for example.

For the present, however, good purchase training is less readily available than that in other functions. Nationally organised professional bodies, for example in the United Kingdom and in Belgium, offer a training service with that of the Institute of Purchasing and Supply being the most comprehensive in Europe. Management Centre Europe caters for the upper end of the market with the International Purchasing Conference well established as the foremost event of its kind.

Many companies seek tailor-made programmes offered by consultants. Generally formats cover three to five days at senior buyer or purchase manager level, aiming to expose participants to the new thinking that changes in technology or the competitive environment demands. From time to time corporations seek comprehensive programmes for practitioners who are in need either of updating or of remotivating in order to escape from the wastelands of the mid-career plateau. The 18-week example was designed for an electronics multinational as part of a major reshaping exercise. It is applicable to a corporation in the strategic mode of purchasing, but its elements can be analysed to provide a framework suited to both the clerical/transactional and the commercial focus. From it can be drawn a flexible training package based upon the current stage of organisational development and the planned programme of continuous development.

Purchasing as a professional activity is in the course of rapid change. As competitive pressures increase so sourcing decisions become more important whilst the technological advances that McKinsey has dubbed 'economics of scope' place additional pressure upon the function. Even to discharge traditional purchasing elements to the higher standards required is a major challenge. To superimpose upon this the dramatic organisational development needs of changed focus is to produce not simply a major training need but also a requirement for a fundamental shift in attitudes.

The premium now placed upon total quality and upon innovation produces a need for entrepreneurs in buying. Purchasing is working in the market-place and purchasing people are exposed to a great many new products and new suggestions. The ability to seek these out and to determine the extent to which they will add to one's own competitive competence, becomes a very important asset. As Andrall Pearson, former president and chief operating officer of Pepsi Co Incorporated, said:

'Many companies such as Pepsi Co have developed major strategic successes by borrowing ideas from the market place, frequently from quite small organisations. It is not just products which must be looked for, it is also company business systems since beyond every process and every product there are mechanisms by which these are bought from the market place. Determining the major competitive strengths of different companies is one way in which one can enhance one's capability. It therefore becomes important to ensure that a dynamic and innovative purchase department is in existence and this implies a continuous drive to raise the level of competency.'

The purchase area is an area where investment in staff training and organisational development produces not just attractive returns but also rapid payback. This will be crucial to success in the 1990s.

## Systems

Finally, systems capability is an essential part of any improvement programme. On-line access by users, is in the industrial sense, a parallel development to electronic point-of-sale in retail distribution, whilst many if not most sophisticated warehouses have computerised inventory systems. Electronic data interchange (EDI) is developing quickly although not as rapidly as its advocates had hoped. The reason for this has been neither technical nor financial but rather a reflection of perceived buyer–seller power relationships. Transmission of basic order, call-off or delivery data should not present a significant problem in the context, but buying organisations frequently either underestimate the extent to which data must be purified or are reluctant to see anything approaching integration. Within limits retail distribution is an exception to this statement whilst third party interchange in other sectors is growing. However, whatever current problems may be, there can be no doubt that the advantages of speed, accuracy and cost will inevitably make EDI the essential communication medium of the future and that no systems of element of continuous improvement is complete without it.

## ● Conclusion

Where purchase departments are positioned depends upon the nature of the purchase environment, upon the criticality of purchase inputs for sustainable competitive advantage, upon the attitude of top management and perhaps, above all, upon the quality of purchasing management itself. In order to change focus towards proactivity, it becomes necessary to develop a marketing plan for the purchase function, and in this context the ability to use such tools as positioning graphs and to point to successful improvement programmes is of major importance. The aims of marketing the function are to gain the support of key decision makers, to change attitudes to and of internal customers, and to change the company culture in respect of purchase.

All these things, of course, are geared to the ultimate aim, which is *maximising the contribution to sustainable competitive advantage*. Purchase can all too easily be the weakest link in the developmental chain. Issues such as just-in-time, partnership with suppliers and functional integration are transforming the face of purchase today. It is quite clear that these movements will continue into the 1990s and no major corporation is going to be immune from their effects. This is why there is an overwhelming need at this stage to examine the profile of the function and to position it appropriately in relation to the organisation concerned. This is a major preoccupation not just of purchase directors and vice presidents, but also in terms of general managers and chief executives.

# ● Appendix: a training package for purchase

The purpose of this Appendix is to set out the various elements in a comprehensive training package for purchase. This can be seen as company specific for in-house use or as a more general vehicle. Elements should be selected from the menu by reference to the departmental focus and a broad indication guide is given.

| Week No. | Clerical/ Transactional | Commercial | Strategic |
|---|---|---|---|
| | MODE APPLICABILITY | | |
| **1. Strategy** | | | |
| Determinants of corporate strategy | | | ★ |
| Environmental factors affecting purchase | ★ | ★ | ★ |
| The purchase mission | | ★ | ★ |
| Devising purchase strategies | | ★ | ★ |
| Benchmarking | | ★ | ★ |
| Formulating objectives | ★ | ★ | ★ |
| Broad measures of achievement | ★ | ★ | ★ |
| **2. Organisation** | | | |
| Manuals of procedure | ★ | ★ | ★ |
| Models of the purchase function | | ★ | ★ |
| Setting up project teams | | | ★ |
| Some key issues: | | | |
| Centralisation/decentralisation | | ★ | ★ |
| Marketing/logistics | | | ★ |
| Independence/integration | | | ★ |
| Managing a world-wide purchase organisation | | | ★ |
| **3. Purchase policies** | | | |
| Standardisation and rationalisation | ★ | ★ | ★ |
| Leverage with flexibility | | ★ | ★ |
| Cost plus contracts | | ★ | ★ |
| The use of competitive tendering | ★ | ★ | ★ |
| Strategic alliances | | | ★ |
| Pre- and post-tender negotiation | | ★ | ★ |
| Global sourcing | | ★ | ★ |
| Supply chain management | | | ★ |
| Using consolidators | | | ★ |
| Countertrade:offset | | | ★ |
| Futures | | | ★ |
| Currency management | | | ★ |

(Continued)

| | MODE APPLICABILITY | | |
|---|---|---|---|
| *Week No.* | *Clerical/ Transactional* | *Commercial* | *Strategic* |
| 4. *Logistics* | | | |
| The total distribution concepts | | | ★ |
| Logistics and ROI | | | ★ |
| Cost elements | ★ | ★ | ★ |
| Coding | ★ | ★ | ★ |
| Inventory models: | | | |
|   Max/Min | ★ | ★ | ★ |
|   EOQ | | ★ | ★ |
|   Cyclical review | ★ | ★ | ★ |
|   MRP | | ★ | ★ |
| Safety and buffer stocks | | ★ | ★ |
| Simulation | | | ★ |
| Logistics information systems | | | ★ |
| Using computers in purchasing | ★ | ★ | ★ |
| 5. *Contracts* | | | |
| Legal framework | ★ | ★ | ★ |
| Forms of contract | ★ | ★ | ★ |
| Warranties | | ★ | ★ |
| Redress | | | ★ |
| Capital equipment procurement | | | ★ |
| 6. *The total quality concept* | | | |
| What is total quality? | | ★ | ★ |
| Quality systems and standards | ★ | ★ | ★ |
| Quality philosophies | | | ★ |
| Quality costs | | ★ | ★ |
| Process capability | | | ★ |
| ISO 9000 | ★ | ★ | |
| 7. *Systems* | | | |
| Transactional systems | ★ | ★ | ★ |
| Purchase databases | ★ | ★ | ★ |
| EDI:third party interchange | | | ★ |
| 8. *Supplier relations* | | | |
| Portfolio analysis | | | ★ |
| Market strategies | | ★ | ★ |
| Purchase research | | ★ | ★ |
| Supplier evaluation techniques | | ★ | ★ |
| Supplier selection | ★ | ★ | ★ |
| Supplier quality assurance | | ★ | ★ |
| Long-term relationships | | | ★ |

(*Continued*)

| Week No. | MODE APPLICABILITY | | |
|---|---|---|---|
| | Clerical/ Transactional | Commercial | Strategic |
| Single sourcing | | | ★ |
| Performance appraisal | | | ★ |
| Co-ownership for shared benefits and risks | | | ★ |
| 9. *Negotiations* | | | |
| The conceptual framework | | ★ | ★ |
| Bargaining ranges and the efficient frontier | | ★ | ★ |
| Behavioural aspects | | ★ | ★ |
| Developing negotiating skills | ★ | ★ | ★ |
| Complex negotiations | | | ★ |
| Cultural impact | | | ★ |
| 10. *Finance* | | | |
| Key concepts | | | ★ |
| Understanding financial statements | | | ★ |
| Sources of finance | | | ★ |
| Budgets | | | ★ |
| Break-even analysis and contribution accounting | | | ★ |
| ROI | | | ★ |
| Cash flow management | | | ★ |
| 11. *Marketing* | | | |
| The marketing mix | | | ★ |
| How markets are vectored | | | ★ |
| The marketing approach to the purchase function: | | | ★ |
| Assessing the marketing strategy of suppliers | | ★ | ★ |
| 12. *Pricing* | | | |
| Views of price | | | ★ |
| How prices are determined | ★ | ★ | ★ |
| Price banding | | | ★ |
| Price changes | | ★ | ★ |
| Transfer pricing | | | ★ |
| 13. *New product development* | | | |
| Integrated purchase and logistics | | | ★ |
| Changes in the role of design | | | ★ |
| Procurement engineering | | | ★ |
| Failure mode and effect analysis | | | ★ |
| Taguchi loss function | | | ★ |
| Quality functional deployment | | | ★ |

*(Continued)*

| Week No. | MODE APPLICABILITY | | |
| --- | --- | --- | --- |
| | Clerical/ Transactional | Commercial | Strategic |
| 14. *Changes in manufacturing technology* | | | |
| Economics of scope | | ★ | ★ |
| Cellular manufacture | | | ★ |
| Set up time reduction | | | ★ |
| Smoothed flows | | | ★ |
| 'Pull' scheduling | | | ★ |
| Multi-skilling | | | ★ |
| Implications for lead time, inventory and marketing | | ★ | ★ |
| Purchase implications | | ★ | ★ |
| Make or buy | | | ★ |
| 15. *Just-in-time* | | | |
| Underlying philosophy:waste:employee involvement JIT as: | | | ★ |
| Corporate strategy | | | ★ |
| Low inventory manufacturing system | | ★ | ★ |
| Profile of JIT suppliers | | | ★ |
| Negotiating JIT agreements | | | ★ |
| Implementing JIT | | | ★ |
| 16. *Developing the purchase team* | | | |
| Effective management and communication | ★ | ★ | ★ |
| Recruitment | | ★ | ★ |
| Team building | | | ★ |
| Developing purchase competencies | | | ★ |
| Motivating plateaued professionals | | | ★ |
| Devising staffing scenarios | | | ★ |
| 17. *Future developments* | | | |
| Key purchase trends for the 1990s | | | ★ |
| Outlook for world trade | | | ★ |
| Assessing for Far Eastern challenge | | | ★ |
| 1992 | | | ★ |
| 18. *Positioning the purchase department* | | | |
| What top management expects of purchase | | | ★ |
| The purchase audit | | | ★ |
| Measures of accountability | | ★ | ★ |
| Determining the optimum purchase position | | | ★ |
| Devising a continuous improvement programme for purchase | | ★ | ★ |

# Index